OUTWARD
SIGN
AND
INWARD
GRACE

Outward Sign

Sign

AND

Inward

Grace

THE PLACE OF SACRAMENTS
IN WESLEYAN SPIRITUALITY

ROB L. STAPLES

BEACON HILL PRESS OF KANSAS CITY
Kansas City, Missouri

Copyright 1991
Beacon Hill Press of Kansas City

ISBN: 083-411-3783

Printed in the
United States of America

Cover Design: Crandall Vail

10 9 8 7 6 5 4 3

To
MARCELLA

We are not Catholics,
but our marriage
has been a
sacrament
anyway.

Contents

FOREWORD

Although the ancient heresy of Gnosticism was repudiated in the early centuries of church history, it continues to lurk in the Christian subconsciousness. This is true not only in the widespread notion that sin somehow inheres in our "flesh" so that true sanctification must await the resurrection but also in the unspoken assumption that true "spirituality" is something achieved apart from such physical acts as being baptized and eating the bread and drinking the cup of the Eucharist.

Furthermore, this less than biblical appreciation for the sacraments is understandable also as a Protestant rejection of the sacramentarianism of the Roman church that attributed to baptism and the Mass an automatic impartation of divine grace, a reaction augmented by a number of other developments. Among these are an Enlightenment stress on reason that separates symbol from reality, a pietistic/revivalistic tendency to view "spirituality" in terms of the individual's relationship to God to the neglect of corporate expressions of faith, and now the widespread influence of existentialism that reduces truth to personal encounter and lends itself easily to Eastern mysticism.

What Professor Staples argues for in this carefully documented, well-reasoned, and often brilliant presentation is a recovery of the biblical wholeness of Christian faith and practice. Christ and the apostles show no Gnostic suspicion of the physical and material. Knowing the earth and all things therein to be part of God's "good" creation, they saw all nature as sacramental, suffused with the grace of the Creator. In such an understanding the sacraments are not empty signs but pregnant symbols. In the New Testament church there simply were no unbaptized Christians, and every Lord's Day the early Christians

11

celebrated Christ's atoning sacrifice by eating His body and drinking His blood in the simple faith that He was present with them at the table.

It is time the Church of Jesus Christ overcame the disjunctions created by the 16th-century Reformation. What is called for is the "evangelical catholicism" of John Wesley's "middle way" in which the two historic Christian traditions were synthesized. In this synthesis the English Reformer not only recovered for the Church a viable doctrine of holiness but also pointed the way to a scriptural view and practice of the sacraments that is both apostolic and catholic.

Such is the thesis Dr. Staples expouses and admirably argues. I am happy to recommend this long overdue plea for the holiness movement to return to its roots in classical Wesleyanism. It deserves careful reading by those who teach and study in college and seminary classrooms, by every pastor who would be faithful to the truth and practice of biblical Christianity, and by all thoughtful laypersons who are concerned about spiritual formation.

—WILLIAM M. GREATHOUSE
General Superintendent Emeritus

PREFACE

An explanation of the terms in this book's title and subtitle may give a helpful preview of what lies ahead in these pages. The title, *Outward Sign and Inward Grace,* is, of course, from John Wesley's definition of a sacrament. The term *Wesleyan Spirituality* indicates the perspective from which the book is written, namely, that spiritual ethos rooted in 18th-century Wesleyanism.

In the book itself the term *Wesleyan/holiness* is used frequently, to indicate the tradition in which I stand and to which this book is mainly addressed. For this, the broader term *Wesleyan,* by itself, would be insufficient. Mainline Methodists have a prior claim to that term; they are John Wesley's ecclesiastical children. But also claiming to be Wesleyan in their theology are Wesley's "grandchildren"—the people whose religious heritage is that of the American holiness movement of the 19th century, which was a revival of early Methodism's emphasis on holiness of heart and life. The term *Wesleyan/holiness tradition* thus serves a dual purpose—the word *Wesleyan* indicating the common theological roots the tradition shares with Methodism, and the word *holiness* distinguishing this tradition from that part of contemporary mainline Methodism that does not identify with the holiness movement. The more cumbersome term *Wesleyan/holiness spirituality* was not used in the subtitle because the sacramental viewpoint herein espoused has more continuity with Wesley's views than with the modifications of those views found in the holiness movement. In the subtitle, therefore, the term *holiness* would have been extraneous.

Spirituality is difficult to get a handle on! In the history of religion, the term has meant different things to different people, due as much to varieties of personality types as to differences in theology. Basically it refers to the way we understand our religious and ethical commitments, and the way we act and react habitually to this understanding. Whatever spirituality is, the need for a renewed interest in it among evangelicals is pointedly portrayed by J. M. Houston in his article on the subject in the *Evangelical Dictionary of Theology:*

> In spite of the renewal movements, there is a dearth today of spiritual leadership and direction in the evangelical world. Catholics can look to Mother Teresa in Calcutta, and the Orthodox to the unnamed martyrs of modern Russia, but evangelical Protestants are largely secularized by their politics, their obsession with growth, and their interests in administration and parachurch activities. The loss of the practice of prayer, the ignorance of the rich traditions of spirituality, and the need to develop a cultural framework for the practice of devotion are challenges worthy of the most serious consideration at the end of the twentieth century.[1]

A sacramental perspective is, I believe, an important component of spirituality, and I hope that a clearer understanding of the sacraments will enhance spirituality among people in the Wesleyan/holiness tradition.

The view of sacraments espoused in this book is *normative* rather than *descriptive*. This means that I have not tried to describe the sacramental beliefs and practices that are current today within the Wesleyan/holiness tradition. I have not sought to find a consensus. To determine that, it would take some careful statistical research—for which I have neither the interest nor the qualifications. The variation is immense; some holiness groups have high regard for sacraments, while some give them very low priority. In its beginning, the Society of Friends (whose understanding of spirituality has some similarities with that of the holiness tradition) did not practice sacraments at all. The Salvation Army gives them little place, although in General Booth's day the reasons were more practical than theological. Among Nazarenes, Wesleyans, Free Methodists, and members of other denominations within the Christian Holiness Association, there is a considerable variety of sacramental views. I have sim-

---

1. Edited by Walter A. Elwell (Grand Rapids: Baker Book House, 1984), 1050.

ply expounded the sacramental vision that I think *ought to* guide the belief and practice of the Wesleyan/holiness churches—if they are to be true to their Wesleyan heritage. Thus *The Place of Sacraments* in the subtitle refers not so much to the place they *have* but to the place they *should have.* That may sound patronizing. Who am I to say what others in my tradition should believe? It is a fair question. I can only reply that mine is simply one opinion, but I hope it is an *informed* opinion. The view expressed in this book is what I believe to be the proper Wesleyan/holiness perspective on the sacraments. I hope I have a valid basis for believing such. So let me state it.

I have already mentioned what, for me, is the key—"being true to our Wesleyan heritage." The headwaters of Wesleyanism lie in the Evangelical Revival in 18th-century England, which sprang largely from the preaching of John and Charles Wesley. The vitality and viewpoint of that revival is what I call classical Wesleyanism. The American holiness movement of the 19th century grew *out of* and was an attempt to *renew* the thrusts of that 18th-century movement. In other words, 18th-century Methodist preaching and teaching was the source and the mainstream. Later like-minded movements simply flowed into that stream, caught up by the current of revivalism and the call to "spread scriptural holiness over these lands." As they did so, they brought with them some unique features that were peculiar to their own time and place in history. In some cases the tributaries differed in content from the mainstream. And here is where my own personal conviction shows up: In many cases, I am persuaded that the tributaries flowing into the mainstream, although enriching it with some new elements, did not always help to purify the stream as a whole. Sometimes they polluted it instead, or (if that word is too strong) at least added elements that, in some respects, served to muddy the waters. For example, in my opinion, Wesley was closer to biblical truth in his doctrine of the Holy Spirit than was Phoebe Palmer, as I have tried to show elsewhere.[2] As for the sacraments, I believe that the Ana-

---

2. Cf. Rob L. Staples, "Wesleyan Perspectives on the Doctrine of the Holy Spirit," in *The Spirit and the New Age,* ed. R. Larry Shelton and Alex R. G. Deasley (Anderson, Ind.: Warner Press, 1986), 199-236; also published under the title "John Wesley's Doctrine of the Holy Spirit," *Wesleyan Theological Journal,* Spring—Fall, 1986, 91-115.

baptist currents that flowed into the Wesleyan stream through the holiness movement served to water down the Wesleyan doctrine of baptism (no pun intended!), and to diminish the significance placed on the Lord's Supper by the Wesleys.

Why should present-day Wesleyans evaluate their sacramental views and practices on the basis of classical Wesleyan theology? Who is to say we have not improved on Wesley and moved closer to a more accurate vision? Again, these are fair questions. I would only suggest that theological truth, although shaped in part by culture, is not culturally bound. I happen to believe that Wesley's perspective on sacraments is more firmly rooted in both Scripture and the historic Christian tradition than are some of the innovations (and the negligence) of his followers. A contemporary theology has lost its moorings when it closes its ears to whispers from the past. I am unapologetically a classical Wesleyan in my theology in general, and in my sacramental theology in particular.

This is not, however, a book about John Wesley's theology of the sacraments. Of that topic, a number of valuable studies have already been made. Nevertheless, I was constantly aware of the ghost of Mr. Wesley looking over my shoulder as I wrote. I hope he was not overly disappointed in what he saw me writing, although I feel quite certain he was as annoyed by my slowness in putting the words together as he was fascinated by the speedy workings of my word processor!

In Christendom at large, much has been written about sacraments. But in Wesleyan/holiness circles, there has been a paucity of literature on the subject. Sometimes one can detect in the contemporary ethos of the holiness movement an implicit fear that too much emphasis on sacraments will turn out to be a mere disguise for "formalism" or "sacramentarianism" or "antievangelism" or some other such bogeyman. I hope my efforts will help to expel such fears.

I am grateful to the administration and trustees of Nazarene Theological Seminary for granting me a semester's sabbatical, which I spent reading, thinking, and writing about sacraments. I am indebted to several persons for helpful suggestions. Theologians H. Ray Dunning and William M. Greathouse read the manuscript in its entirety. Large parts of it were read by New

Testament scholars Alex R. G. Deasley and Richard E. Howard, liturgist Donald Boyd, and my former graduate assistant Von Unruh. Cecil Paul, former director of Nazarene Communications, strongly encouraged me in this project, even teaching my adult Sunday School class for several weeks in order to give me more time for writing. Bonnie Perry smoothed out many of my awkward sentences. The students in my seminary course on the theology of sacraments had access to the manuscript in rough draft and gave valuable feedback. I am especially grateful to my many theology students across the years whose questions and spirited discussions about the sacraments have helped to sharpen my perspectives. I take a special "fatherly" satisfaction in their expanding sacramental vision.

Although this book was birthed during a semester's sabbatical, the notion that it needed to be written was conceived long ago and has gestated during almost three decades of teaching theology. I must confess that I have not always held the views I now hold regarding sacraments. Before beginning my teaching career, I spent some years in the pastorate. During that time, I regarded both baptism and the Eucharist as having only minor importance in the life of faith. I favored infant dedication over infant baptism and practiced immersion more than sprinkling or pouring. And I nonchalantly rebaptized some who felt dissatisfied with their previous baptism. Across the years some of my views have changed, as I have come to understand better the meaning of the gospel, of grace, of the Church, of what it means to be a Christian, of the historic Christian tradition, and of my own Wesleyan heritage. Isn't that what the Christian journey should be—a continual reexamination of our past so that we may better serve the present age and more clearly perceive the direction we should take in the future?

The book develops inductively rather than deductively. Therefore some questions that may be raised in the reader's mind in early portions of the book will, I hope, be answered in subsequent sections. All biblical quotations are from the *New International Version* unless otherwise indicated. Following common practice, I have used the word *wine* when speaking of the Communion elements. But it should be understood that we teetotaling Wesleyan/holiness folks use grape juice![3] On the printed page, however, in a discussion of sacraments, *grape juice* looks as bland as it is said to taste by those accustomed to real wine in the Eucharist! If I am guilty of linguistic fudging, I trust I may be forgiven.

My intention was to avoid theological technicalities. I found it impossible to avoid them altogether, but I hope they do not detract from the book's central purpose, which is to help my fellow Christians in the Wesleyan/holiness tradition to better appreciate the sacraments, and to show that a clear sacramentalist vision can be a help to holy living.

—Rob L. Staples
Nazarene Theological Seminary
Kansas City

---

3. The reason for this will be found in chapter 9.

ACKNOWLEDGMENTS

Sources from which materials have been reprinted are all listed in the footnotes and bibliography.

We acknowledge permission to reprint the following copyrighted materials:

Augsburg Fortress Publishers: Excerpts from *Experience and Faith: The Significance of Luther for Understanding Today's Experiential Religion*, by William Hordern. Copyright © 1983 by Augsburg Publishing House. Used by permission.

William B. Eerdmans Publishing Company: "The Idea of Sacrament: An Approach," by Thomas Howard in *Reformed Journal*, February 1979.

"Imagination, Rites, and Mystery: Why Did Christ Institute Sacraments?" by Thomas Howard in *Reformed Journal*, March 1979. Used by permission.

Chapter One

THE WESLEYAN DILEMMA:
"SPIRIT" VS. "STRUCTURE"

What *is* a sacrament? "A visible word," said Augustine in a succinct metaphor. "An outward sign of an inward grace, and a means whereby we receive the same," said John Wesley, abridging the definition given in the catechism of the Anglican *Book of Common Prayer.* "An outward and visible sign of an inward and spiritual grace given unto us; ordained by Christ himself, as a means whereby we receive the same, and a pledge to assure us thereof," reads the full Anglican definition without Wesley's abridgments.

How many sacraments are there?

"Seven," declares Roman Catholicism. "Only two," most Protestants insist. "An indefinite and unlimited number," some theologians, both ancient and modern, have suggested.

What do we believe and practice with regard to the sacraments?

For the Wesleyan/holiness tradition, *that* is the salient question. In attempting to answer it, we find ourselves impaled on the horns of a dilemma.

A. THE DILEMMA DEFINED

The Wesleyan/holiness tradition has always embraced a degree of uncertainty about the place of sacraments in the cultivation of the holy life. The American holiness movement was

21

largely a child of 19th-century revivalism. This resulted in a tendency to turn away from the more formal and structured Christianity found in the mainline churches, especially the Methodist church, which had mothered the greatest number of those who identified with the holiness movement. Revivalism stressed the religion of inward experience, of John Wesley's "warmed heart." When such "heartfelt" religion became a reality in people's lives, they saw less need for churchly structures and liturgies. Structured worship services were sometimes spurned as a sign of "formalism" in which the Holy Spirit was not given room to operate freely. Salvation was a condition of the heart, and the Christian life was not a matter of following certain prescribed rituals. This religious outlook, with its emphasis on freedom and spontaneity, is referred to as *spirit* in the title of this chapter.[1]

In such an environment, sacraments could easily become devalued by one whose religious experience was believed to transcend the need for such formality. Those groups who had affinities with the Methodist emphasis on inward religion (such as the Quakers), and those with actual roots in Methodism (such as the Salvation Army), viewed sacraments as hindrances to the inner life of the Spirit. But that viewpoint was the exception. In most of the groups making up the holiness movement of the late 19th century, the sacraments of baptism and the Lord's Supper were administered sincerely and with some degree of regularity, not only in local churches but also at such gatherings as camp meetings and conferences. The sacraments were practiced mainly because Christ had commanded them, but also because they were part of the Methodist heritage. Despite its practice, the holiness movement never worked out for itself any thoroughgoing theology of sacraments. Its adherents merely appropriated the sacramental practice of their Methodist progenitors, even as they generally gave it less theological significance. Baptism was viewed more or less as a public testimony on the part of the baptized to his or her salvation, which was already an accomplished fact with or without the rite. The Lord's Supper

---

1. The word *spirit* is used here, rather than *Spirit,* to designate a mood, tenor, tone, temper, or attitude, although the advocates of *spirit* believe that it is in their kind of worship that the (Holy) Spirit is most present.

was mainly a memorial that served to kindle remembrance of Christ's sacrificial death, but it was not perceived as a means whereby *present* grace is conveyed, except in the sense that simply remembering the Lord's sacrifice is a helpful aid to Christian living.

H. Ray Dunning, Nazarene theologian, suggests that the difficulty of many of Wesley's more evangelical successors to relate to his sacramental teaching and practice derives in part from the fact that the cultural milieu in which they live is different from that of Wesley. He says:

> Whereas Wesley worked in the context of an established church, the present situation in most areas of the world reflects a denominational form of church structure with the loss of the sense of unity that follows from such a fragmented situation. There is furthermore the influence of the Enlightenment and American frontier individualism, which has exalted the lone individual as the locus of meaning, so the corporate dimensions of human existence seem unreal. This has contributed largely to a loss of the awareness of the significance of the church in constituting the Christian life, an awareness that Wesley keenly felt.[2]

To this must be added the influence of the concept of religious conversion that developed out of American revivalism. "The emphasis on dramatic, emotion-laden, will-oriented experience that resulted in a marked and sudden transformation has resulted in a depreciation of the sacraments."[3]

These trends in the American holiness movement were not developed in a vacuum. In these respects, the holiness movement merely reflected the "spirit of the age." The same trends were characteristic of Free Church Protestantism as a whole, in which baptism and the Eucharist had lost much of their sacramental meaning.

Indeed, in the voluntaristic, congregationalist, democratic American environment, corporate worship was often

---

2. H. Ray Dunning, *Grace, Faith, and Holiness: A Wesleyan Systematic Theology* (Kansas City: Beacon Hill Press of Kansas City, 1988), 549.

3. Ibid. Dunning adds: "The reality of radical conversion cannot be questioned, but it must be recognized that the shape and expression of it is culturally influenced." Pp. 549-50.

sacrificed to aggressive individualism in American religious life as had been the case in American business life. In claiming to be not of the world, American evangelicalism with its pragmatic, utilitarian, businesslike crusades and Madison Avenue-like revivals had begun to look very much like the surrounding culture.[4]

The pattern of the 19th-century revivals had become institutionalized in Sunday worship. The sermon was central and the sacraments were peripheral. Preaching was generally more evangelistic than pastoral. Thus the holiness movement was nurtured in an environment that was deeply suspicious of "ritualism" and "formalism" as opposed to "spontaneity" and "freedom" in worship.

On the other hand, and not without some irony, the holiness movement came into being perceiving itself as the rightful heir of early Methodism. It originated as a revival of John Wesley's teaching, particularly his doctrines of sanctification and Christian perfection. These holiness bodies saw themselves as called into being to be the exponents of those early Methodist emphases that mainline Methodism was deemed to have allowed to fall into disrepair.

Now it so happened that the Wesley of the "warmed heart" was none other than Wesley the "High Churchman, the son of a High Churchman," to use his own words.[5] This latter Wesley, the lifelong Anglican, had an enduring appreciation for the established church, and for him the Anglican liturgies and sacraments were of immense importance for the cultivation and propagation of holiness.[6] This "catholic" side of Wesley and of his followers—the side that loves tradition, appreciates order in worship, and gives high priority to the sacraments—is what we are referring to as "structure" in this chapter's title.

---

4. William H. Willimon, *Word, Water, Wine, and Bread* (Valley Forge, Pa.: Judson Press, 1980), 112.

5. *The Journal of the Rev. John Wesley, A.M.,* ed. Nehemiah Curnock (London: Epworth Press, 1916), 325 (hereafter cited as *Journal*).

6. This is evidenced by (to mention just three examples) his *Sunday Service of the Methodists in North America,* Methodist Bicentennial Commemorative Reprint (United Methodist Publishing House and the United Methodist Board of Higher Education and Ministry, 1984), which Wesley prepared sometime during the last decade of his life; by the *Covenant Service,* which he published in 1780; and by his lifelong love for the *Book of Common Prayer.*

These two sides of Wesley, which we are designating "spirit" and "structure," constitute what we are calling "the Wesleyan dilemma." They appear, on the surface at least, to be in tension with each other. The dilemma of the American holiness movement of the 19th century had roots in Wesley's own theology and practice, as he struggled to harmonize his high churchmanship and his evangelical experience. In turn, the American holiness movement passed the dilemma on to its late-20th-century offspring.

We will first review the present situation and then examine its roots in the Wesleyan Revival of the 18th century.

B. THE PRESENT SITUATION

In the Wesleyan/holiness churches today the dilemma is still with us, if in a slightly modified garb. On one hand there is an emphasis on the "freedom of the Spirit," a desire for spontaneity in worship and in religious expression. In some congregations the preferred form of worship approaches a "charismatic" style (albeit without speaking in tongues) including handclapping, spontaneous vocal praise, and a preference for gospel songs and choruses over hymns and anthems. The emphasis here is on *experience*, the importance of feeling, the religion of the heart. Prescribed forms of worship sometimes appear extraneous and unnecessary to those who have breathed the clear mountain air of spiritual freedom.[7] Formal religion can appear foggy and oppressive and sacraments may seem a waste of time.

This is not to imply that the "religion of the heart," with its accent on experience, is devoid of intelligent thought. In fact, the advocates of "spirit" over "structure," who would disparage sacraments, often appeal not only to the authority of experience but to that of reason as well. To many devout persons deeply committed to the Christian faith, there is something strange and incomprehensible in the phenomenon of sacramental practice in the life of the church. Why should not intelligent and educated Christians be content with the more reasonable and rational ele-

---

7. Such congregations may not have discerned the ritualistic elements in their own patterns of worship, e.g., the rituals of singing, witnessing, praying, or visiting each other during the service.

ments in public worship—preaching, praying, reading Scripture, and expressing praise in music? Why should they perpetuate such nonrational practices as the sprinkling of water on the head of an uncomprehending child, or the dipping of an adult under the water, or the consuming of tiny quantities of bread and wine to the accompaniment of solemn words? Whether it comes from an interest in experience or from a concern for reasonableness, sacraments are looked upon as relatively unimportant by a sizable number of persons in the Wesleyan/holiness churches today. They are considered to be unnecessary structures that fail to enhance true spirituality.

But there are others who see dangers in such trends and perspectives, and who agree with Reinhold Niebuhr, who said:

> It may be possible to have a brief period of religious spontaneity in which the absence of such disciplines does not matter. The evangelism of the American frontier may have been such a period. But this spontaneity does not last forever. When it is gone a church without adequate conduits of traditional liturgy and theological learning and tradition is without the waters of life.[8]

There is a growing conviction in some quarters that many people within the holiness movement do not really know how to worship. Focusing particularly on the Church of the Nazarene, General Superintendent Emeritus William M. Greathouse, writing shortly before his retirement, warned against what he called a "crisis" in worship. He said, "There seems to be in many churches confusion as to what really constitutes worship." He deplored "the growing tendency to crowd out congregational singing with special music" and "the drift toward religious entertainment" in church services. "This practice represents an invasion of the church by the spirit of this age. A narcissistic culture demands entertainment, and we can be religiously entertained and left untouched by the Spirit of Christ."[9]

Concerned about such trends, many in the Wesleyan/holi-

---

8. Reinhold Niebuhr, *Essays in Applied Christianity*, ed. D. B. Robertson (New York: Meridian Books, World Publishing Co., 1959), 62.

9. William M. Greathouse, "The Present Crisis in Our Worship." Address delivered in the chapel of Nazarene Theological Seminary, November 16, 1988, and subsequently published in the *Preacher's Magazine*, December, January, February 1989-90, 4 ff.

ness movement yearn to hear the note of eternity in the sanctuary. Some are calling for worship renewal and a recognition that worship can be enhanced by incorporating traditional forms such as use of the lectionary, preaching the Christian year, and a more meaningful appropriation of the sacraments. A number of individuals and congregations have responded to this call and have learned to appreciate the sense of historical continuity that comes from following a time-honored liturgy. They have experienced meaningful spiritual formation through the Scripture readings from the Old Testament, the Gospels, and the Epistles, as prescribed in the New Common Lectionary. They have exulted in the singing of hymns directed to God and away from oneself and have appropriated the sacraments as a means of grace. Most of these individuals and congregations testify to a spiritual satisfaction they never found in the less-structured kind of worship that stressed "spirit" above "structure."

Ironically, the "spirit above structure" kind of worship is often wedded to an ecclesiastical organizational and administrative polity that by contrast is extremely "structured." In 1854 the renowned Swiss-born American theologian and church historian, Philip Schaff, in analyzing American Christianity for a German audience, said:

> [American Christianity] is more Petrine than Johannean; more like busy Martha than like the pensive Mary, sitting at the feet of Jesus. It expands more in breadth than in depth. It is often carried on like a secular business, and in a mechanical or utilitarian spirit. It lacks . . . the true mysticism, an appreciation of history and the church, . . . the substratum of a profound and spiritual theology; and under the mask of orthodoxy it not infrequently conceals, without intending or knowing it, the tendency to abstract intellectualism and superficial rationalism. This is especially evident in the doctrine of the church and of the Sacraments, and in the meagerness of the worship . . . [wherein] nothing is left but preaching, free prayer, and singing.[10]

Some elements in Schaff's indictment of American Christianity almost a century and a half ago bear an uncanny resem-

---

10. Quoted in *Christianity Today*, February 17, 1989, 53.

blance to the ecclesiastical life of some Wesleyan/holiness denominations today. We often see the ironic phenomenon of a tightly *structured* denominational government whose administrative leaders proclaim the need for "keeping the glory down" by maintaining an *unstructured* worship wherein the "freedom of the Spirit" reigns supreme! There are some parallels between this and Schaff's description: (1) A strong emphasis on church planting and church growth with a comparatively weak emphasis on worship ("busy Martha," "expands more in breadth than in depth"); (2) a burgeoning ecclesiastical bureaucracy ("carried on like a secular business"); (3) a statistically defined concept of ministerial success ("utilitarian spirit"). This takes us less than halfway through Schaff's analysis, but the parallel between the remainder of his statement and present-day Wesleyan/holiness ecclesiastical life and polity is self-evident.

C. THE WESLEYAN ROOTS

In a fascinating way, the present dilemma is the reflection of a similar dilemma in John Wesley. Over the years of Wesley's ministry, especially in the earlier decades, several changes took place in his concept of the church and its worship. These changes involved both his practices and his doctrines, and the two were mutually influential. "His practices modified his theology, and his changed theology led him into new practices."[11] Regarding his doctrine of the *church*, Wesley worked throughout most of his adult life with two fundamentally different concepts and responded to each of them with varying degrees of enthusiasm. These two views of the church correspond roughly to what historical theologian Ernst Troeltsch, early in this century, called "church-type" and "sect-type" Christianity.[12] (We are calling it a "rough" correspondence because in making the distinction, Troeltsch used sociological criteria that may or may not be significant in understanding Wesley.) Troeltsch, borrowing from sociologist Max Weber, described "church" and "sect" as *ideal types*, or

---

11. Frank Baker, *John Wesley and the Church of England* (Nashville: Abingdon Press, 1968), 137.

12. Ernst Troeltsch, *The Social Teaching of the Christian Churches*, trans. Olive Wyon, 2 vols. (New York: Harper and Brothers, 1960).

conceptual models that are helpful in understanding Christianity and its various institutional forms.[13] As such, the distinction is instructive for understanding the beginnings of early Methodism.

Leaving aside the sociological subtleties of Troeltsch's two types, and looking only at their broad outlines, one can see something similar in Wesley's views of the church. He held *two* different views, which are lucidly described by Frank Baker. The first view (Wesley's "church type") was that of "an historical institution, organically linked to the apostolic church by a succession of bishops and inherited customs, served by a priestly caste who duly expounded the Bible and administered the sacraments in such a way as to preserve the ancient traditions on behalf of all who were made members by baptism."[14] Wesley's other view (similar to Troeltsch's "sect type") was that of "a fellowship of believers who shared both the apostolic experience of God's living presence and also a desire to bring others into this same personal experience by whatever methods of worship and evangelism seemed most promising to those among them whom the Holy Spirit had endowed with special gifts of prophecy and leadership."[15] Again, Baker compares the two views as follows:

> The one view . . . would see the church as an institution aspiring to represent and include all humanity, on whose behalf its ministers discharge a mainly sacerdotal function. The other . . . regards the church as a company of like-minded people who believe themselves called apart by God for some special purpose, and whose ministers . . . are regarded as prophets rather than priests.[16]

And still again:

> The first view saw the church in essence as an ancient institution to be preserved, the second as a faithful few with a mission to the world: the first was a traditional rule, the

---

13. Cf. Claude Welch, *Protestant Thought in the Nineteenth Century* (New York: Yale University Press, 1985), 2:293-94; Wilhelm Pauck, *Harnack and Troeltsch: Two Historical Theologians* (New York: Oxford University Press, 1968), 78-79. The phrase "ideal types" means that they are constructs of which examples may be, but are not necessarily, found in existing ecclesiastical structures.

14. Baker, 137.

15. Ibid.

16. Ibid., 158.

second a living relationship. In the church as an institution Wesley had been born and reared and ordained: into the church as a mission he was gradually introduced . . . by a growing awareness of God's calls upon him as an individual.[17]

These two models of the church existed side by side in Wesley's ecclesiology, and each played a part in the shaping of Methodism. Wesley's Methodist "societies" separated from the Church of England after his death, and the forces leading to such separation were partly set in motion during Wesley's lifetime.[18] Consequently, one could say that from the standpoint of ecclesiastical organization, Wesley's odyssey was generally from "church-type" to "sect-type." But in terms of spirituality and Christian nurture, both types were deeply and quite equally ingrained in Wesley throughout his entire life.[19]

When we turn to his view of *sacraments,* we find a similar dual model with regard to *one* of the sacraments but not in regard to the other. As for the Lord's Supper, we fail to find the kind of two-sidedness that characterizes his view of the church. His Eucharistic ideas were fairly unified, and little change can be seen in them over the course of his ministry. This is evident from the fact that in 1787 he published a sermon titled "The Duty of Constant Communion," which was almost identical to a version of the same sermon he had written 55 years earlier for his students when he was a fellow of Lincoln College. In a preface he stated: "I thank God, I have not yet seen cause to alter my sentiments in any point which is therein delivered."[20]

On the surface at least, this seems not to be the case with regard to baptism, particularly in its relationship to regeneration. Wesley worked with two different models in this doctrinal area.

---

17. Ibid., 137-38.

18. Frank Baker's book, quoted above, is an excellent examination of these forces leading to separation.

19. It should be remembered that Wesley insisted strongly that members of the Methodist societies depend on the Church of England for the sacraments and for the doctrinal interpretation thereof, and that they go there regularly for Holy Communion. He also insisted that Methodist preaching services be scheduled to avoid conflict with stated hours of worship in the Anglican churches.

20. *The Works of John Wesley,* 3rd ed., 14 vols. (London: Wesleyan Methodist Book Room, 1872. Reprint, Kansas City: Beacon Hill Press of Kansas City, 1978), 7:147 (hereafter cited as *Works*).

To some students of Wesley, this illustrates the difficulty he had reconciling his high churchmanship and his evangelical experience. Wesley advocated infant baptism, believing that Jesus instituted it as the New Testament successor to the Old Testament rite of circumcision. He believed that in some way objective grace was conferred upon a child in baptism. Along with this viewpoint, which Albert Outler calls Wesley's "mild allowance of the doctrine of baptismal regeneration,"[21] he also insisted that in adult experience another form of regeneration was possible quite apart from the sacramental rite. It has been widely assumed by Wesley scholars that he never completely reconciled these two views and continued to espouse both. The most succinct treatment of his view of baptismal regeneration is found in his *Treatise on Baptism*, while in his sermon on "The New Birth" the emphasis is on conversion as a conscious adult experience of regeneration. In discussing the two views, Outler says: "The point is that Wesley held to both ideas."[22]

But this is "the point" only if it means that Wesley held two different views concerning the *time* when regeneration may be experienced. He believed it was experienced by some in infancy, at the time of baptism, and by others in adult years. With some adults it may be at the time of baptism, but this is not *necessarily* so. His views may not be as self-contradictory as some scholars have assumed, and in chapter 6 we will examine these assumptions more closely. But whether or not Wesley was torn between two views of baptism as it relates to regeneration, there did exist a dilemma in his concept of the church. As noted above, he worked with two models, one emphasizing "spirit" and the other placing great importance on "structure." This broader ecclesiological dilemma was difficult for Wesley to resolve. Wherever it continues to exist, there remains a degree of uncertainty about the place of sacraments in the cultivation of spirituality.

In gathering up the strands of the discussion to this point, this much seems clear: In the theology and practice of Wesley, in that of the 19th-century holiness movement, and in that of present-day Wesleyan/holiness churches, some uncertainty ex-

21. Albert C. Outler, *John Wesley* (New York: Oxford University Press, 1964), 318.
22. Ibid.

ists in the proper way to strike a balance between the claims of "spirit" and those of "structure." How those claims are balanced will affect one's sacramental perspective. The dilemma can be understood even better if we examine the meaning and role of experience in Christian theology and life.

D. THE DANGER OF EXPERIENCE

In the above section it was noted that the present Wesleyan/holiness dilemma of "spirit" versus "structure" reflects a similar dilemma in Wesley's own understanding of church and sacraments. But its roots may be traced back even further. At the time of the Protestant Reformation of the 16th century, a similar polarity existed in the understanding of the nature of true Christianity.

It is a little misleading, however, to speak of *the* Protestant Reformation, because there were actually four Reformations, or four *wings* of the one Reformation. In continental Europe there were the Lutheran and the Reformed (Calvinist) wings. In England there was the Anglican wing. Both in England and on the Continent there was a fourth wing, variously named the "Anabaptist," "spiritualist," "sectarian," "radical," or "left" wing.

This fourth wing was not homogeneous or monolithic. Quakers, Mennonites, and Baptists are some of its modern descendants. It was a mixed bag, to say the least. Politically, there were, oddly enough, both pacifists and revolutionaries in this left-wing Reformation, and many of these groups had great differences with one another. But a common theme that ran through them all, and enables us to put them in a class together, is the emphasis on religious experience. This stress on experience provides an interesting parallel between three movements: (1) the left-wing Reformation, (2) the "sect-type" side of Wesley's understanding of the church, and (3) the "spirit above structure" side of the Wesleyan/holiness tradition.

It is not only in the Wesleyan/holiness churches that experience has been elevated to a place of high honor in recent years. In the 1970s, experience was a central theme in North American religion.[23] Following a decade of social activism in the

---

23. Cf. William Hordern, *Experience and Faith: The Significance of Luther for Under-*

60s, a chief concern in the 70s, in both the churches and the counterculture, was inner experience. In the churches it expressed itself in charismatic renewal, the popularity of "born again" religion, "possibility thinking" and other self-help gospels, and a turning away from social activism toward "spiritual formation" in the theological seminaries. Meanwhile, the counterculture embraced such things as Eastern mysticism, mind-expanding drugs, belief in reincarnation, and transcendental meditation as roads to deeper truth. Today the so-called New Age movement incorporates many of these themes. This is not to say that the trends in the church and those in the counterculture were consciously and intimately related. Rather, both are part of a wider trend in recent culture to place high priority on the development of the inner life.[24] One thesis of this book is that such an emphasis on subjective experience may result in a one-sided Christianity to which a proper sacramental theology may help to restore balance.

The current fascination with experience is not a new phenomenon. For the past two centuries theology has given much attention to the role of experience in religion. It was a central theme of 19th-century liberalism. Early in that century, German theologian Friedrich Schleiermacher, known as the "father of modern theology," taught that true religion is not an intellectual belief in doctrines but a matter of experience—"the feeling of absolute dependence." About a century later, Rudolf Otto found the basis of religion in the experience of the "numinous"—the sense of awe, wonder, and mystery by which we are overwhelmed in our most "religious" moments. Standing between Schleiermacher and Otto chronologically, Ludwig Feuerbach carried the emphasis on experience to its logical conclusion, claiming that if we start with human experience, we end up with nothing more than human experience. If, as Schleiermacher said, religion is rooted in the feelings, then, said Feuerbach, doctrines are but symptoms of felt needs. Theology is

---

standing *Today's Experiential Religion* (Minneapolis: Augsburg Publishing House, 1983), for an excellent analysis and critique of the recent and current interest in experience. The discussion in the present section is heavily indebted to Hordern's stimulating book.

24. Interesting, but outside the scope of the present study, is the fact that liturgical renewal was occurring in many mainline churches during this same time.

therefore nothing but anthropology. God is merely a projection of our own humanity onto a heavenly screen. To talk of God is merely to talk about our own wishes and ideals.

Karl Barth, early in this century, pointed out that if one attempts to gain a knowledge of God through subjective experience, he is always vulnerable to Feuerbach's criticism. Barth called for a return to the more "objective" emphases of the Reformation, particularly its Lutheran and Reformed wings. It would be instructive, then, to consider Luther's perspective on experience as it contrasted with that of the Anabaptist, or radical, wing of the Reformation.

The majority of Reformation studies have concentrated on Luther's debates with the Roman Catholic and the Reformed (Calvinist) traditions as being the forums in which his own views took shape. But to a great extent his theological position took shape as he debated against the views of the Anabaptists.[25] This is particularly true with respect to Luther's stance on religious experience.

In a real sense, the Reformation was born in Luther's experience. Searching diligently for a "gracious God," and seeking to find inner peace and forgiveness, he confessed his sins to a confessor several times a day. But he failed to find peace. He finally saw that his search for salvation was itself an expression of self-centeredness. He saw that he was *incurvatum in se* ("curved in upon self"), and that every human effort at self-salvation only intensified his sin.

He finally discovered through Hab. 2:4 and Rom. 1:17 ("The righteous will live by faith") that the gospel is the Good News. This was religious *experience,* but it was experience turned away from itself to God. Luther saw that our peace is based, not on anything we can do, but on what God has done for us in Jesus Christ. It was personal experience—but experience of an *objective* reality outside the self.

In one sense, therefore, Luther had set the authority of his own experience over against that of the medieval Catholic church. Salvation was "by grace alone," or "by faith alone," or

---

25. Cf. the work of the Canadian Mennonite scholar, Harry Loewen, in *Luther and the Radicals* (Waterloo, Ont.: Wilfrid Laurier University Press, 1974).

"by Christ alone," or through "Scripture alone." For Luther these were not contradictory; he was saying the same thing in four different ways, each highlighting a different facet of the gospel. In this context, his doctrine of the "priesthood of all believers" seemed to encourage each person to find in himself or herself the reality that could not be granted by pope, councils, priests, or sacraments.

The Anabaptist, or "radical," Reformers agreed with this aspect of Luther's thought and made it their main emphasis. But Luther soon concluded that they had taken it too far. As a result he ended up doing battle on two fronts—against Roman Catholicism and against the left-wing Reformers. As for the latter, the battle was waged over a number of issues, including the nature of the Church, the understanding of scriptural authority, the work of the Holy Spirit, and the meaning of the sacraments. The last of these is our interest here, and the difference between Luther and the Anabaptists is graphically epitomized in their respective views on baptism.

The term Anabaptists (or "rebaptizers," who insisted on baptizing again as adults those who, under the Roman Catholic system, had been baptized as infants) can be misleading, giving the impression that water baptism was of utmost importance to them. In reality, their faith was not of the sacramental kind. The important thing to them was not the baptism of water but the baptism of the Holy Spirit.[26] This meant that before one could be baptized by water, there had to be evidence of sanctification.[27]

> When a person had been baptized by the Holy Spirit, it was also a good thing to be baptized by water, for Jesus commanded his followers to do so. But its purpose was not to bring salvation—the baptism of the Spirit already had brought that; its purpose was rather as a public witness to what God had done and could do for others.[28]

In his opposition to Roman Catholic sacramental doctrine,

---

26. The term *baptism of the Holy Spirit* did not carry the connotations of a second work of grace that it came to have in the American holiness movement.

27. Like Spirit baptism, sanctification did not refer to a second work of grace but to the ongoing life of obedience to Christ that should follow one's conversion.

28. Hordern, 57.

Luther himself could even declare that faith is sufficient for salvation even without the sacraments, especially baptism. If we can be baptized, we should be, he insisted, but if baptism is not available, we can still be saved if we believe the gospel. For Luther, faith must accompany the sacraments, and it is the faith, rather than the outward sign, that saves. The Anabaptists seized this teaching of Luther and emphasized it to the point of despising the outward sign of the sacrament. As Paul Althaus says, "They took everything they had learned from Luther about the fact that faith alone saves and used it to devaluate the sacraments."[29]

There are obvious parallels between the teachings of the left-wing Reformers and certain themes in recent American religion. Good examples are the concept of Spirit baptism in the charismatic revival and doubts about infant baptism by many persons in denominations that have traditionally practiced it. As Hordern says,

> The radical reformers who identified the kingdom with the inner experience naturally argued that outward or objective things cannot be of decisive importance. The important thing is what happens in the heart, for salvation is an inward process, initiated by God through the divine Word and through the Christ who dwells within. Thus, the Bible, water baptism, eating bread and wine at the Lord's Supper, the church as an institution and liturgical actions, all being external things, are not of decisive importance.[30]

In the face of the Anabaptist challenge, Luther was forced to define and refine his understanding of experience. He did so by clarifying two major concepts that became fundamental aspects of his theology. First, he insisted on the final authority of Scripture (sola scriptura). All religious experience is to be tested by the Bible. In this, John Wesley was to agree. Although Wesley placed much importance on experience as a confirming source for theology, it was never the primary source. Since experience is variable from person to person, no experience can be made normative for theology. Instead, "The Scriptures are the touchstone

---

29. Paul Althaus, The Theology of Martin Luther, trans. Robert C. Schultz (Philadelphia: Fortress Press, 1966), 350.
30. Hordern, 58-59.

whereby Christians examine all, real or supposed, revelations."[31] Colin Williams states that for Wesley "experience is the appropriation of authority, not the source of authority."[32] For Luther (and for Wesley as well), the Holy Spirit will never reveal to us anything that is contrary to Scripture. Important as personal religious experience was, it could not be the decisive matter, but must always be tested by an authority outside oneself, namely, the Scriptures.[33]

The necessity for this lies in the second of the concepts by which Luther clarified his understanding of experience—the doctrine of original sin or total depravity. If our depravity is total in the sense that *every aspect* of life has been affected by sin (which is what total depravity means), then our self-understanding is faulty. Any interpretation we make of our own religious experience is less than completely reliable. Although forgiven and cleansed, the believer carries scars from sin that are not completely erased this side of the final resurrection. Consequently there is always the danger that we will interpret our inner experiences from a perspective of self-interest. Self-deception is a danger that continually lurks at the heart's door of a fallen but redeemed human being.

Luther came to see that we cannot have an assurance of salvation from looking at ourselves and our works, but only by looking at God's work for us. He saw in the Anabaptist emphasis on personal experience a new form of salvation by works. As he saw it, the person who finds the basis of salvation in inward experience, or feelings, or a consciousness of the Spirit's presence in the heart, is as much engaged in finding salvation within the self as the person who performs outward works in order to earn salvation. It is another way of putting the self, instead of God, at the center.

The danger Luther saw in the left-wing Reformers' position is the same danger to which the Wesleyan/holiness tradition has

---

31. *The Letters of the Rev. John Wesley, A.M.*, ed. John Telford, 8 vols. (London: Epworth Press, 1931), 7:298 (hereafter cited as *Letters*).

32. Colin Williams, *John Wesley's Theology Today* (New York: Abingdon Press, 1960), 33.

33. Neither Luther nor Wesley advocated some kind of literal proof-texting but understood that Scripture must be interpreted in its context. This context ultimately stretches out to include the whole of Scripture. Cf. Hordern, 64.

been susceptible, whenever that tradition has leaned too far in the direction of becoming a "theology of experience." Although experience is certainly one valid aspect of the tradition, it needs to be kept in check. John Wesley saw the danger of a one-sided emphasis on the "religion of the heart" even as he strongly insisted that it was *one* valid component of a vital faith. In his sermon titled "Salvation by Faith," he gives his classic definition of faith: "[Faith] is not barely a speculative, rational thing, a cold, lifeless assent, a train of ideas in the head; but also a disposition of the heart."[34]

Joseph Butler, bishop of Bristol, who wrote *The Analogy of Religion,* was a great philosophical defender of orthodoxy in Wesley's day. To Wesley's understanding of faith as an inward disposition of the heart (which he based on the Anglican Homily on Salvation), and his belief in the inward witness of the Holy Spirit, Butler protests: "Sir, the pretending to extraordinary revelations and gifts of the Holy Ghost is a horrid thing —a very horrid thing!"[35] In effect, Butler held that true faith is *not* a disposition of the heart, but a speculative, rational thing, a train of ideas in the head. Wesley's definition takes not an either/or but a both/and position. Faith is *"not barely . . . a train of ideas in the head; but also a disposition of the heart."*[36] For Wesley, the *balance* was the important thing. Both head and heart were involved in faith. In the above sermon, he opposed an overemphasis on the head. At other times he just as strongly urged against the "enthusiasm"[37] of those who ignored the head in the interest of the heart. For Wesley, this was the danger to which a theology of experience could lead unless kept in careful balance.

The danger of experience, then, is the danger of *subjectivity,* which is not altogether unlike being "curved in upon oneself," which was Luther's understanding of sin. Wesley also viewed sin in this manner. He said: "Man was created looking directly to God, as his last end; but, falling into sin, he fell off from God,

---

34. *Works* 5:9.
35. *Journal* 2:257.
36. *Works* 5:9, italics mine.
37. In the 18th century, "enthusiasm" meant essentially what today we mean by fanaticism, emotionalism, etc.

and *turned into himself.*[38] This is why a vital sacramental theology is important. Sacraments underscore the *objectivity* of our faith—what God has done for us prior to and apart from our own doings. "This is my body, which is broken *for you*" (1 Cor. 11:24, KJV, italics mine). "Don't you know that all of us who were baptized into Christ Jesus were baptized into *his death?*" (Rom. 6:3, italics mine).

But the sacraments, which can ignite and fuel this faith in what God has done for us, are not mere outward forms that are cold, lifeless, speculative, rational, dispassionate, and nonexperiential. On the contrary, they are alive and teeming with *imagination.* We will give that idea some thought in the next chapter.

---

38. *Works* 9:456, italics mine.

Chapter Two

THEOLOGY AND IMAGINATION

NOTE: This chapter is basically an essay in theological method. It is therefore foundational to the theology of sacraments expressed throughout the book. However, the remainder of the book can be assimilated apart from this background material. Therefore, those readers with no special interest in methodology may wish to move on to chapter 3.

* * *

When Paul says we are buried with Christ through baptism into death, how are we to understand his assertion? When Jesus says of bread, "This is my body," and of wine in a cup, "This cup is the new covenant in my blood" (1 Cor. 11:24, 25), how are we to interpret such strange statements? When He tells us to eat and drink "in remembrance" of Him (v. 24), what kind of mental recall is it that requires a bite of bread and a sip from a cup? Why can't we simply remember in our heads without this strange business of consuming portions of food and drink so tiny as to provide practically no physical nourishment at all? Answers to such questions are what a sacramental theology is all about.

A. LOGOS AND MYTHOS

In the ancient Greek mind, two modes of thinking functioned side by side—*logos* ("reason") and *mythos* ("myth"). Unfortunately, we moderns have a tendency to set the two against

41

each other as opposites, but in Hellenic culture they were not perceived as antithetic modes of thought. When we reflect on the way we moderns think, we can see that the Hellenic perception was correct. We think in both modes, sometimes moving quickly from one to the other, mixing the two in our discourses and our dialogues. Practically all activities of the thinking mind sooner or later involve both *logos* and *mythos*.

Logos, for the Greeks, meant "reason." It could also mean "word," not as a grammatical form, but the thought lying behind the word, or the content that is conveyed when the word is spoken or written. *Logos*, or reason, includes all that can be stated in rational or propositional terms. It refers to "objective" truth that appears the same to all rational minds. For example, the simple formula "2 + 2 = 4" is true in every culture, in every country, on every continent, and presumably on every planet, as well as in heaven (2 angels plus 2 angels equals 4 angels!). The other kind of thinking, namely *mythos*, concerns the imagination. This mode of thought cannot be subject to verification but contains its truth in itself. Its truth lies in its powers of persuasion that arise out of its own beauty.

Both *logos* and *mythos* were highly developed in ancient Greek culture. It is astonishing that the civilization often considered to be the most rational in history (a civilization that could produce an Archimedes and an Aristotle) was the selfsame civilization that believed in, and may even have invented, the most imaginative fables.[1]

Even the philosopher Plato, as "rationalistic" as anyone, was an accomplished mythmaker. For example, in *The Symposium* he constructs the myth of Androgyny, in which human beings were first created in a spherical form, with two heads, four arms, and four legs. This enabled them to see in all directions at once and, catlike, to land on two feet if they should slip or stumble. Because they were exceedingly strong, their creator decided to make them weaker; for this purpose he split them into two halves. This split was the origin of the sexes; one half was male, the other female. Ever since, the two halves, sensing their in-

---

1. Pierre Grimal, ed., *Larousse World Mythology* (London: Hamlyn Publishing House, 1973), 97.

completeness, have been trying to get back together, to regain their lost wholeness. This was Plato's way of describing the meaning of love *(eros)*. Is it true? Of course not, in any literal sense. And certainly from a biblical viewpoint, it is unacceptable, for in the Bible sexuality is part of the created order as God made it, not a result of some divinely ordained split. A partial "truth" comes through Plato's story, nevertheless, namely the truth of Gen. 2:18, that "it is not good for the man to be alone." It is one way of describing, in mythical language, the attraction of male and female for each other. This is just one example of *mythos* in Greek culture.

Consider the great Hellenic epic myths. How much poorer would Western civilization be without the *Iliad* and the *Odyssey?* These great epic poems are the products of the human imagination, particularly the imagination of the ancient wandering Greek minstrel, Homer (or whoever wrote the poems that have been ascribed to him). Without imagination, such literary treasures would not exist. It would be useless to ask whether the Greeks actually believed such mythological tales to be true. It would be as pointless as to ask if Michelangelo's sculpture of David in Florence is a true representation of the young shepherd preparing to fight Goliath, or if his sculpture of Moses in Rome is a true image of Israel's great lawgiver. Such questions would be meaningless. Michelangelo's David and Moses are beautiful, and such ingeniously creative works of the imagination have induced in many a contemplative soul a sense of the meaning of perfection, a sort of intuition of the divine. Both reason and imagination were part and parcel of ancient Greek culture. Both were ways of "knowing."

A similar observation can be made regarding the Hebrews. The Hebrew word *dabar,* translated as *logos* in the Septuagint, refers to the content of revelation, that is, to the thought or idea lying behind spoken or written words. Although "knowledge" to the Hebrews was not something abstract, rational, and intellectual as it was to the Greeks, they did believe in the objectivity of "truth," of "word," of "Torah." They had commandments that embodied this truth—propositional, rational statements that communicated to persons through "the hearing of the ear." To be sure, knowledge was not coldly intellectual and abstract but intensely and intimately personal (sexual intercourse was described as "knowing" one's wife!), but they knew how to conceptualize and verbalize and convey meanings by the use of *words.* In some of their great thinkers, such as Philo of Alexandria, a contemporary of Jesus, the concept of *logos* was very similar to the Greek understanding. If Philo was philosophically closer to Plato than were most of his Jewish predecessors (or successors for that matter), it would nevertheless be a mistake to assume that the Hebrews were strangers to rational thinking, even if their kind of "reasoning" was different from that of the Greeks.

But, just as with the Greeks, there was another mode of thought common among the Hebrews, which involved imagination more than reason. We may justifiably refrain from calling it "myth," because the Hebrews were radically monotheistic, and monotheism was not fertile soil for mythology.[2] Furthermore, in recent times *myth* is a controversial word, used in different senses by different writers, and it "conveys discordant overtones suggesting unreality to many people."[3] Still, in the cultures that created them, myths were not considered falsehoods but attempts to explain the transcendent in terms of the earthly, the other-worldly in terms of the this-worldly. Such "explanations" were to be taken seriously but not literally. At any rate, although the term *myth* might be misleading when discussing Hebrew thought, the Hebrew people could exhibit great descriptive powers and speak of God in ways that were not to be taken literally but seriously. In Hebrew culture, imagination was everywhere. Although the second of their Ten Commandments prohibited the making of "any graven image" of the Deity (Exod. 20:4, KJV), lest they become idolaters by worshiping the image instead of God himself, they used pictorial language about God that oozed with imagination: God was a Rock, a Fortress, a Shield, a Light, a Shepherd. He had eyes and ears and a face and a right arm and even "back parts" (Exod. 33:23, KJV).

---

2. Cf. One meaning of *mythos* is "stories of the gods." Cf. G. Stählin, "Mythos," in *Theological Dictionary of the New Testament,* ed. Gerhard Kittel, trans. Geoffrey Bromiley (Grand Rapids: Wm. B. Eerdmans Publishing Co., 1967), 4:782. This is the meaning adopted by Paul Tillich in *Dynamics of Faith* (New York: Harper and Brothers, 1957), 48 (hereafter cited as *DF*).

3. Dunning, 120 n. 49.

Such anthropomorphisms did not bother them in the least. They knew God was Spirit and therefore infinitely greater than all created beings, but they also knew that such concrete expressions could communicate divine truth more effectively than the most profound abstractions.

Consider the example of God's call to Jeremiah:

> "*See,* today I appoint you over nations and kingdoms to uproot and tear down, to destroy and overthrow, to build and to plant."
> The word of the Lord came to me: "What do you *see,* Jeremiah?"
> "I *see* the branch of an almond tree," I replied.
> The Lord said to me, "You have *seen* correctly, for I am *watching* to *see* that my word is fulfilled."
> (Jer. 1:10-12, italics mine)[4]

Of course, the Hebrews understood that God communicated with human beings by His "Word." "Hear, O Israel!" "Thus *saith* the Lord." But the prophets who proclaimed that Word were also called "seers," persons with in*sight* who could fore*see.* Both modes of thought existed side by side.

Today, the distinction is often referred to as "left brain" and "right brain" activity. Recent physiological research has suggested that the different modes of thinking are based in different sides of the brain. That which we call *logos* is mainly an activity of the left side of the brain, and *mythos* emanates predominantly from the right side. Although some persons are more proficient in one type of thinking than the other, we all engage in both "left brain" and "right brain" modes of thinking.

Both in the Bible and in the historic Christian tradition, truth is communicated to human beings in two ways. On one hand, truth is contained in "left brain" rational statements, laws, commands, propositions, and creeds: "In the beginning God created" (Gen. 1:1). "Thou shalt not bear false witness" (Exod. 20:16, KJV). "Choose you this day whom ye will serve" (Josh. 24:15, KJV). "Jesus was born in Bethlehem in Judea" (Matt. 2:1).

---

4. There is a play upon words here. The Hebrew word for *watching* sounds like the Hebrew for *almond tree*—perhaps because, in the springtime, the almond was the first tree to awake from its winter sleep.

"I believe in God the Father Almighty, Maker of heaven and earth" (Apostles' Creed). "Very God of Very God, begotten, not made; being of one substance with the Father" (Nicene Creed).

But these constitute just one of the forms in which truth is received. The divine word of address comes to us also in other forms. One of these is the "right brain" imaginative story that requires us not only to *hear* something but also to "*see* something" as we listen. Such stories were a staple of Jesus' teaching method. We call such stories parables. Even the blind person can "see" when he or she hears the parables. Such stories deal not merely in abstractions but in concrete, picturesque, living scenes from human existence that our earthly experience enables us to recognize: "A sower went forth to sow" (Matt. 13:3, KJV). "A certain man had two sons" (Luke 15:11, KJV). "A woman has ten silver coins and loses one" (v. 8). "A certain man went down from Jerusalem to Jericho, and fell among thieves" (10:30, KJV).

Besides the parables, there are the miracles of Jesus, reported in vivid language by the Gospel writers: "Jesus then took the loaves, gave thanks, and distributed to those who were seated" (John 6:11). "He touched her hand and the fever left her" (Matt. 8:15). "Then he touched their eyes" (9:29). "He spit and touched the man's tongue" (Mark 7:33). "About the fourth watch of the night he went out to them, walking on the lake" (6:48). "He got up and rebuked the winds and the waves, and it was completely calm" (Matt. 8:26).

And besides parables and miracles there are happenings in the lives of Jesus and His disciples that are decidedly more ordinary than miracles, but vividly rich with meaning nevertheless: "After fasting forty days and forty nights, he was hungry" (Matt. 4:2). "When they landed, they saw a fire of burning coals there with fish on it, and some bread" (John 21:9). "When he was at the table with them, he took bread, gave thanks, broke it and began to give it to them. Then their eyes were opened" (Luke 24:30-31). Such accounts may be told to us *audibly*, but as we hear them, our imagination gives birth to *visible* images that involve the senses of sight, and smell, and touch, and taste—not merely sound alone. The truths heard and comprehended by our left brain are colored by our right brain in vivid patterns. As hearers, we become seers.

Parables. Miracles. Happenings. And this also: "Jesus came
. . . to the Jordan to be baptized" (Matt. 3:13). "While they were
eating, Jesus took bread, gave thanks and broke it, and gave it to
his disciples" (26:26). "Go and make disciples of all nations,
baptizing them" (28:19). "Whenever you eat this bread and
drink this cup, you proclaim the Lord's death until he comes" (1
Cor. 11:26). Water . . . bread . . . wine. Touch, taste, smell, and
see! "Visible words!" Sacraments! But more about that later.

B. ELEMENTS OF THEOLOGICAL THINKING

What we are saying in all this is that both reason (logos) and
imagination (mythos) have a place in religious faith. In fact, those
three—reason, imagination, and faith—are basic elements in all
theological thinking. Each is involved in the act of knowing.
"The conceptualizing act of the reason, the creative construction
of the imagination, and the assurance of faith are all indispensable for the living of a full human life and the apprehension of
truth."[5] Reason is dominant in science, imagination in the arts
and industry, and in religion faith is central. But in every form of
human activity they are all involved.

Pure science is largely rational; it is a matter of logic and the
ratio of ideas. And yet "pure" science seldom comes about simply by reason alone. The great scientists have great imaginations
—the ability of the seer to visualize the various possibilities to
which scientific investigation may lead. Writing about science,
Albert Einstein said: "Imagination is more important than
knowledge."[6] As a pure scientist, he could understand the formula $E=MC^2$, which was the theoretical basis of the atomic
bomb, but he could also foresee the devastation the bomb made
possible. Pure science thus merges into technology, which is the
use the imagination makes of reason in constructing mech-
anisms and processes by which the results of the purely theoretical may be put to use in the actual world.

In the fine arts "pure" imagination seems to be dominant,

5. Hugh Vernon White, Truth and the Person in Christian Theology (New York: Oxford University Press, 1963), 28.
6. Quoted in Burton Stevenson, ed., The Home Book of Quotations, 5th ed. (New
York: Dodd, Mead, and Co., 1947), 961, no. 12.

but the artist must have brushes, canvases, paints, sounds, musical instruments, tablets, pen, stone, or chisel. These are the products of technology (i.e., of applied science). There is also a *philosophy* of art, called *aesthetics*, and its very existence demonstrates that even art does not thrive in the realm of imagination alone totally apart from reason.

Each of the three fields—science, art, and religion—incorporate all of the three elements: reason, imagination, and faith. As for faith, it may be almost wholly implicit in the work of the scientist, but it is there nevertheless. The scientist believes the universe has some kind of order, which gives meaning to scientific exploration and experiment. It is this faith in the orderliness of nature, and in some degree of predictability, that makes science possible. Likewise in art, faith may seem only implicit, but the artist has faith in something—perhaps in the beauty or meaning that he or she wishes to express through music, painting, drama, or literature. Even if, instead of beauty and meaning, only ugliness and chaos are perceived, the artist believes that these conform to reality. It should be clear that when we speak of the faith that is involved in science and art, we are using the word *faith* in a general (one might say, secular) sense, and not in a specifically Christian, or even theistic, sense. But when we consider the field of religion, it is necessary to keep in mind the more specific sense of the word. In the religious person as he or she engages in the act of worship, *faith* seems dominant and the *rational* structure of thought may appear to be obscured. Nevertheless, reason is present; otherwise worship is nonsense, a mere mumbo jumbo. And *imagination*, which is present in the activity of the scientist and the artist, is abundantly present in religion. It is the latter, the place of imagination in religious worship, that is the concern of this chapter.[7]

And now, in theological thinking, these three abide: *reason, faith,* and *imagination*—but the greatest of these is imagination! This claim may, at first glance, seem grossly irreligious. Shouldn't the priority be given to faith? Or it may seem grossly irrational. Shouldn't the priority be given to reason? The cate-

---

7. For my understanding of the place of imagination in theology, I am largely indebted to my former teacher, Hugh Vernon White. Cf. his *Truth and the Person,* chap. 3.

gory under discussion here is the way we do theology and the way the human being is grasped by divine revelation, even before faith is exercised or reason is convinced. From that perspective, imagination is fundamental and prior. We may even say that imagination is the window through which the light of reason is first glimpsed and the warmth of faith is received. With that in mind, we can more precisely define each of the three elements of theological thinking and the part they play in theological work.

a. Reason. In the 17th century (in thinkers such as Descartes, Spinoza, and Leibniz), and in much of modern thought since then, reason has been considered to be an objective and fixed structure. This is what we mean when we speak of *rationalism*. By examining the inner structure of reason (or the mind), one could come to a knowledge of all reality, including God. Such rationalism has proven inadequate, and in most 20th-century theological thinking the claims of reason are much more modest. Reason is simply "reasoning," which connotes ordered and coherent thought. The interpretation of data and the structuring of ideas are functions of reason. Reason is logical thinking, but logic essentially means "order," and thus logical thinking is orderly thinking. For theology, therefore, reason means orderly, systematic, and critical thinking. By the use of reason, theology is able to explicate the content of religious faith and express it "in the clearest and most coherent language available."[8] Such explication and expression is the task and goal of theology.

b. Faith. Theology is the rational or systematic interpretation and expression of a religious *faith*. But what is faith? On a popular psychological level it means a hopeful, positive attitude. That alone would make it little more than sentimentalism. An attitude toward what? Faith must have an object. A person's religious faith is usually connected, at least loosely, to some religious tradition. Faith is thus belief—belief in the claims and creeds of the given tradition. But faith is more than belief. It is also trust, and in *Christian* faith such trust "lives and moves and has its being" in what Buber called the "I-Thou" relationship.

---

8. John Macquarrie, *Principles of Christian Theology*, 2nd ed. (New York: Charles Scribner's Sons, 1977), 1.

Thus at its highest level faith includes a cognitive element; faith is a way of "knowing," an apprehension of reality by a personal being. Theology is but "the elaboration of a rational structure of meanings derived from the primary act of faith."[9]

c. Imagination. "The primary act of the thinking mind is imagination; in it are both reason and faith, i.e. order and a sense of reality."[10] Imagination is not daydreaming nor the irresponsible play of fancy. It is the serious and responsible way the thinking person consciously deals with the real world. Of course, it is possible for imagination to become pathological, and in such cases a completely unreal world may be imagined. But in its normal functioning, imagination is the person's most pristine way of thinking and of dealing with that portion of reality that is not immediately present in experience. The greater part of any person's "world" is not present in time and space. For example, my parents are no longer living; my children have "left the nest" and are making homes of their own; I live many miles from where I was born; and several decades separate me from the scenes of my childhood. It is imagination that enables me to make all those times and places "present" and hold them together, along with myriads of other times and places (including times that are still yet to come and places where I have never been), in a unified "world." The making present of that world is accomplished first in pictorial form, or, in a word, mythologically. Then as abstract reason works with this same material, the details are filled in, and a more orderly world is conceptualized.

In considering the place of imagination in theology, we must not be misled. There is certainly a symbiotic relationship between the human imagination in general and the Christian imagination in particular, but the latter must be kept under the control of divine revelation. Therefore between the imagination that produced Homer's *Iliad* or Plato's "Androgyny" on the one hand and the Old Testament narratives and New Testament parables and miracle stories on the other, there is a difference. We assume God's revelation in history and a doctrine of biblical inspiration that prevents the Christian imagination from run-

---

9. Hugh Vernon White, 32.
10. Ibid.

ning wild. Liturgy, worship, and sacraments must express the consensus of the historic Christian tradition. The latter establishes a boundary beyond which imagination and story must not be allowed to go. Nevertheless it is the human imagination that God uses in revealing himself to human beings. The human imagination, darkened by sin (Rom. 1:21), can be redeemed and sanctified by grace, and what God uses we must not despise.

However, neither the world as construed by imagination nor that constructed by reason is ever complete. Neither can encompass the whole of reality. At best, both reason and imagination can only hint at the nature of reality in general and of Ultimate Reality in particular. Therefore both imagination and reason (myth and metaphysics) are *symbolic* representations of reality. Although such representations are only partial and incomplete, this does not mean that they are *false* representations. The issue is the adequacy and appropriateness of the symbolism. But if imagination has the kind of priority we have been claiming for it, then symbolism is of crucial importance in understanding and proclaiming the gospel.

C. RELIGIOUS SYMBOLISM

Sacramental theology draws deeply from the well of symbolism; therefore any treatment of sacraments must necessarily say something about the meaning and nature of symbols. The word *symbol*[11] refers to an object or pattern that is used to represent an invisible metaphysical reality and that also participates in the reality it represents. Symbols are conceived by vision or intuition and not by means of rational thinking. Theology finds symbolic thinking to be essential. Of necessity theology, like philosophy, deals heavily in abstract rational concepts. But it often finds conceptions in symbolic or "imaginal" form to be more adequate for the expression of its true meaning. This is especially true of *Christian* theology, whose basic symbols are taken from history and from the person and work of Jesus Christ. When our Lord took a piece of bread and a cup and said, "This is my body. . . . This is my blood," He was creating a sym-

---

11. Derived from the Greek *symbolon*, which meant a sign or token by which a thing is inferred, which in turn is derived from *symballein*, "to throw together."

bol. He was also using, and inviting us to use, the divinely given gift of imagination without which all such symbolism is meaningless.

Augustine referred to sacraments as "visible words." This is without doubt the shortest, and possibly the best, description of sacraments ever given. More will need to be said about it later. But here it can be observed that the term *visible words* joins together the two modes of thought we discussed at the beginning of this chapter, *logos* and *mythos* (or reason and imagination). Sacraments are *words*, but they are not merely spoken words to be heard. They are words that are *seen*. They are words that can be tasted, touched, and smelled. They are visible words that can be "heard" even as water and wine are poured and as bread is broken. They are words that "speak" to all the senses.

This highlights the meaning of religious symbolism. Biblical as well as other religious literature uses seeing, feeling, and tasting almost as often as hearing in describing the experience of the Divine Presence.[12] It is not only through the ear that we are to hear the divine address. *"Taste* and *see* that the Lord is good," urges the Psalmist (34:8, italics mine). It was only when Job's faith reached the level of *seeing* that he was reconciled to the ways of God. "My ears had heard of you but now my eyes have seen you" (42:5). Isaiah heard the Lord say, "This has *touched* your lips; your guilt is taken away and your sin atoned for" (6:7, italics mine). It was by His *touch* that Jesus did most of His healing.

As we looked at two different modes of thought common in ancient Greek culture, we also pointed out that Hebrew culture likewise had two ways of thinking. By the time we come to the Christian concept of *Logos*, which early Christianity borrowed from Greek philosophy and reinterpreted, it can be seen that the line of demarcation between the two modes has largely disappeared. The New Testament reinterpretation of the Greek philosophical term has widened the concept of *Logos*, so that in Christian theology it is now broad enough to include what we have called the mode of imagination. "Reason" and "Imagination" therefore can both be subsumed under the rubric of *Logos*.

---

12. Paul Tillich, *Systematic Theology*, 3 vols. (Chicago: University of Chicago Press, 1951-63), 1:123 (hereafter cited as *ST*).

We can see how this is true when we note that in Christian theology, *Logos* or "Word" stands for the whole of God's revealing activity. The divine revelation does not occur solely in the form of spoken or written words, or of rational propositions. It also happens by way of events, visions, ceremonial rites, and supremely in the Christ event. At the climax of God's revealing activity, "The Word became *flesh*" (John 1:14, italics mine). "The Christian doctrine of the Incarnation of the Logos includes the paradox that the Word has become an object of vision and touch."[13] "That which was from the beginning, which we have heard, which we have seen with our eyes, which we have looked at and our hands have touched—this we proclaim concerning the Word of life" (1 John 1:1). "Incarnation" is the strongest argument for "sacrament." Jesus Christ is the supreme "Visible Word." And in the Church's understanding of sacraments, the bread that is His body and the wine that is His blood are "visible words" proclaiming Jesus Christ.

John Wesley defined a sacrament as "an outward sign of inward grace, and a means whereby we receive the same."[14] H. Ray Dunning suggests that "perhaps what Wesley meant by signs might be more appropriately conveyed by the concept of symbol, as proposed by Paul Tillich."[15] This is a helpful suggestion as long as we understand that the "sign" is not merely the physical element (water, bread, wine) of the sacrament, but the entire action surrounding its proper use. Dunning considers Tillich's idea of symbol to be "perhaps the most adequate proposal in contemporary theology for an understanding of religious language."[16] Let us pursue this idea by taking a brief look at Tillich's concept of symbol.

For Tillich, symbols have several characteristics.[17] First, they point beyond themselves to something else. In this respect, symbols are like signs. But there is a difference between symbols and signs. The second characteristic of a symbol is that it participates in that to which it points. "While the sign bears no neces-

---

13. Ibid.
14. *Works* 5:188.
15. Dunning, 543.
16. Ibid., 121.
17. Cf. Tillich, *DF,* 41-43.

sary relation to that to which it points, the symbol participates in the reality of that for which it stands."[18] A fever may be a *sign* that I should see a physician. Pottery fragments found in an archaeological dig are a *sign* of human habitation. A red face may be a *sign* of anger. "Wars and rumors of wars" are *signs* of the times (Matt. 24:6; Mark 13:7). But a nation's flag is more than a sign; it is a *symbol.* The flag is not the same thing as the nation, but it shares in the reality of that nation. In other words, it cannot be said that the flag is something separate from the nation that it symbolizes. We acknowledge this when we pledge allegiance to the flag. To pledge allegiance to the symbol is to pledge allegiance to the thing symbolized. Conversely, at least in the minds of many citizens, to desecrate the flag is to show disrespect to the nation.[19] Symbolism is a kind of shorthand. Although not identical with the real thing as a whole, it participates in the reality of that real thing to which it points.

Another characteristic of a symbol is that it opens up levels of reality otherwise closed to us. "A picture and a poem reveal elements of reality which cannot be approached scientifically."[20] Further, a symbol "unlocks dimensions and elements of our soul which correspond to the dimensions and levels of reality."[21] A great play or a symphony uses symbols to unveil new dimensions in each of us. Finally, symbols cannot be produced intentionally or invented. "Like living beings, they grow and they die. They grow when the situation is ripe for them and they die when the situation changes."[22] This underscores another difference between symbols and signs.

> The sign can be changed arbitrarily according to the demands of expediency, but the symbol grows and dies according to the correlation between that which is symbolized and the persons who receive it as a symbol. Therefore, the symbol which points to the divine, can be a true symbol only if it participates in the power of the divine to which it points.[23]

---

18. Tillich, *ST* 1:239.
19. At the time of this writing, the United States Supreme Court and some members of Congress are in sharp disagreement over this issue.
20. Tillich, *DF,* 42.
21. Ibid.
22. Ibid., 43.
23. Tillich, *ST* 1:239.

Although Tillich has done much to clarify the meaning of symbol for 20th-century theology, it would be a mistake to assume that such an understanding was unknown previously. Actually Tillich has merely recovered the meaning of symbol as it was understood in most of Christian history until modern times. Paul M. Bassett points out that the Early Church did not believe, as most moderns commonly do, that although

> a symbol stands for or represents something, [it] is itself an abstraction from the thing symbolized. In the early Church, in fact in much of the Graeco-Roman world, a symbol was not an abstraction at all but was a way into the very essence of a thing or an event or an idea. The symbol participated, as it were, in the character of the thing or event or idea as authentically as the thing or event or idea itself did.[24]

Bassett says the Reformed tradition also understood *symbol* in this classical sense—"not as an abstraction from reality but as a window into reality that participates in the reality itself."[25]

The philosophical basis of such a view is what is known as the *analogia entis* ("the analogy of being"), which is the assumption that there is a relationship between the infinite and the finite, or between God and human being. In the light of this, Dunning's suggestion that what Wesley meant by "sign" is nearer to what Tillich means by "symbol" appears to have validity, even though Tillich's term is loaded with more complex philosophical freight than Wesley's. In discussing Wesley's view of sacraments, Ole E. Borgen says:

> Following traditional conceptions, Wesley maintains that God in his wisdom did not pick the material elements at random. No, the natural qualities of the significative elements reveal a definite parallelism or analogical relationship with the thing signified. The cleansing and purifying qualities of water, the matter of Baptism, symbolize analogically the inward washing of the Holy Spirit. . . . Likewise, as bread and wine nourish our bodies, so the partakers of the Lord's Supper will be fed with the Body and Blood of Christ. As the

---

24. Paul M. Bassett and William M. Greathouse, *The Historical Development*, vol. 2 of *Exploring Christian Holiness* (Kansas City: Beacon Hill Press of Kansas City, 1985), 36.
25. Ibid., 182, n. 68.

grain is cut down, bruised and baked with fire, so was Christ
bruised, and suffered agony and pain for us.[26]

One can see here a kind of *analogia entis* in Wesley's view of
sacraments. The material elements (water, bread, wine) have an
analogical relation to the objective reality that they signify.

Not only are symbols different from signs (if we accept Tillich's distinction), but they are also to be distinguished from *signals*. "Symbolism, as that language of the mind which expresses
what is beyond rational recognition, serves to distinguish the
human from the animal world. Animals react to signals, not
symbols."[27] Humans also react to signals, but such reactions
serve to demonstrate our kinship with the animals rather than
our difference from them. It is symbols that demonstrate the difference. Only human being has created "a symbolic universe of
which language, myth, art, religion are part."[28] The ringing of a
bell was a signal to Pavlov's dogs that food was on its way,
while the ringing of a bell in a high school building is usually a
signal that the class is over. A red light at an intersection is a
signal for traffic to come to a halt. Signals are not nearly as complex and profound as symbols. "To the extent that the symbol
hints at the divine, it forms a link between the human and the
superhuman."[29]

Sacraments are not signals. Neither are they signs, in the
sense described above. They will be called signs in much of this
book (as well as in the book's title) because there is a long tradition of using the word in historical and creedal treatments of
sacraments, one example being Wesley's definition quoted
above. One can hardly avoid the term *sign* when discussing the
history of sacramental doctrine, and in this book we will not
presume to rewrite the vocabulary of Church history by substi-
tuting *symbol* for *sign* in the traditional formulations. But in sac-

---

26. Ole E. Borgen, *John Wesley on the Sacraments* (Nashville: Abingdon Press, 1972),
52.

27. Erika Dinkler-Von Schubert, "Symbol," in *Handbook of Christian Theology*, ed.
Marvin Halverson and Arthur A. Cohen (New York: World Publishing Co., 1958), 359.

28. Ibid., quoting Ernst Cassirer, *The Philosophy of Symbolic Forms: Language and
Myth*.

29. Dinkler-Von Schubert, 359.

ramental doctrine, *sign* does not have the meaning it has in the examples used above. Rather, what is meant by *sign* in our treatment of sacraments is closer to the understanding of symbol held by classical theology, by the Reformers, and by some contemporary theologians.

We have used the flag as an illustration of the difference between signs and symbols. The difference can be further clarified by considering the Cross—the supreme symbol of Christianity. To a first-century traveler in Judea, an empty cross on a hillside would be a *sign* either that a crucifixion had recently taken place or that one would soon occur. But when Christ died on such a cross and was raised from the dead, and when this Good News was spread, the Cross became, for Christians, a powerful *symbol*.

This understanding of symbol differs from the meaning given the term in some discussions of sacraments, both past and present. Often symbol has been used to describe a "low" or "weak" view of sacraments, whereas sign (often used in conjunction with *seal*) is seen as depicting a "higher" understanding. In such usage, symbol merely means an abstract pointer or indicator. Such an understanding of symbol is quite opposite to the meaning given to the term in this book. For example, G. C. Berkouwer, in his book *The Sacraments*,[30] has a chapter titled "Symbol or Reality?" in which he argues that sacraments are not mere symbols. The issue is posed in terms of "symbolism" versus "realism." Of course Berkouwer is defending the Reformed (Calvinist) doctrine of sacraments, which, as he correctly points out, has been attacked by both Lutherans and Roman Catholics as being too similar to Zwingli's position that was viewed as only "symbolic." Both Catholics and Lutherans believe that in the Eucharist we meet the "real presence" of Christ, as opposed to a merely "symbolic" presence. Berkouwer claims that the Reformed position also believes in the "Real Presence." To him and to those against whom he defends the Reformed view, a "symbolic" doctrine would be one where baptism and the Lord's Supper are seen as only outward signs having illustrative value and

---

30. (Grand Rapids: Wm. B. Eerdmans Publishing Co., 1969), 202 ff.

significance to be sure, but less than a "reality" because as signs they only *point to* a reality.[31]

This is only partly a problem of semantics. Important theological issues are involved, and a fuller discussion of them must be left to chapter 7. Here it is necessary only to state that we believe the meaning of symbol developed above (with help from Tillich), applied to sacraments, at least comes close to expressing what John Wesley meant by an "outward sign of an inward grace." For Wesley these "signs" were not mere dispensable pointers. He believed that baptism was far more than a human testimony to one's faith, and the Eucharist was far more than a memorial of Christ's death. A sacrament was *a means whereby we receive* inward grace. A mere sign, in the sense described above, can only be an *indicator* pointing to grace, not a *means* whereby it is received. But a symbol can be such a means, because a symbol participates in the power of that which it symbolizes.

The meaning of *symbol* developed here is essentially the opposite of the meaning given the term in discussions such as that of Berkouwer, where symbol is contrasted with reality. In that usage, a symbol is merely an accidental and *dispensable* "*pointer*" to a reality. Applied to sacraments, this would mean that baptism is merely a human confession of faith (the faith being the real thing whose existence is not dependent on the baptism). And the Lord's Supper is merely an aid helping us remember and celebrate the Lord's death and His coming again (these events, and the salvation they bring, being the real things). But in our usage, a symbol is actually an *indispensable participant* in the reality to which it points, so that God *really* gives himself to us in, by, and through the sacraments. In the sacraments the symbol cannot be abstracted or divorced from His self-giving.

At the same time, sacramental theology must guard against an opposite error. Although the symbol participates in the reality to which it points, it is not synonymous with that reality. To the extent that a symbol points to the divine, it participates in the power of the divine; it forms a link between the human

---

31. Ibid., 202.

and the divine. But it is not itself the divine. Thus the meaning of symbol adopted in these pages guards against the view that the sacraments convey grace *ex opere operato* ("by the work performed"). This view, found in medieval Roman Catholic theology, is often perceived by Protestants as teaching that grace is given through the sacraments apart from any necessary faith on the part of the recipient. This confuses symbol and reality, virtually making them one and the same. This is seen most graphically in the Roman Catholic doctrine of transubstantiation, where the eucharistic bread and wine become the actual body and blood of Christ.

We believe an understanding of sacraments as symbols (in the sense developed above) guards against both the error of transubstantiation, which transforms the symbol into a thing to be handled, and the "memorialist" view, which sees the symbol only as abstract and dispensable pointers that do not participate in the power of the divine to which they point.[32]

*   *   *

In bringing to a close this discussion of "Theology and Imagination," it should be clear that imagination, far from being a flight of fancy, a daydreaming escapism, or the conjuring up of mental images that cannot possibly be true, is the mode of perception that may come closest to defining what it means to be human. As far as we can tell, animals do not have imagination. As we have noted, animals react to signals instead of symbols, being moved by instinct rather than imagination. One might presume that the angels in heaven do not need symbols, since they behold reality more directly than is possible for us mortals; but about that we can only conjecture, for divine revelation has given us very little knowledge about the experience of the angels. It could also be conjectured that the departed saints in the Church Triumphant no longer need imagination; but that would surely be a misguided notion. If imagination is part of the *imago Dei*, as it surely must be, and not a result of the Fall, is there any reason why it should ever cease? If, in Kipling's words,

---

32. Cf. Tillich, *ST* 3:120-24.

> *Each for the joy of the working,*
> *And each, in his separate star,*
> *Shall draw the Thing as he sees It*
> *For the God of Things as They are!*[33]

then in eternity, our imaginations shall be set loose to be forever creative!

But we can be certain of this: As for us human beings still on earth, who do not yet see "face to face" (1 Cor. 13:12), reality is mediated through myriads of oblique angles and colors and shapes and textures in the fabric of creation. And, unlike animals and angels, we are forever trying to catch sight of a meaningful and comprehensive pattern by relating all the angles and colors and shapes and textures to each other. Imagination makes us human, and it is our humanness that makes sacraments both possible and necessary.

This is tremendously important for a sacramental theology. It is for us human creatures that the sacraments have been designed. Jesus did not call them sacraments, of course, nor do the biblical writers. That is the name we have given them. But our Lord commanded water, bread, and wine—not for the angels, and not for the beasts, but for us.

---

33. From Rudyard Kipling, "L'Envoi."

Chapter Three

THE
SACRAMENTALIST VISION

What is sacramental theology? Is it essential for a vital faith or is it an optional frivolity? Does it represent a distortion and adulteration of the pure gospel? Does it enrich personal faith or impoverish it? Was Roman Catholicism unfaithful to the gospel by having embroidered the plain fabric of New Testament Christianity with an elaborate sacramentalism? Was the Protestant Reformation justified in sweeping from the medieval churches their images, statues, shrines, and relics—visual objects that aided the popular imagination in focusing on the mysteries of the faith? Is evangelical Protestantism richer or poorer for having taught that divine truth is embodied more in rational propositions than in material elements such as bread and water and wine? Is the Wesleyan/holiness tradition richer or poorer whenever it presumes to appropriate the "inward grace" of the sacraments while giving only perfunctory attention to the "outward sign," thereby giving its quest for "spirit" (i.e., experience) priority over its concern for "structure"? Before such questions can be adequately answered, or judgments soundly made, it is important to understand the vision that inspires the sacramentalist.

Wesley's definition of a sacrament as "an outward sign of inward grace, and a means whereby we receive the same"[1] sug-

---

1. *Works* 5:188.

gests that a sacrament is not only a symbol that is *said* but also one that is *seen* and *done*. In Protestant theology, a sacrament involves the performance of an *action*, the utterance of *words*, and the use of a physical *substance*. Let us consider the latter.

A. THE BASIC INSIGHT

Underlying all sacramental theology is the fundamental insight that *God may accomplish spiritual ends through material means*. Divine truth can certainly be communicated through spoken or written words, and such sacred words may often be powerfully expressive. But, if the well-known adage is true, that "a picture is worth a thousand words," then a symbol that is seen and done usually has more power to move the imagination of human beings than has the spoken word alone.

In the preceding chapter we considered a nation's flag as an example of a symbol. In fostering patriotism, there is a place for inspirational speeches or instruction in the meaning of *country*. But, as John Lawson reminds us,

> if for the sake of his country a man has to take his life in his hands upon the field of battle, the season has passed for a lecture upon the principles of the Constitution! He requires a flag—a vivid visual symbol which can in a moment focus to his imagination all that he has been taught about the idea of "country."[2]

Of course, a flag can make no such appeal to one's patriotism if there is no understanding of what a flag is in the first place. Lessons, lectures, or sermons may be necessary to instruct in the meaning of any given symbol. But once understood, the symbol can have a power that goes far beyond the word that is merely spoken. In great crisis moments in human history or in our own personal lives, we resort instinctively to visual and acted symbols.[3]

Jesus Christ implanted this insight in the very heart of Christian faith. Of course, He taught about God by spoken

---

2. John Lawson, *Comprehensive Handbook of Christian Doctrine* (Englewood Cliffs, N.J.: Prentice-Hall, 1967), 163.
3. The well-known photograph of American soldiers raising the flag on the island of Iwo Jima during World War II, and the patriotism it inspired, is a good example of the power of a symbol.

words, and spoken words are still necessary for the propagation of the faith. But when our Lord wanted to focus His disciples' attention on that which lies at the center of redemption, namely, His atoning death and His coming again,[4] He gave them a different symbol—a nonverbal one.[5] He told them to *do* something, to "act out" something, to eat and drink something. And because He desires that faith in Him as the Son of God be more than a mere intellectual assent, He told them that in making new disciples, they were to immerse them in something, or to sprinkle or pour something on their heads.[6] *Something.* Some THING! As we shall presently see, "thingness" has far-reaching significance for Christian faith.

Sacramental theology, therefore, may be understood as the theological perspective that sees the *physical* as potentially the vehicle of the *spiritual.* It is the view that God can work the spiritual through the material. It is the perspective that sees matter not as essentially evil nor as the enemy of spirit, but as a carrier of divine grace.

Sometimes the perspective that we are here calling sacramental theology, or "the sacramentalist vision," is referred to as "sacramentalism" or "sacramentarianism." Those terms are acceptable whenever they connote belief in the efficacy of the sacraments as means whereby divine grace is conveyed to human being. But "evangelical rationalists"[7] have sometimes overreacted to the terms, assuming them to carry the connotation that sacraments are absolutely necessary as the sole means whereby *salvation* is conveyed. Such connotation was much truer of Roman Catholicism before Vatican II than of Catholicism today. The Wesleyan/holiness tradition stops short of that meaning, and the terms will not be used in this book. God does give grace through the sacraments. A sacrament is "an outward sign of inward grace,

---

4. Cf. "For whenever you eat this bread and drink this cup, you proclaim the Lord's death until he comes" (1 Cor. 11:26).

5. It is of interest to sacramental theology that in the fourth Gospel, the miracles of Jesus are called "signs." James F. White refers to sacraments as "sign-acts" or "acted signs" that convey meaning in a nonverbal way. *Introduction to Christian Worship* (Nashville: Abingdon Press, 1981), chap. 5.

6. The question of the mode of baptism will be discussed later.

7. The term is used here with the meaning it has in Robert E. Webber, *Evangelicals on the Canterbury Trail* (Waco, Tex.: Word Books, 1985).

and a means whereby we receive the same," according to Wesley. Certainly, to Wesley, forgiveness and the new birth may well be included in the "inward grace" received through sacraments. But Wesley did not make the sacraments absolutely necessary for salvation. Salvation is possible without them, although they are the *ordinary* means through which God accomplishes His saving purpose.[8]

Therefore the Wesleyan/holiness tradition does not often speak approvingly of "sacramentarianism" or "sacramentalism" in the above sense; but it does seek to maintain the "sacramentalist vision." The one who holds such a vision can be called a "sacramentalist," even though his or her overall theological stance is *evangelical.* Perhaps we could say that Wesleyans are "evangelical sacramentalists." In other words, in their understanding of the gospel, they are evangelicals as opposed to sacramentarians, but within their evangelical commitment they share the sacramentalist vision. At its minimum, the term *sacramentalist* would refer to one who believes that God may accomplish spiritual ends through physical means, that "thingness" as mentioned above is not antithetical to spiritual life. Wesleyans heartily believe this truth.

But "thingness" may be mishandled, as it was by a particular segment of Christianity in one era of Christian history. Roman Catholicism in the late Middle Ages interpreted the great mysteries of the faith for the popular mind by locating these mysteries almost entirely in external forms such as shrines, pilgrimages, sacred relics, and the sale of indulgences. The Reformation attempted to relocate these mysteries in the place New Testament Christianity insisted was their rightful locale—the human heart. The mood of the Reformation is described by Thomas Howard:

> It will do you no good to trek to Santiago de Compostella, or to the shrine of Blessed Thomas at Canterbury, or even to the Holy Sepulchre itself. What is needed is a pilgrimage of the heart, from unrighteousness to purity. Again, your money and your beads will have not the slightest effect on your soul's account (and you may be sure there is no tally

---

8. Cf. *Works* 10:190-93, 198; *Letters* 2:227.

being kept in any such place as Purgatory). What is needed is repentance, which means only one thing in the gospel, namely a turning away from sin and the pursuit of holiness from your heart. This alone will put you in the way of salvation. And again, nothing at all is achieved by your simply being under the roof where a Latin mass is being said. What is needed is not miracles of chemistry up there on the stone slab, full as it is of dead relics, but rather the miracle whereby your own heart becomes the altar of which sacrifices of righteousness are offered in faith to God. All these external acts and objects, far from being helpful, are positively destructive. They nullify the very evangel of grace itself.[9]

Out with such external forms, objects, and actions that cannot save or nurture! The Protestant broom swept clean.

Perhaps *too* clean! In times more recent—and more sober—Protestantism has recognized that "external objects" may have power to focus the religious imagination on the things of the Spirit. Ironically, Protestantism practiced this all along with regard to objects like water, bread, and wine.

But in medieval Catholic thought, divine grace was understood as a "substance," elaborately dispensed through the sacramental practice of the church. Grace was a divine "medicine," a kind of heavenly "vitamin," an energy-giving "virtue" automatically[10] infused into the soul through the administration of the sacraments by a priest empowered to do so by his ordination (which was itself a sacrament). Divine grace—this mysterious substance that Catholics received through sacraments—was constantly thought of in impersonal terms, as a quasi-material "stuff" channeled to the soul as water flows through a pipe, or electricity travels over a wire. The presuppositions behind such a conception were those of Stoic philosophy, mixed with the ves-

---

9. Thomas Howard, "The Idea of Sacrament: An Approach," *Reformed Journal,* February 1979 (hereafter cited as "IS"). This article and its sequel, "Imagination, Rites, and Mystery: Why Did Christ Institute Sacraments?" *Reformed Journal,* March 1979 (hereafter cited as "IRM"), both written by a teacher of English, constitute a beautiful apologetic for the sacramentalist vision. I have borrowed heavily from these articles in the writing of the first three sections of this chapter.

10. As noted in chapter 2, the Latin term is *ex opere operato* ("by the work performed"), which refers to the assumption of medieval Catholicism that the correct and churchly performance of the rite conveys grace to the recipient, with or without faith on the part of the recipient.

tiges of primitive religion and Mediterranean folk-piety to which the medieval Roman church, consciously or unconsciously, made large concessions and accommodations. Roman Catholic theology today is far removed from this medieval mentality, and Protestant sacramental thought intersects at many more points with Catholic understandings than in the days following the Reformation. But it was this "substance" kind of sacramental thinking that Martin Luther rebelled against.

To it all, Luther said, "No!" Divine grace is not a substance but a new *relationship* that God offers to the unworthy sinner. It is the personal attitude of God in Christ toward sinful human beings. It is forgiveness, pardon, and reconciliation. Away, then, with papal superstition! Grace is not a medicinal substance that can be magically infused into the soul through some "intravenous feeding tube" called a sacrament. To Luther, grace was not a "thing."

But here we must be careful. The rejection of the Roman Catholic conception of sacramental grace as "substance" was not a denial by the Reformers of the significance of "thingness" for faith. Although grace was not a thing, it could be conveyed *by way of* things, and by actions, and by eating bread and drinking from a cup in obedience to Christ, and being baptized in His name. The use of material symbols does not signal a lack of spirituality. Christian theology considers it erroneous to suppose that the invisible (i.e., the purely mental or the spoken) is somehow more spiritual than the visible and the acted. For this reason, William Temple could insist that Christianity is "the most avowedly materialist of all the great religions."[11] The use of material objects (water, bread, and wine) in the most sacred acts of Christian worship is an affirmation of the Trinitarian God who is Creator, Redeemer, and Lover of the world that He has made. The physical may be a domicile, a residency, of the spiritual. That is the basic insight in the sacramentalist vision. It is the fundamental sacramental principle. As such, it is identical to the "incarnational principle," by which the Word could become flesh, and flesh could become the residency of God. The same

---

11. William Temple, *Nature, Man, and God* (London: Macmillan and Co., 1949), 478.

principle that made Incarnation possible also makes sacraments possible.

B. MYSTERY AND METAPHOR

In the centuries since the Reformation, the idea of sacrament has not been the most crucial issue in evangelical Protestant thought. To be sure, great battles have been fought between various sectors of Protestantism over the proper meaning and mode of baptism and the Lord's Supper. One of these battles (that between the Lutherans and the Anabaptists regarding baptism) was discussed in chapter 1. In the Marburg Castle, Luther and Zwingli argued bitterly over how we are to understand what is happening in the Lord's Supper when the bread and wine are being consecrated. Luther and Calvin disagreed on the way Christ's presence in the Eucharist was to be conceived. As for the Church of England, all manner of sacramental views had currency within her ranks during the first decades of her separation from Rome.

Despite the intensity of these issues, other concerns have occupied the greater part of evangelical Protestant attention for almost half a millennium. The historical reasons for this are clear enough. The Reformers rejected the authority of pope, councils, and church. They replaced it with the authority of Scripture alone (sola scriptura). Such a revolutionary idea had to be defended. As the classical period of the Reformation (the era of Luther and Calvin) gave way to the period of Protestant orthodoxy, Continental Protestantism became strongly propositionalist. Protestantism remains so to a great extent, especially in its more evangelical sectors. This can be seen typically in the evangelicals' doctrine of Scripture, systems of theology, preaching, and piety of which Bible study, testimony, and other verbal exercises are important parts. In terms of our discussion in chapter 2, logos became more important to Protestantism than mythos. Of course, in the Protestant ethos it is recognized that the great mysteries of the faith cannot finally be contained in rational categories. Nevertheless, this recognition gets shoved aside in the overwhelming effort to articulate the Christian faith in satisfactory propositions.

This is not to say that the sacramentalist is opposed to propositions. Sacraments make no sense if they are not approached with understanding. As Thomas Howard says,

> Orthodoxy can never be maintained by waving wands and thuribles about. Somewhere in there an Athanasius or an Augustine needs to pick up his pen and spell out what is wrong with the wrong view, and why it is that the right view alone is to be held by everyone.[12]

But after the essential theological work has been done, every Christian knows that "on every single point of the Faith we come eventually to the place where we must say, 'It is a mystery, I cannot press my explanation any farther than this.' Creation, fall, redemption—who is equal to these topics?"[13]

That is the key to sacramental theology—*mystery*. There are no propositions, rational statements, or logical syllogisms that can fully explain what happens in the sacraments. No church father, council, theologian, or pope has ever found the precise language to adequately state exactly what sort of spiritual transaction is taking place in baptism and the Eucharist. After every attempt at explanation has run its course, sacramental theology chooses to simply find meaning in the celebration of the mystery.

But *what* meaning? The material elements in a sacrament must be understood at two levels. First, they are just what they appear to be—water in a baptistry (or a river, creek, or lake) or in a baptismal font, and a loaf of bread or small pieces of it on a plate, and some wine in a common chalice or small quantities of it in tiny individual cups. Second, they constitute a means by which something beyond water, bread, and wine is made real and present to us.[14] In the sacramentalist vision, the sacraments are more than souvenirs, helping to jog the memory with a picture of something that happened in the past. When the Lord commanded us to "do this in remembrance" (1 Cor. 11:24), He intended more than a mere mental "remembering" of something past. Indeed, the sacraments make that which is remembered

---

12. Howard, "IS," 10.
13. Ibid.
14. Cf. ibid.

real to us in the *present.* It is to this kind of "remembering" that the sacramentalist believes the Lord calls us—a remembering that makes the past real in the present. How? *That* is the mystery.

But we need not be put off by mystery. In the Early Church fathers, the word *sacrament* (Latin *sacramentum*) was closely related to the word *mystery* (Greek *mystērion*). In fact, the Greek *mystērion* was usually translated by the Latin *sacramentum.* Of course, *mystērion* was not used in the New Testament to denote specifically those actions commanded by Christ, which the church came to call sacraments. Nevertheless, there is a correspondence in meaning between the two. In Paul, a mystery was not a perplexing puzzle. The word meant something hidden in God's eternal and inscrutable will, which could not be discovered by human searching, but which has been *revealed to believers through Jesus Christ* (Rom. 16:25-26; 1 Cor. 2:7-10; Eph. 1:9; 3:9; Col. 1:26). Paul saw Christ as the great demystifier, a solver of mysteries rather than a maker of them. But it is only for the person of faith that they are truly solved. To the unbeliever the sacraments are just meaningless human activity, but to the person of faith they become a revelation of the inner meaning of the gospel. "Can anything really significant happen to us in the sacraments?" the nonsacramentalist might ask, as Nathanael of old asked if any good could come from Nazareth. Like Philip, the sacramentalist replies, "Come and see" (John 1:46). What is Christ doing for us in the sacraments? Only His loved ones know!

Beyond that, however, the solution to the mystery involved in sacraments lies, perhaps, in *metaphor.*[15] Metaphor is the basic unit of creative thought. Gail Ramshaw-Schmidt says:

> In metaphor the mind expands in a fresh way, imagining
> the new and renovating the old. Metaphor does not label: it
> connects in a revolutionary way. Metaphor is not merely an

---

15. The word is from the Greek *metapherein,* meaning "to carry over," and is a figure of speech containing an implied comparison, in which a word or phrase ordinarily and primarily used of one thing is applied to another. Examples of biblical metaphors: "God . . . is a rock" (2 Sam. 22:32; Ps. 18:31, both KJV); "The Lord is my shepherd" (Ps. 23:1); "Ephraim is a cake not turned" (Hos. 7:8, KJV).

image, the look-alike, the reflection in a mirror. Rather, metaphor forms a comparison where none previously existed.[16]

A metaphor alters one's perception by superimposing images
that are dissimilar and logically incompatible.

> What shall we call the four sticks holding up the chair
> seat? How about "legs"? We speak scarcely a single sentence
> without relying on the metaphoric quality of language. Hid-
> den inside our prosaic talk about chair legs is an ancient per-
> sonification of the simple chair, a metaphor of lively limbs on
> dead wood.[17]

How does metaphor aid our understanding of sacraments?
Bread, wine, and water (the material components of sacraments)
stand at the juncture between the seen and the unseen. They
form a link, as it were, between that which we can see (and
touch and taste) and that which we cannot. Sacraments represent explicit meeting points where we come in contact with the
transcendent. At the very center of the Church's life as the Body
of Christ are actions that "tune us in" to the mystery of the gospel. In baptism we are buried with Christ (Rom. 6:3-4), and in
the Eucharist we eat His flesh and drink His blood and thereby
have eternal life (John 6:53-56). On the face of it, it sounds as
absurd to us as it did to the Jews who argued about it among
themselves (v. 52). It baffles our imagination and bridles our cre-
dulity how mere physical stuff can have this exalted and central
place in the Christian's relationship to the One who is

> *Immortal, invisible, God only wise,*
> *In light inaccessible hid from our eyes.*
> —WALTER C. SMITH

But we are brought up short when we recall that "mere
physical stuff" has precisely this exalted and central place in every great event in the history of salvation. Thomas Howard
states it beautifully:

> Look at these events: creation, fall, redemption, in-
> carnation, passion, resurrection, ascension, Pentecost, and
> eucharist. Is there one of them that occurred in a purely "spir-

---

16. Gail Ramshaw-Schmidt, *Christ in Sacred Speech* (Philadelphia: Fortress Press,
1986), 7.
17. Ibid., 8.

itual" realm? The whole drama was played out, to the confusion and outrage of gnostics, Manichaeans, and rationalists of all time, in starkly, embarrassingly physical terms. He *made* something (water and rock and whales) and it all praised him; we botched it by making a grab and trying to call it our own, and everything fell into corruptibility; he planned a rescue and a restoration, and chose a man and a tribe and demanded lamb's blood; then he took on this flesh himself; in the suffering of that flesh he effected the redemption of the world; that flesh came out of the grave, the sign and guarantee to all heaven and hell that victory was won; that flesh ascended into the midmost mysteries of the triune godhead; the godhead came down on the tongues and into the flesh of men and women; and, for them, at the center, for as long as history would go on, bread and wine.[18]

The sacramentalist takes his or her inspiration from these historical realities. God's whole redemptive scheme was carried out in terms physical, material, fleshly. To the Western rationalist who would point us to the world of abstract thought as the place where truth is found, the sacramentalist insists that the God of truth is none other than the God who created this material world and became incarnate in it for us. To the Eastern mystics whose siren song would entice us to escape from this world of water and woods and soil and flesh and blood and bread and wine into an ethereal realm of pure spirit, the sacramentalist insists that the Christlike God returns to His world and returns the world to us and offers us something infinitely greater than escape; He offers *redemption*.[19] "All things in heaven and on earth," says the apostle, will be gathered "together under one head, even Christ" (Eph. 1:10). Nothing—no "thing"—is to be left out!

A sacramental theology, then, takes seriously the biblical doctrine of creation. This doctrine holds that the world and all things in it are *real* and not illusory. Sticks and stones and broken bones—all are real. So are stars and suns, and seeds dying in the soil and bringing forth a hundredfold harvest. The beasts of the field, the birds of the air, and the fish of the sea—all these

---

18. "IS," 11.
19. Ibid.

are very real. The Lord God made it all and looked at it and pronounced it "good."

But something else is true about this created world. Not only is it real, but also it is *metaphorical*. This means that the world, besides being simply itself, points us to something beyond itself. The material and visible world has the capacity to show us something about transcendent reality in a mode suited to our mortal eyes. The world brings to us, news from beyond the world. It acts as a messenger or herald, much like the knight of the Middle Ages, cloaked in the colors of the king whom he represented and wearing the king's coat of arms. The colors were beautiful in themselves, as worn by the herald, but beyond that, they reflected the design and colors of the king whose herald he was. Just so, the shapes and colors and design of the material creation, to the sacramentalist, reflect the pattern of the Sovereign who is beyond them and whose herald they are.

It is not that the created world has been given an extra job to do—the job of being a herald from beyond this material world just for the benefit of us humans—in addition to its regular job of just being itself. For those who have eyes to see, the pattern observed in the fabric of this world is true on all levels, beginning with God. For example, we see seeds of corn planted in the springtime soil only to die and decay. But not *only* to die, for out of that death springs the shoot, then the stalk, and then the ear, and then a harvest. That is the natural way that seeds and soil and sunlight work. But it is also a metaphor of what is true throughout the universe, up and down the scale from God to subatomic particles. It is the truth that life springs from death, that the one who loses his or her life shall find it, that the person who buries self-interest in the principle of self-giving love discovers an abundant harvest of true self-fulfillment. It is the truth that the One who was crucified, dead, and buried was raised again on the third day. It is the truth of *kenōsis*—that the One who emptied himself and became a servant was exalted to God's right hand.[20]

---

20. The word *kenōsis* is from the Greek "to empty" and is used by Paul in Phil. 2:7, whose context, verses 5-11, is known as the "kenosis passage," where Christ is said to have "emptied himself" (RSV, cf. NASB) or "made himself nothing" (NIV).

This is what it means to say that this world is *metaphorical* as well as *real*. Material things have their own value but also serve as metaphors of something greater. The Rock of Gibraltar, Switzerland's Matterhorn, and Yosemite's El Capitan have their own majesty, but to the Christian, sensitive to the beauty of creation, they may bespeak the Rock of Ages and fairly shout:

> *The Lord's our Rock; in Him we hide,*
> *A Shelter in the time of storm.*
> —VERNON J. CHARLESWORTH

A lamb has value just as a lamb, but it may remind us of the Lamb slain to take away the sin of the world. The rippling of a waterfall, the murmur of the wind in the trees, the variegated song of the mockingbird in the morning, or the call of the whippoorwill at twilight—in all this we may detect faint intimations of a greater song. We may hear strains of a chorus of angels "numbering thousands upon thousands, and ten thousand times ten thousand" encircling the heavenly throne and singing, "Worthy is the Lamb, who was slain, to receive power and wealth and wisdom and strength and honor and glory and praise!" (Rev. 5:11-12). The sacramentalist has ears to hear!

A metaphor may be described as a "visual parable." As with the spoken parables of Jesus, the visual parables may both conceal and reveal. When the Master spoke "many things in parables," He knew that among His hearers only those who had "ears to hear" would get the message (Matt. 13:3, 9, KJV; cf. 3-17). With the visual parable also, only the one who has "eyes to see" will comprehend. For those with such seeing eyes, a metaphor has the capacity to bridge the distance between the "far away" and the "right here." G. A. Studdert-Kennedy has expressed this thought in the following poem:

> *How far above the things of earth*
> *Is Christ at God's right hand?*
> *How far above yon snowy peaks*
> *Do His white angels stand?*

> *Must we fare forth to seek a world*
> *Beyond that silent star?*
> *Forsake these dear familiar homes*
> *And climb the heights—how far?*

As far as meaning is from speech,
As beauty from a rose,
As far as music is from sound,
As poetry from prose,

As far as art from cleverness,
As painting is from paints,
As far as signs from sacraments,
As Pharisees from Saints,

As far as love from friendship is,
As reason is from Truth,
As far as laughter is from joy,
As early years from youth,

As far as love from shining eyes,
As passion from a kiss,
So far is God from God's green earth,
So far that world from this. [21]

In the sacraments, received in faith, the "far away" becomes the "right here." The metaphorical nature of the world is one of the assumptions underlying sacraments, regardless of what theological view one takes of them. "This is my body" assumes there is something about grains of wheat that have been crushed, baked, broken, and shared around a table that is a metaphor of the "living bread that came down from heaven" who was "bruised for our iniquities" and given for the life of the world. "This is my blood" assumes that there is something about wine in a cup, squeezed from grapes grown on a rocky hillside, that is a metaphor of the Blood trickling from "five bleeding wounds . . . received on Calvary" (Charles Wesley) and spattering on Golgotha's rocky crest as an atonement for our sins. "Buried with him in baptism" assumes that there is something about going out of sight under water and coming up again that is a metaphor of dying to the old life of sin and being raised to newness of life. The washing imagery of baptism assumes that there is something about having water poured or sprinkled on a person that is a metaphor of having our sins washed away. Mys-

---

21. G. A. Studdert-Kennedy, "Set Your Affections on Things Above," in *Rhymes* (London: Hodder and Stoughton, 1929), 61-62.

tery? Yes. Who can comprehend it? But through metaphor we have a clue.

Thomas Howard makes two important observations about metaphors.[22] First, the sacramentalist would insist, the metaphors are not chosen or imposed arbitrarily. The human imagination perceives an inherent "fitness" in the chosen metaphor that makes it appropriate for the message it conveys. For instance, there is an appropriate (not arbitrary) connection between high ceilings and kings. Why? Because both carry the notion of exaltedness. Mountain peak and not swamp is the right metaphor for joy. Lamb and not coyote is the right metaphor for innocence. Now if someone should urge that tunnels are better metaphors for kings than high ceilings or that swamps are better metaphors for joy than peaks, then the human race would have to reply that we need to erase everything and start over!

Second, two or more metaphors may be appropriate for the same truth. For instance, Christ is pictured in Scripture as both King and Servant. The "king" metaphor will capture one aspect of Christ, and the "servant" metaphor will capture another. Both are valid and necessary for a full-orbed picture. The same is true of the "lion" and "lamb" metaphors; in some ways, Christ is like a lion, and in other ways He is like a lamb (Rev. 5:5-6). But we may not speak of Christ as snake or butcher. This is not to denigrate either snakes or butchers; snakes are a part of God's creation, and butchers may be saints. But the human imagination knows there is nothing in those metaphors that adds anything to our knowledge of who Christ is. In the biblical story, as well as in the literature of numerous ancient cultures, the snake is a symbol of evil. As for butcher, if slaughter is the category, then Christ is the victim of the slaughter, not the one who wields the knife.

To those two observations of Howard regarding metaphors we may add another, namely, that the same metaphor may be used for two or more different truths. For example, water is sometimes used in Scripture to represent danger or trial, as in Isa. 43:2. But in the sacrament of baptism, water represents *salvation from* danger and the beginning of new life. In Prov. 4:17,

---

22. Cf. "IRM," 16-17.

bread and wine are metaphors of wickedness and violence. But in the Eucharist they represent the body and blood of the Lord. Important, therefore, for the interpretation of a metaphor is the context in which it is used.

Given these three parameters in the understanding of metaphor, the sacramentalist believes a metaphor can often capture for the Christian imagination the *mystery* of salvational truth far better than any scheme of logic.[23]

C. PROCLAMATION AS PLAY

In Protestantism there are two major ways of proclaiming the gospel—preaching and sacraments. Having rejected as the only true Church the institution headquartered in Rome with the pope as its head, the Reformers had to redefine the Church. To them the Church was found wherever the Word was preached and the sacraments were administered. Both had to do with proclamation; the Church was defined by what she proclaims. Preaching was the *audible* proclamation of the gospel, and sacraments were the *visible* proclamation. Just as there are different ways of proclaiming the gospel audibly, so there are various ways of proclaiming the gospel visibly.

In addition to the principle discussed in the previous section—that the metaphorical nature of the created world is a portal into the mystery of the transcendent—there is another idea at work in sacramental theology. We might call it *playacting*. "All the world's a stage," wrote Shakespeare, "and all the men and women merely players."[24] Rejecting the determinism implied in such a statement, we can say that in a sense the Church is a stage also, especially in the drama it plays out in its sacraments, and we worshipers are the players.

How so? In baptism and eucharist we "act out" what we believe. As C. K. Barrett writes, "The church is never more clearly the church than when it is enacting its faith in such rites as baptism and the Lord's Supper."[25] But far from being some esoteric

---

23. But see again the quote from Howard on p. 68.
24. *As You Like It*, act 2, scene 7, lines 139-40.
25. C. K. Barrett, *Church, Ministry, and Sacraments in the New Testament* (Grand Rapids: Wm. B. Eerdmans Publishing Co., 1985), 54-55.

or occult behavior peculiar to these most special religious occasions, such acting out is of one piece with other phenomena that are universally characteristic of the human race since the beginning of its recorded history. We human beings are creatures of ritual in much that we do in everyday life.

One example is a *greeting*. Practically all cultures have some customary ritual for greeting people. Depending on the given culture, it may be a handshake, a bow, a curtsy, a salute, or a nod of the head. Whatever the ritual of greeting, it is an acting out of our wish to signal the ideas of friendship, peace, respect, or welcome. Instead of giving an eloquent oration on welcome or friendship, we do a physical thing. We instinctively feel that the physical gesture will carry the message we wish to convey.

Or take *praying*. When we kneel to pray, or bow the head, we signal the ideas of reverence and humility. Instead of explaining verbally to our fellow worshipers (or to God) that we wish to be reverent now, we do something physical to send the signal. Or take this: Some people will lower their voices in a church building, even when it is largely vacant, or in a mortuary when they go to pay respects to the dead. Why? It is their way of making a point in a physical way of something significant that they want to acknowledge, even though they might not be able to explain it to a bystander if one should inquire.

Or take a matter as mundane as *eating*. Thanks to modern medical technology, we could get the needed nutrition much more quickly and efficiently by swallowing vitamin pills. But who could enjoy that for very long? When we want to make a meal really memorable, we go through the rituals of cooking, and garnishing, and setting tables with candelabra and centerpiece and linen napkins and silverware and crystal goblets and our best china. Why? Because we are ritual creatures. We recognize that eating together with family or friends is something much more significant than merely transferring nutrients from beans or broccoli to one's bloodstream.

Thomas Howard, whom we have already quoted considerably in this chapter, makes the important point that in the great intractable mysteries of human life (birth, sex, and death), we ritualize our responses to them.[26] Each of these events is

---

26. Cf. "IRM," 16.

"merely" a routine biological event, yet in all tribes and societies they are adorned with elaborate ritual.

Howard first considers *birth*. He says:

> In our own culture the decking tends to run along white, yellow, pink, and blue lines, with bows, ruffles, silver spoons, and pretty blankets as the tokens. Horses don't bother with this; yet they have the same experience biologically, foaling away merrily just as we do.[27]

Why do we humans add all the extra accoutrements? Because the mere obstetrics will not cover the topic. "Something has happened, and we must do something beautiful about it, something beyond the forceps and thermometers and diapers and charts."[28] The bows and frills indicate something much deeper in our humanity.

And there is *sex*. Howard says:

> The approach of a man to a woman is again "simply" a biological event, and a time-worn one at that. Nothing unusual. But all of us set this approach about with very high hedges. (At least we did: the present Western experiment in "free" sexual congress arises from time to time in history, and nothing lasting is ever built on it.) We festoon it all solemnly.[29]

Depending on the particular culture, the festooning may take the form of puberty rites or shared milkshakes, and then dowries or engagement rings. In America the festooning may involve a processional with bridal gown and veil, bridesmaids and ushers, the taking of vows, the giving and receiving of a ring, a wedding cake, a reception, and whatever else weddings entail. All this is part of our human desire to mark the significance of the event by ritual tokens.

And *death*. "When we have filled in our medical reports and made our sociological analyses of the dynamics of dying and have staved off corruption with embalming fluid and copper vaults, we set it all about with long palls, drawn hearses, and sung requiems (or whatever)."[30] The floral tributes, the eulogies, and the kind words spoken to the bereaved are ways in which

---

27. Ibid.
28. Ibid.
29. Ibid.
30. Ibid.

we proclaim that a person's death is something more significant than the mere cessation of breath or heartbeat or brain wave activity.

In each of these events, as we mortals confront the great mysteries of human life, we inevitably ritualize them. This creates a paradox: As we come to the most serious events in human existence, we discover that we have moved beyond the place where techniques and methodologies are effectual—where no "work" we can perform will suffice to adequately mark the occasion. Consequently we find that we must *play!* Ceremony and ritual are really a form of playacting.

> We are doing what children do with their dolls' houses and toy trucks: we are saying, *let this represent that.* With children it is, *let this doll represent Mummy or Queen Eleanor,* or *let this Dinky Toy be my Mack truck.* With adults it is, *let this gowned procession represent the bride's approach to her lord,* or *let this rite bespeak our honor to the dead person.*[31]

Playacting, ritual, ceremony, enactment. These are all forms of play, and they touch upon what we human creatures really are.

Now the most significant *salvational* events in human life, for the Christian, are (1) the forgiveness of sins and the receiving of new life in Christ, and (2) the subsequent and continued growth of the holy life. In different theological terms we call the first justification and regeneration (which are concomitant), and the second sanctification.[32] The Protestant sacraments may be understood as a ritualizing of these events. The Church, with the authority of her Lord behind her, has developed a way for us to engage in "playacting" to mark these events. She has said: Let this act of being immersed in water (or having water poured or sprinkled on our heads) represent our having our sins washed away and being given a new life in Christ. And let this act of eating and drinking represent our continual need for nourishment by the grace vouchsafed to us by Jesus Christ. It is PLAY! And there is rejoicing in heaven when we enter the game, and a "great cloud of witnesses" (Heb. 12:1) in eternity's grandstand cheers us on!

---

31. Ibid.
32. Sanctification here is used in its broadest sense, without being broken down into initial, progressive, entire, etc.

All this may sound strange and irreverent to those accustomed to think of the Lord's Supper as a solemn and somber occasion, or even a sad and gloomy one. Unfortunately, such a mood has often been fostered by the way Communion services have been conducted in local congregations, with a solemnity that is unnatural and forbidding. This is not to say that levity and frivolity should prevail, or that solemnity is altogether out of place. But insofar as she has allowed the somber atmosphere to become the exclusive one, the Church has failed in her teaching. The Eucharist, you see, is a *supper.* For happy families, that is a joyful time. The Lord's Supper is a *fiesta*—not a funeral![33] In early Christianity, the Eucharist was as much a celebration of Easter as of Good Friday, and for many centuries this remained truer of Eastern Orthodoxy than of Roman Catholicism. The Lord's Supper is also a foretaste of the Heavenly Banquet in God's everlasting kingdom, and as such it should be a harbinger of that ultimate joy.

Until recent times, to think of sacraments as playacting probably would have sounded strange to many Christians. But during the decade of the 1970s a novel theological approach came on the scene, known as "play theology." It has already proven itself to have been a passing theological *fad.* But even short-lived fads sometimes make a lasting contribution to theological understanding. Play theology made one point that is worth preserving. It is not our purpose here to explore this theme in any depth.[34] But the point it made may be useful for the sharpening of the sacramentalist vision.

Before we proceed, let us be sure we do not confuse play theology with "a theology of play." The latter is an attempt to offer guidelines to Christians in the use of their leisure time, to acknowledge play as necessary for a well-rounded life, and to give

---

33. In chapter 9 we will attempt to show how we sometimes tend to make it a "funeral" and discuss ways to avoid doing so.

34. The following are some suggestions for further reading on the subject of play theology: Harvey Cox, *The Feast of Fools* (New York: Harper and Row, 1969); Hugo Rahner, *Man at Play* (New York: Herder and Herder, 1972); David L. Miller, *Gods and Games* (New York: Harper and Row, 1973); Michael Novak, *The Joy of Sports* (New York: Basic Books, 1976). And for a survey of the literature, see chapter 6 of Lonnie D. Kliever, *The Shattered Spectrum* (Atlanta: John Knox Press, 1981).

what might be called a "religious interpretation of play."[35] Play theology, on the other hand, seeks to give a "playful interpretation of religion." It reinterprets the Christian faith in the light of the phenomenon of play.

In spite of the faddish nature of play theology, its contribution to North American religion comes because play is such an important aspect of the culture. The spectacle of Super Bowls, World Series, and U.S. Opens, the insatiable appetite for professional and amateur sports, the thirst for entertainment, and the enormous salaries paid to movie stars, rock musicians, and athletes all testify that we are a play-loving and play-worshiping society. This fact, deplorable as it may be from the standpoint of what it says about our cultural value systems, provides models, paradigms, and metaphors even for the work areas of life. Financiers "play the stock market," politicians devise "game plans," and military leaders engage in "war games." Play is an activity that can be found in every sector of human culture and at every stage of an individual's life.[36]

On reflection, this universal experience bears some similarity to *religious* experience. Play is a voluntary and exhilarating activity that is separated in time, space, logic, and value from other activities.[37]

> In playing we step out of one world and into another—a world that usually demands serious effort and often delivers unfettered joy. Play is thus a form of transcendence that all human beings can and do experience in the everyday world of ordinary life. As such, play closely resembles religious forms of transcendence at virtually all of these points.[38]

Play offers a metaphor of faith, especially as faith expresses itself in the sacraments. By participating in the sacraments, we experience transcendence. We draw apart from the ordinary workaday world in which the greater portion of our lives is

---

35. Robert K. Johnston, *The Christian at Play* (Grand Rapids: Wm. B. Eerdmans Publishing Co., 1983), is an example of the "theology of play" rather than of "play theology," as we are using the terms here.

36. For a more technical treatment of the phenomenon of play in culture, see Wolfhart Pannenberg, *Anthropology in Theological Perspective*, trans. Matthew J. O'Connell, (Philadelphia: Westminster Press, 1985), 315-39.

37. Cf. Kliever, 150.

38. Ibid.

spent and transcend it by entering into the exhilaration of the holy. Of course, this is true of all worship to a degree. But in many public worship services, especially in nonliturgical churches, it is easy to simply become spectators. When we act out our faith in baptism, Eucharist, or other liturgical actions, we become participants in the game, not mere spectators in the stands. Of course, sacraments, like play, demand effort (if we are to benefit from them), but they can deliver unspeakable joy! For many persons play is a way to transcend the humdrum tedium and monotonous existence in which they find themselves trapped. Likewise the sacraments (especially the Lord's Supper), when understood as play, provide a way for the believer to transcend the ordinariness into which religious expression may too easily drift.

This experience of transcending the tedium of daily life must not be understood as *escape*. Actually, sacraments are an experience of the transcendence and mystery of God precisely because they bring the holy into our mundane lives through ordinary concrete symbols. Through the use of the common life-essential elements of water and bread, and the wine that symbolizes blood, we are assured of God's presence in our everyday existence. Thus in the very encounter with divine transcendence through the sacraments, understood as play, we come to experience the mysterious *immanence* of the God who is Immanuel, God with us. The transcendence we experience is not escape; it is the "real presence" of God in our lives.

Play, then, is the means by which we breathe life and vigor into our mundane lives rather than an escape from the real world. Of course, play is only one of the ways in which we may think of sacraments, but, for some, it may be a helpful way.

D. A Sacramental Universe?

A word of caution is now in order regarding "the sacramentalist vision," which we have been considering in this chapter. What has been discussed here is, for the most part, akin to what has been called a "sacramental universe."[39] This term indi-

---

39. See, for example, Temple, lecture 19, and Donald M. Baillie, *The Theology of the Sacraments* (New York: Charles Scribner's Sons, 1957), 42-47.

cates "the idea that the sacraments in the specific sense are but concentrations of something very much more widespread, so that nothing could be in the special sense a sacrament unless everything were in a basic and general sense sacramental."[40]

This idea may at first seem to be in conflict with an important principle of Protestant theology, that "the existence of a sacrament depends entirely on the word of promise, so that it is not anything in the material element, but entirely the divine Word that can make water or bread and wine sacramental."[41] H. Ray Dunning suggests that theologically the idea of a sacramental universe would be a witness to God the *Creator*, rather than a witness to God's redemptive work in history.[42] But this would seem to put too great a gulf between the God of creation and the God of redemption. Creation and redemption are not two separate divine activities disconnected from one another. This is the clear message of Rev. 13:8 ("the Lamb that was slain from the creation of the world") and of Matt. 25:34 ("the kingdom prepared for you since the creation of the world"). God in Christ is reconciling *the world* (2 Cor. 5:19; cf. Col. 1:20). It is the Creator God who redeems and the redeeming God who creates.

Thus a truly Christian theology of sacraments need not exclude the broader idea of a sacramental universe. Consider Baillie's implied answers when he asks:

> Is the divine Word entirely absent from the wider world from which it singles out special elements for a specially sacred use? Is there not a basic reason why material things should be taken by the Word and consecrated to be instruments of divine grace? Do they not lend themselves to such a use because God made them, because they are His creatures?[43]

This is fully in keeping with Wesleyan theology's doctrine of prevenient grace, even more so than with Baillie's own Reformed tradition. The doctrine of prevenient grace holds that there is a continuity between nature and grace rather than a radical discontinuity. John Wesley made no sharp divorcement be-

---

40. Baillie, 42.
41. Ibid., 43.
42. Dunning, 543.
43. Baillie, 43.

tween nature and grace, as Luther and Calvin were prone to do.
He taught that all human existence is enveloped by the wooing
activity of God, who enlightens everyone coming into the world
with some knowledge of himself—a knowledge that allures and
disquiets. Wesley could believe in a sort of "sacramental universe" because he rejected what Robert E. Cushman calls "the
practically absolute disjunction between nature and grace—that
philosophical and theological ineptitude of the Reformation."[44]

When Christianity took the common elements of water,
bread, and wine and made sacraments of them, it was because
the universe is the kind of place in which that can fitly happen.
These same sacraments were born also because the human imagination, as we have seen, has the capacity to see in the metaphorical nature of the world a probe into the mysteries of the
faith.

At the same time, it is important to remember that the sacraments do not arise out of nature alone. The metaphorical
power of nature does not of itself make a sacrament. A necessary component of a Christian sacrament is its relation to God's
special revelation in history. The idea of a sacramental universe
is a good background for understanding the Christian sacraments, but it is not the central focus. Although there is continuity between nature and grace, the sacraments focus ultimately on grace, and speak authoritatively only to faith.
Therefore, to the question, "Is the idea of a sacramental universe
a legitimate background for an understanding of the doctrine of
sacraments?" the answer is "Yes, but . . ." And for a *Christian* sacramental theology, the "but" must greatly qualify the "Yes."

---

44. Robert E. Cushman, "Salvation for All," in *Methodism*, ed. William K. Anderson
(Nashville: Methodist Publishing House, 1947), 115.

Chapter Four

WHAT ARE SACRAMENTS?

An understanding of the meaning of sacraments will involve several considerations—the definition of the term, the question of the number of sacraments the Church should have, the way the Church has understood them, the question of what sacraments are supposed to accomplish, and what safeguards they offer for the preservation of Christian truth. These matters will be addressed in the following sections.

A. DERIVATION AND DEFINITION

The word *sacrament* is thought to have come originally from the Latin *sacramentum,* which in ancient times referred to a sum of money that two parties to a lawsuit deposited with a third party—something like putting money in "escrow," as we would call it today. This foreshadowed one aspect of the idea of a Christian sacrament, especially as understood by Protestants, namely, that a sacrament involves the use of some physical element—a "sign" or "symbol." Later *sacramentum* came to refer to the oath of allegiance taken by a Roman soldier as he promised to serve and defend the empire. This anticipated yet another element inherent in a sacrament, as emphasized by Protestants, namely, the word of promise that accompanies the sign and without which the sign would not have its sacramental character. When we put together these two early meanings of *sacramentum* in the Latin tongue, the term bequeaths to us two important aspects in the idea of a Christian sacrament. First, the action involves a physical element used as a symbol, and second, a word of promise accompanies the use of the symbol, the latter being both the divine word of grace and the human confession of faith.

As alluded to previously, the Latin *sacramentum* was used by some of the Early Church fathers to translate the Greek word *mystērion.* It was used in the Latin Vulgate to translate *mystērion* in Eph. 5:32, but there Paul is not speaking about what the church later came to call "sacraments."[1] The word *mystērion* is used in various other contexts in the Greek New Testament, and in none of them does it designate what we know as sacraments today. Nor did it carry the meaning *mystērion* had in the Greek "mystery religions" (although there is one point of similarity— baptism and the Eucharist do not reveal their meaning to unbelieving eyes). Nevertheless, the Christian sacraments contain elements of meaning derived from both the Latin and Greek words. *Sacramentum,* as a soldier's oath of allegiance, became the ancestor of our word *sacrament,* which is both our pledge of allegiance to the gospel and God's covenant promise to us. *Mystērion* made its contribution too; as *mystērion,* the meaning of a Christian sacrament is not fathomed by unbelievers.[2] But that is not the only contribution of *mystērion* to our understanding of sacraments. In our discussion in chapter 3, we saw that Christian faith necessarily includes the element of "mystery." Rational categories alone are not sufficient to contain the wonder and glory of the gospel. Although the word *mystērion* in the New Testament is not synonymous with *sacrament,* Paul's *idea* of mystery connects with the Church's understanding of sacrament nevertheless. The mystery Paul proclaims is the unexplainable "depth of the riches and wisdom and knowledge of God" (Rom. 11:33, RSV). For Paul,

---

1. However, some Roman Catholic theologians use Eph. 5:21-33 (Paul's discussion of husbands and wives) as a scriptural basis for including marriage among the sacraments.

2. Cf. Alan Richardson, "Sacrament, Sacramental Theology," in *A Dictionary of Christian Theology,* ed. Alan Richardson (Philadelphia: Westminster Press, 1969), 300.

mysterion . . . denotes the ineffable way or pattern of God (Rom. 11:25; 16:25; Eph. 3:3; Col. 1:26) or the means or medium by which the hidden intentionality of God is revealed in specific intentions, as made known in Christ (Eph. 1:9, 3:4; Col. 2:2, 4:3), in the gospel (Eph. 6:19), through the church (Eph. 3:9), or in individual believers (Col. 1:27).[3]

Paul's expression of Christ as a *mystērion* disclosed by God to the believer is a profound and consistent development of the word of Jesus, "To you has been given the *mystery* of the Kingdom of God."[4] It is a mystery that cannot be known by human reason alone. One of the ways we receive the mystery is through sacraments.

The English word *sacrament,* etymologically the child of *sacramentum* and grandchild of *mystērion,* has come into use in theological language to indicate certain specifically religious events. The term has been "baptized" into the Christian vocabulary! Although the word *sacrament* is not found in Scripture with the specific meaning assigned to it by the Christian tradition, it is a legitimate term for the actions that the consensus of the Church has found to be practiced in Scripture and bequeathed to us by the Lord. It is important, when investigating the biblical foundations of the theology of the sacraments, to make an adequate distinction between the history of the *word—sacrament—*and the *thing* signified by the word. The latter has been at work in the Church from the beginning (although at different levels of intensity), as the response of the believing community to the grace it receives from God and mediates to the world.[5]

The title of this book is taken from John Wesley's definition of a sacrament as "an outward sign of inward grace, and a means whereby we receive the same."[6] Wesley, of course, was abridging the definition given in the Anglican Catechism of the *Book of Common Prayer:* "An outward and visible sign of an in-

---

3. Robert L. Browning and Roy A. Reed, *The Sacraments in Religious Education and Liturgy* (Birmingham, Ala.: Religious Education Press, 1985), 38.

4. Ibid., 39; cf. Mark 4:11, NASB.

5. Cf. Raphael Schulte, "Sacraments," in *Encyclopedia of Theology: The Concise Sacramentum Mundi,* ed. Karl Rahner (New York: Seabury Press, 1975), 1477-78.

6. *Works* 5:188.

ward and spiritual grace given unto us; ordained by Christ himself, as a means whereby we receive the same, and a pledge to assure us thereof." The Anglican definition was, in turn, influenced by the thought of Augustine.[7] Such definitions have been criticized as being actually "anti-sacramental" in that they seem to set "outward" and "visible" against "inward" and "spiritual," implying that the latter pair of terms is more important than the former pair. It is suggested that "what is operating primarily in this definition is the platonic tradition which sees the heavenly world distinct from the earthly and views the whole world of sensible realities as image and shadow and the *real* world as that of the invisible, heavenly realities."[8] It is plausible to read these definitions in this way, since Augustine stood in the tradition of Plato. If such a Platonic dualism is necessarily connoted by such definitions, the latter should be abandoned. As we shall see later in this chapter, biblical thought understands the world as permeated with God's presence and purposes, and it sees the outward and the visible as God's good creation and the residency of grace. One may wonder if Wesley's *abridgment* of the Anglican definition, in which he omits the words "visible" and "spiritual" while retaining "outward" and "inward," was an attempt, conscious or unconscious, to sift out some of the Platonism. In any case, Wesley's definition of a sacrament as "an outward sign of inward grace" in no way demands such a dualistic worldview. Rather, it may be seen as a way to bridge the unfortunate gulf that Christian thought has sometimes made between God and His world, between nature and grace. Wesley's doctrine of prevenient grace holds that there is a continuity between nature and grace. And he classified sacraments as "means of grace," thus implicitly dispelling such a Platonic dualism.

We have been discussing the origin of the *word* sacrament, and a long-standing definition. We still need to inquire what a sacrament *is*.

B. The Protestant Criteria

Historically, Catholics and Protestants have differed in their

---

7. Cf. *City of God,* book 10, chap. 5.
8. Cf. Browning and Reed, 32-33.

understandings of sacraments. The difference is seen most clearly when we consider the *number* of sacraments. The question, What *is* a sacrament? is tied to the question, How many sacraments *are* there?

For many centuries, the number of sacraments was not precisely defined. Roman Catholic theology during the Middle Ages identified seven vital actions the church considered efficacious for salvation. Peter Lombard was the first Catholic writer to definitely catalog the sacraments as seven; this was done about A.D. 1150 in his *Four Books of the Sentences,* which became a basic textbook in theology in western Europe for hundreds of years. According to Lombard, the seven sacraments are baptism, confirmation, penance, Eucharist, extreme unction, ordination, and marriage. The understanding of sacraments taught by Lombard was characteristic of Roman Catholic theology until the Second Vatican Council in the middle of the 20th century.

Baptism was to be performed by a priest, unless that was impossible, usually by aspersion (sprinkling). It was believed to be a cleansing from original sin, which thereby changed the recipient's character and admitted him or her into the church.

Confirmation completed the Christian initiation begun in baptism, and prepared one for the full communion of the Eucharist. It was performed through the laying on of hands and anointing with chrism (consecrated oil) and conferred on the baptized person the power of the Holy Spirit for participation in the responsibilities of the church.

Penance was the performance of some act specified by the priest after he had heard one's confession of sin. Its central purpose was the removing of sins the repentant believer had committed after baptism.[9] It was the condition of receiving absolution in which the priest declared God's forgiveness and restored the sinner to fellowship in the church.

Eucharist, or Holy Communion, was the partaking of bread and wine. The church believed that by a prayer of consecration the substance had been changed into the actual substance of the body and blood of Jesus. Through this sacrament the church offered again to God the one acceptable sacrifice through which the soul is renewed in spiritual strength.

---

9. Karl Rahner, *Encyclopedia of Theology,* 1189. See n. 5 above.

Extreme unction, otherwise known as the "last rites" or the "anointing of the sick," was a sacrament administered to persons believed to be dying. It was believed to bring about the remission of sins and to fortify the soul for the life beyond.

Ordination, or "orders" as it is often called, was a sacrament in Catholicism, unlike its Protestant counterpart. In Protestantism the ministry is a functional office rather than a sacramental one; a person is ordained to exercise the functions and the authority of a minister. But in Catholicism, ordination was understood to confer a special measure of the Holy Spirit on the priest and mark him with a permanent and indelible character. Even if he became an unfaithful priest, he would always stand in this special relationship to God, a relationship not available to the layperson. Ordination was to be performed by the laying on of hands by a bishop, with appropriate words conferring power to exercise the office of priest.

Marriage also was a sacrament for the Catholic. In marriage, as in the other six sacraments, the recipients were believed to be infused with grace.[10] Appeal was made to the "great mystery" *(mystērion)* in Paul's discussion of marriage in Eph. 5:32, although, for medieval Catholic theology, biblical exegesis was not decisive in designating marriage a sacrament.[11]

It should be reiterated that the above summary is of the sacramental thought of medieval and pre-Vatican II Roman Catholicism. In present-day Roman Catholic thinking, these views have been modified in various ways. But we have presented the above in order to make clear what it was the Protestant Reformation objected to and why Luther developed different criteria for sacraments.

Obviously, and interestingly, an individual Roman Catholic cannot normally receive all seven sacraments, but only six at the most. This is because the church insists on a celibate priesthood —priests cannot marry, and married persons cannot be priests!

---

10. See the discussion of grace as a "substance" in the first section of chapter 3.

11. Cf. the remark in Berkouwer, "It is noteworthy that in Ephesians 5 Paul appeals to Genesis, while according to Rome only New Testament Christian marriage may be called a sacrament. Catholic theology tries to escape this paradox by saying that already in Genesis 'the sacramentality of marriage is prefigured in a rather profound manner.' Christ supposedly took up marriage into the sacramental order."

The choice is between the sacrament of marriage and that of ordination; one cannot have both.

Why did the Roman Catholic church teach seven sacraments? Her theology did not pretend to rest finally on scriptural proofs for this number, beyond a certain sacredness of the number seven in the Scripture. The decision lay, instead, with the tradition and authority of the church. The tradition saw a meaningful parallel between the seven sacraments and the natural course of a person's life. Thomas Aquinas, perhaps the greatest Roman Catholic theologian, pointed to a certain similarity between "spiritual" and "natural" life and applied it to the sacraments.[12] Baptism, he noted, corresponds to birth, confirmation to the growth of the body, the Eucharist to nourishment, penance to healing, and extreme unction to dying. In addition to these five, which parallel the life of an individual, two others are added that relate to the perfection of life in community—ordination (the power to exercise spiritual rulership) and marriage (necessary for natural propagation). Thus the number of sacraments in medieval Roman Catholic theology was based not on biblical foundations but on the view that they constitute a series of supernatural acts that infuse divine grace into all of life, individual and social, from beginning to end. There is undeniably a certain beauty and harmony in this scheme. But as we mentioned in our discussion of A Sacramental Universe, this consideration cannot be the ultimate and decisive one for a biblical view of sacraments. As Berkouwer says, "There is beauty, to be sure, in the sacraments, but the beauty lies in the majesty with which God goes his way in history, making earthly elements to become sacraments by his word."[13]

Protestantism has generally recognized as sacraments only baptism and the Eucharist.[14] Why the smaller number for Protestants?

---

12. *Summa Theologica*, pt. 3, ques. 65, art. 1.

13. Berkouwer, 30.

14. Although in certain periods and in some churches confirmation has had status or near-status as a sacrament, and in the first stages of the Reformation Luther counted penance among the sacraments, but he soon ruled it out. Cf. *Luther's Works*, ed. Jaroslav Pelikan and Helmut T. Lehmann, 55 vols. (Philadelphia: Muhlenberg Press, 1959), 36:18, 124.

The answer is determined by three specific criteria, as developed by the Protestant Reformers. First, only those rites should be considered sacraments that, according to the New Testament, Jesus himself established or initiated. In theology this has been called "dominical institution," meaning they were begun or "instituted" by the Lord himself.

This should not be misunderstood. The New Testament clearly shows that Jesus was not the first to propose the act of baptism. John the Baptist was already practicing it when Jesus began His public ministry, and before John it was practiced in Judaism to signify the purification of Gentile converts before becoming members of the community of Israel. But Jesus *did* put it in a new context by commanding it in the Great Commission as the way His new disciples from all nations were to be initiated into the faith, and this may be called "dominical institution." The appropriateness of the word *institution* is clearer with regard to the Lord's Supper, even though it was probably "instituted" at the celebration of the Jewish Passover, where something new was built upon something old. Still, instead of claiming "dominical institution" as a criterion of sacraments, it might be better to say that Protestantism recognizes as sacraments only those rites in which Jesus directly participated either as ministrant or recipient, and, by so doing, placed His authority behind them. "Dominical authorization" might be a better term. Whatever the term, this is one of the criteria by which Protestantism generally rules out all but two of the Catholic seven. "We seek sacraments that have been divinely instituted," said Luther.[15]

The second criterion is that a sacrament must have a physical "sign" or element (water, bread, wine). Luther said there were many things it might seem possible to regard as sacraments, namely those things to which a divine promise has been given, such as prayer (Luke 11:5-13), the Word (v. 28), and suffering ("who can recount all the times he promises aid and glory to those who are afflicted, suffer, and are cast down?").[16] But, he insisted, it was proper "to restrict the name of sacrament to

---

15. *Luther's Works* 36:92.
16. Ibid., 123-24.

those promises which have signs attached to them."[17] On that basis, he could find only two sacraments in the church—baptism and the Eucharist—"for only in these two do we find both the divinely instituted sign and the promise of forgiveness of sins."[18]

The third criterion, as already indicated, is this: The physical sign must be accompanied by a biblical word of promise. For Luther, a sacrament consists in the *combination* of sign and promise. The element (water, bread, or wine) by itself is not a sacrament. Luther explains that every visible action can naturally be understood as a figure or allegory of something invisible, "but figures or allegories are not sacraments, in the sense in which we use the term."[19] "Our signs or sacraments, as well as those of the fathers, have attached to them a word of promise which requires faith, and they cannot be fulfilled by any other work."[20] "We have said that in every sacrament there is a word of divine promise, to be believed by whoever receives the sign, and that the sign alone cannot be a sacrament."[21]

In summary, the Protestant criteria, as developed by Luther, and followed by most Protestants since the Reformation, are these three: (1) dominical institution, as loosely defined above, that is, a sacrament must have Christ's explicit authority behind it, (2) a physical or material element or sign, and (3) the divine word of promise that requires the response of faith. Reformation theology held that only those actions meeting these criteria could properly be considered sacraments.

On this threefold basis, Luther and Protestantism ruled out, as sacraments, the other five rites taught by the Catholic church. Confirmation, with its sign of laying on of hands, was believed to have no divine promise connected with it.[22] Penance, in which a promise might be inferred from Matt. 16:19 and John

---

17. Ibid., 124.
18. Ibid.
19. Ibid., 92.
20. Ibid., 65.
21. Ibid., 92.
22. Ibid., 92. John Calvin also argued against confirmation on the grounds that it devalued and impoverished the significance of baptism. Cf. *Institutes of the Christian Religion*, ed. John T. McNeill, 2 vols., 4.19.8 (hereafter cited as *Institutes*). This edition of the *Institutes* appears as volumes 20 and 21 in *The Library of Christian Classics* (Philadelphia: Westminster Press, 1960, hereafter cited as *LCC*).

20:23, had been turned into a meritorious act that required no faith, but only works.[23] Extreme unction falls at the point of "dominical institution," for Jesus gave no word on it at all.[24] Ordination has neither authority from the Lord nor promise of grace attached to it. Thus, although Luther had high regard for the work of ministry, he did not consider ordination a sacrament. Finally, marriage fails to meet any of the three criteria. Certainly marriage is accepted as an extremely important divine order by all Christians. But since it has existed from the beginning of the world (thus not instituted by Christ) and is practiced with great respect in non-Christian religions, there is no reason why it should be called a sacrament of the Church. With characteristic overstatement, Luther says:

> Nowhere do we read that the man who marries a wife receives any grace of God. There is not even a divinely instituted sign in marriage, nor do we read anywhere that marriage was instituted by God to be a sign of anything.[25]

How many sacraments are there? For the majority of Protestant Christians there are two. A sacrament must be a divinely given action in which there is a divinely given physical sign that carries with it a divinely given promise of grace to the recipient. Only baptism and the Lord's Supper meet the qualifications. Wesley agreed with the Reformers on the number of sacraments, pointing out that the numbering of seven sacraments was not defined before Peter Lombard, and agreeing with Augustine that only baptism and the Lord's Supper are of divine institution.[26]

---

23. *Luther's Works* 36:81-91. Calvin opposed penance on the same grounds on which he rejected confirmation, namely, that it devalued baptism. Cf. *Institutes* 4.19.17.

24. The main scriptural basis used to defend unction as a sacrament was James 5:14-15, and Luther had little appreciation for the Epistle of James, as is well known. He said: "No apostle has the right on his own authority to institute a sacrament. . . . For this belongs to Christ alone." *Luther's Works* 36:118.

25. Ibid., 92. Luther's argument against the Catholic view of sacraments may be at its most ambiguous at the point of marriage. In Eph. 5:22-33, Paul could be interpreted as saying that the love between husband and wife is a sign or symbol of Christ's love for the Church. There is no divinely ordained physical sign, of course, unless it be sexual union, and the institution of that is in Genesis and not in Jesus' words. And Luther is correct in holding that marriage brings to the married couple no special grace other than the grace available to everyone.

26. Cf. *Works* 10:112-13.

Some churches closely aligned with the Wesleyan/holiness tradition consider foot washing to be an "ordinance" (the term usually preferred instead of "sacrament" by those who practice it) on the basis of John 13:14. The practice seems to meet two of the Reformation criteria—dominical institution ("you also should wash one another's feet") and the physical sign (the basin, water, towel, and the act of foot washing itself). The third criterion might seem to be met in the words "Now that you know these things, you will be blessed if you do them" (v. 17). Furthermore, the account of foot washing stands in the Gospel of John precisely at the place where one would expect to read about the Eucharist.

Against the placing of foot washing on the same level with baptism and Eucharist as sacraments are two arguments: First, although there is the promise of "blessing," it is not a new covenant promise of grace for the forgiveness of sins grounded in Christ's atonement, as are baptism (Rom. 6:3-4) and Eucharist (Matt. 26:28). Second, the practice of foot washing in biblical times was a common courtesy performed for guests in the home. Although this courtesy was sanctified by Jesus' words and actions, its value was intrinsic. That is, the act had value simply as the washing of hot, tired, dusty feet. But in baptism and Eucharist the signs have little intrinsic value in themselves. Baptism is not an especially efficacious way to take a bath, even if by immersion, and the bread and wine of Communion offer little nourishment for the body. Their value lies mainly in their *symbolic* meaning. Of course foot washing may be a symbol or sign of humility and servanthood. But in modern society those virtues may be better put into practice by the washing of dishes, or clothes, or floors, for someone in need of help, than by the ceremonial washing of feet. Still, respect should be shown toward those for whom the ordinance of foot washing is meaningful, although it is not in the mainstream of Christian tradition, nor a part of the classical Wesleyan heritage.

How many sacraments are there? In one sense, that is the wrong question. There are as many sacraments as we define the word to cover. Nevertheless, this book follows the Protestant tradition (which is not completely unambiguous), and the classical Wesleyan tradition, in limiting the number to two.

As we consider the question, How many sacraments are there? our task is to discover and carry out our Lord's intention as to what is essential in the structure of His Church. The "dominical institution" of baptism and Eucharist may not be incontrovertibly established by proof-texting.[27] But the New Testament seems to show that Jesus wanted the Good News proclaimed by His Church to involve the verbal proclamation of the gospel and two "visual parables" or "action parables" (baptism and Eucharist).[28] If this is a correct reading of His intention, then the Church should recognize these two sacraments. It matters not how sacred and useful other rites may be, the New Testament does not command them for the Church with the same soteriological intensity as prevails in these two particular rites. We should not attempt to enlarge upon those things Christ seems to have made central. The name *sacrament* is not worth contending about, but baptism and the Lord's Supper should together have a name that is not given to any other feature of the Church's life, or to any other rite in sacred ceremony.

The more one's faith is shaped by classical Protestantism, the stronger these two sacraments will be insisted upon as both the minimum and the maximum the Church should have. It should be pointed out, however, that many Protestants today are showing increasing openness to the Catholic idea of having more sacraments than two. And many Catholics are open to the idea of enlarging the number from the traditional seven. Some theologians, both Protestants and Catholics, speak of rites that are not sacraments, but are *like* sacraments in that they are "sacramental in tone and effect."[29] Protestants tend to call them "ordinances." Catholics employ the term "sacramentals" to refer to any kind of action that may be used to further the notion that God is at work in His world conveying grace to those who seek it. Both sacraments and "sacramentals" should be open-ended as to number, some insist. Browning and Reed, for example, in

---

27. The attempt to do so is even described by Browning and Reed as "a specious bit of scholarly quackery," 47.

28. Specifically, see the Great Commission (Matt. 28:19) and Jesus' institution of the Lord's Supper (1 Cor. 11:23-26).

29. H. Grady Hardin, Joseph D. Quillian, and James F. White, *The Celebration of the Gospel* (Nashville: Abingdon Press, 1964), 110.

their excellent study of sacraments, challenge the assumption "that there should be a fixed number or even a definite designation of what is a sacrament."[30] However, the reader is disappointed when in the final chapter the question of new sacraments is discussed, and the only "new" one that is given extended attention is foot washing! James White attempts to mediate the situation by proposing three classes of sacraments, which he calls *dominical, apostolic,* and *natural.*[31] But such distinctions seem forced.

Although there is merit in the notion of open-endedness regarding the number and definition of sacraments, we believe a prior consideration should be to guard against a *trivialization* of sacraments. It is true that many things in the world besides water, bread, and wine may become emblems of the eternal and vehicles of grace. But two world wars, the Holocaust, and many other modern atrocities have shown us that both the Enlightenment expectation for a harmonious and rational world order and the romantic ideal that "everything that lives is holy" were naive and arrogant assumptions about human capability. Is it wise for the Church to take just any thing or action that may legitimately be considered a vehicle of grace and lift it to the same sacramental level with those things about which our Lord gave explicit instructions? It would seem that if an infinite number of things be considered sacraments, then nothing is a sacrament in the most meaningful sense of the term.

The answer to the question, How many sacraments are there? gives us part of the answer to the question, "What *is* a sacrament?" But only a part. The question, "What *is* a sacrament?" involves another question, namely, "What does a sacrament *do?*"

C. MEANS OF GRACE

Sacraments are often discussed under the broader category

---

30. Browning and Read, 290.
31. James F. White, *Sacraments as God's Self Giving* (Nashville: Abingdon Press, 1983), 70-92. Baptism and the Eucharist are listed as the dominical sacraments. Apostolic sacraments are those things that the Lord did not institute but that the apostles practiced in a continuation of the actions and intentions of Jesus, namely, reconciliation, healing, and ordination. The natural sacraments are listed as Christian marriage and Christian burial.

of "means of grace." This term refers to what John Lawson calls
"the means by which the general saving action of God is mediated to particular congregations and to individual believers."[32]
Gustaf Aulén refers to the means of grace as "the constitutive
factors of the church" through which "the activity of the Holy
Spirit which creates the church takes place."[33] In the Book of
Acts certain actions, which may be called "means of grace," are
mentioned as constituting the Earliest Church: "They devoted
themselves to the apostles' teaching and to the fellowship, to the
breaking of bread and to prayer" (Acts 2:42).

In his sermon on "The Means of Grace," John Wesley gives
this definition: "By 'means of grace' I understand outward signs,
words, or actions, ordained of God, and appointed for this end,
to be the ordinary channels whereby he might convey to men,
preventing, justifying, or sanctifying grace."[34] He distinguishes
between the "instituted" means of grace and the "prudential"
means.[35] The former are those specifically grounded in Christ's
instructions, and include prayer, searching the Scriptures, the
Lord's Supper, fasting, and Christian fellowship. The prudential
means of grace were the disciplines of the bands and classes
into which he organized the Methodist societies for the purpose
of promoting spiritual growth. We may note that whereas the
Lord's Supper is mentioned in Wesley's list of instituted means,
baptism is not. This is to be explained by the initiatory character
of baptism—its function as a singular event at the beginning of
the Christian life, not to be repeated. Wesley's enumeration of
means of grace, on the other hand, consists of those things that
promote the subsequent ongoing development of the holy life.
When he urges his listeners and readers to make use of the ordained means of grace, he speaks to adults, most of whom have
been baptized. Nevertheless in his treatments of baptism, it is
clear that he believes grace is conveyed through that sacrament
also, when it is accompanied by faith, and thus it may properly
be called a means of grace.[36] Baptism is a "means of grace, per-

---

32. Lawson, 155.
33. Gustaf Aulén, *The Faith of the Christian Church*, trans. Eric H. Wahlstrom (Philadelphia: Muhlenberg Press, 1960), 318.
34. *Works* 5:187.
35. Ibid. 8:322 ff.
36. Cf. ibid. 6:73-74; 10:191-93.

petually obligatory on all Christians."[37] The concept of "means
of grace" is embodied in Wesley's very definition of a sacrament-
—"an outward sign of inward grace, and *a means whereby we
receive the same.*"[38]

In noting what different theologians have designated as
means of grace, it becomes clear that there is a certain "elas-
ticity," as Aulén calls it, in the concept. "Christian faith has no
interest in circumscribing the compass of the means of grace."[39]
God can work through many and various means. On the other
hand, there is also a "stability" in the concept. "Just any old
thing" cannot be passed off as a means of grace. The stability
rests on the fact that Christ is Lord of the divine revelation and
that the establishing of the Church by the Spirit signifies the
realization of the reign of Christ. All means of grace must be
defined by the Christ event. The Word (both written and
preached) is a means of grace because its center is in Christ, the
Living Word. Prayer is a means of grace because it is prayer in
Christ's name. Certainly the sacraments are inseparable from the
work of Christ. Baptism in the name of the Father, Son, and
Holy Spirit is an identification with Christ (Rom. 6:3-8). The
Lord's Supper receives its content from the sacrificial life and
death of Christ. Christ is thus the ruling power of the means of
grace. In other words, the means of grace are the modes of the
Holy Spirit's activity in creating the Church, since the Holy
Spirit is also the Spirit of Christ.[40]

In relation to the means of grace, Christian faith is con-
fronted by two dangers. First is the possibility that the means of
grace will be understood in a mechanical way. The phrase
"means of grace" may be distorted to mean that there is something standing *between* the Spirit and the Christian, and that the
Spirit can only be given through such mechanical means. This is
the danger in the conception of the sacraments developed in the
medieval Catholic church. We overcome this by emphasizing
that the Spirit is not separate from the means of grace but constitutes their inner dynamic, and also that grace is to be under-

---

37. Ibid. 10:188.
38. Italics mine.
39. Aulén, 321.
40. Ibid.

stood in terms of the personal relationship God's grace offers to us. The second danger is a spiritualizing tendency that would abolish the means of grace altogether, seeing them as a barrier in our relation to God. It is argued that we must come to God directly and "immediately" in subjective mystical experience. This is the danger we discussed in the last section of chapter 1. Immediacy is gained at the price of surrendering the means of grace. The relation between God and human beings loses its content, and we are trapped in our own ego.[41]

Wesley was careful to make clear that the means of grace are not meritorious. They have no intrinsic power by virtue of their simply being performed. They have value to us only when we see that our salvation, from its inception to its consummation, is the work of God alone. That is the meaning of grace—God does for us what we cannot do for ourselves. Nevertheless, there are divinely ordained means by which this unmerited grace may come to us, and the sacraments are among the most important of these means.

The importance Wesley placed on the means of grace is clearly shown in the definition of the church as stated in the Methodist Twenty-five Articles of Religion. Article XIII, "Of the Church," was copied from the Church of England's article by the same title. It states: "The visible Church of Christ is a congregation of faithful men, in which the pure Word of God is preached, and the Sacraments duly administered according to Christ's ordinance, in all those things that of necessity are requisite to the same." Here the church is not defined in terms of its organization or ministry, but in terms of the means of grace. The means of grace are thus constitutive of the church. In this, Wesley is in agreement with the Protestant Reformers who defined the church in similar terms.

In a letter to William Law, Wesley unequivocally rejects any inward mystical way to holiness that would neglect the outward means:

> All the externals of religion are in order to the renewal of our soul in righteousness and true holiness. But it is not true that the external way is one and the internal way another.

---

41. Ibid., 320.

There is but one scriptural way wherein we receive inward grace—through the outward means which God hath appointed.[42]

We have been looking at the definition of "means." We now need to look into the definition of "grace" in this context. We have already noted that medieval Catholic theology conceived of grace in "substantial" or quasi-material terms, and that Luther rejected this conception and understood grace as the mercy of God, or the personal relationship of forgiveness that God offers to the unworthy sinner. In this sense grace is often described as "God's unmerited favor."

At the time of the Reformation, the debate about the number of sacraments was also a debate about the *nature* of the sacraments. Furthermore, differing views of sacraments reflected a difference in the understanding of grace. The numbering of the sacraments (seven) by the Roman Catholic church, which came to be fixed only through a long process of doctrinal development, was connected with the concept of the infusion of grace (understood as a divine "substance") that occurred by means of the sacraments. Understood in this way, grace needed to be replenished again and again throughout life, and since sacraments were the channels through which supernatural grace was infused into the soul, a sacrament was erected at each stage or aspect of life. The Reformers saw this as an error, insisting, for instance, that the sacraments of penance and confirmation were admissions that the grace given in baptism was insufficient and had to be continually replenished. Of course, Rome also knew that God's grace is favor or mercy, but she had come increasingly during the Middle Ages to stress grace as the infusion of a supernatural, impersonal, quasi-material substance.

John Wesley's theology, rooted as it is in the Anglican tradition, is a kind of *via media* (middle way) between Catholic and Protestant thought. With the Reformers, he understood grace as the unmerited personal favor of God, or as mercy, which addresses the *guilt* of sin. But he also understood grace as the divine enablement that is necessary for deliverance from the *power* of sin. The latter meaning of grace as enablement was not

---

42. *Letters* 3:366-67.

understood in the medieval Catholic sense of impersonal substance, however, but as the working of the Holy Spirit in the heart. Both meanings of grace, for Wesley, are encompassed by the Atonement. The grace of God manifested in the cross of Christ brings both justification and sanctification. The sacraments, then, are "the means by which the Holy Spirit applies the atonement of Christ in all its ramifications."[43]

When we classify the sacraments as "means of grace," it is important to assert that they do not mediate a special kind of "grace," or any other grace than that which comes to us also through the Word. "Christian faith knows of no other grace than that which consists in the self-impartation of divine love, or, in other words, the fact that God gives himself."[44] There is no greater gift than God himself. It is precisely *this* gift, the grace of the self-giving God, that is promoted and amplified in the sacraments.

In the foregoing we have discussed the sacraments under the category of "means of grace." But that category is broader than sacraments. Some things are classified as means of grace for which the Christian tradition has never claimed sacramental status. Baptism and the Lord's Supper are just *two* of the means of grace. But if the three Protestant criteria discussed in the first section of this chapter are considered significant, then the sacraments of baptism and the Lord's Supper are two of the most important means of grace. This claim can be made because in each of those two sacraments converge these three realities: (1) Christ's own authority, (2) the use of a physical sign (which has tremendous implications for our understanding of both creation and redemption), and (3) the word of promise granting us the forgiveness of sins. In none of the other means of grace do all three of these realities converge so powerfully.

We must now turn from the general category to look specifically at the sacraments and ask *what they are.*

D. VISIBLE WORDS

As stated previously, perhaps the best description of sacra-

---

43. Dunning, 541.
44. Aulén, 332.

ments ever given is that of Augustine, bishop of Hippo in North Africa, who lived from A.D. 354 to 430. It is certainly one of the shortest descriptions. Probably antiquity's greatest theologian, Augustine referred to sacraments as "visible words" *(verbum visible)*. In discussing sacraments, he said: "The word is added to the element, and there results the Sacrament, as if itself a kind of visible word."[45] Although Augustine was not attempting to give a formal definition of the word *sacrament* but was explaining the theological meaning of those acts performed when Christians gathered together, such as baptism and the Eucharist, his phrase "visible word" became "the sacramental slogan of the Western church."[46]

What did Augustine mean by "visible word"? He was mainly contrasting the visible word with the *invisible* word. By the latter he meant the inner reality of God himself that became "visible" in the Incarnation. The divine Word is itself inaccessible to our senses ("No one has ever seen God" [John 1:18]), but in the Incarnation He is revealed. As the Incarnate One speaks, "Therefore go . . . baptizing" and "Do this in remembrance of me" (Matt. 28:19; Luke 22:19), and when we obey by doing those things, God's inner truth becomes "visible" to our senses. We can agree with Jenson when he points out that in Augustine's sense of the word, all churches have sacraments.

> To someone who denied it, I would have little argument to present: I could only say, "Go and *watch* the church for a while." Church groups that themselves claim not to have sacraments are only indulging a semantic prejudice—though it may prove a disastrous indulgence, tempting them to discard necessary sacraments and create vacuums that will be filled somehow, perhaps most inappropriately to the gospel.[47]

In Augustine's understanding of sacraments as "visible words," it would be practically impossible to engage in any kind of worship without using sacraments.

---

45. "Tractus on the Gospel of John," 80.15.3, *Nicene and Post-Nicene Fathers*, 1st ser. (Grand Rapids: Wm. B. Eerdmans Publishing Co., 1978), 7:344.

46. Robert W. Jenson, *Visible Words: The Interpretation and Practice of Christian Sacraments* (Philadelphia: Fortress Press, 1978), 3.

47. Ibid., 5.

In the theology of the Reformation, however, more than a millennium later, the context of Augustine's phrase was shifted. In the teachings of the Reformers, "visible" was contrasted not so much with "invisible" as with "audible." A distinction was made between the Word that we hear and the Word that we see. Preaching, teaching, and all other forms of communication that are carried on in the sentences of language were called "audible" words. But, said the Reformers, God speaks not only in such audible ways but also by the kinds of signs that can be seen and touched and tasted and smelled. This should not be surprising, because we humans speak to each other in varied ways. Consider touching: If, by words, we speak to one another in God's name, in the sacraments we often *touch* each other in God's name. We act for God in acting toward each other. Our worship is full of hands: baptizing, pronouncing benediction, uniting the hands of lovers, anointing the sick, sprinkling a coffin with dust, and giving the bread and the cup. The actions are powerful symbols that complement what can be said with words.

Augustine's description of sacraments as "visible word" in contrast to the "invisible" Word, and the Reformation use of the term in contrast to the "audible" Word, should be seen not as mutually exclusive meanings, but rather as a difference of emphasis. Both aspects are central to the gospel. The invisible Word became visible in the Incarnation and becomes visible again as we partake of the sacramental elements. And in the preaching of the Church the Word becomes audible, and in the sacraments it again becomes visible. Again we can agree with Jenson when he says:

> The basic Augustinian-Reformation interpretations of the Christian sacraments as "visible words" of the gospel, seem to me so profoundly and primitively and obviously biblical that I have no special way to argue for them. To someone who attacked their theological rightness, I could only say, "Go and read the whole Bible yet again!"[48]

When the church speaks of sacraments as "visible word," the adjective, "visible," should not cause us to overlook the

---

48. Ibid.

noun, "word." The Reformation's concentration on the preaching of the Word in no way implied a depreciation of the sacraments. Sacraments are not in competition with the Word but are one of the ways the Word is proclaimed. The phrase "visible *word*" emphasizes that the sacraments have the character of a *message*.

It may help us to understand more clearly what we mean when we define sacraments as "visible words" if we will but look around us and take note of the way we communicate by means of visible words in everyday life. One example of a visible word is a handshake. More than once I have stood in a mortuary during visitation hours and watched as a bereaved person was greeted by an old friend with a warm handshake, watery eyes, and a quivering chin. No words were spoken, but a message of sympathy, caring, and understanding was communicated—probably much more effectively than if words had been attempted. That is one example of "visible word."

Another is a kiss. When a man kisses the woman he loves, he is sending a message that "speaks louder than words." He is saying, "I love you," without uttering the words. A message is being sent by way of a visible word.

Let us consider this scenario: A father comes home from work, sees in the playpen his infant son, not yet walking or talking, picks him up, holds him lovingly in his arms, and plants a kiss on the child's cheek. I submit that a message of love has been received by the child—far more meaningfully than if the father had merely looked across the room and said, "Hello, son, Daddy loves you." Furthermore, the mother, looking on, also understands by the action that love is being spread through the "community" (family). As for the infant son, he may not have conceptualized very clearly what hugs and kisses are. He may have no theology of love, so to speak, and no rational understanding of the sociology of the family or human relationships. But he *gets the message!* The message has been transmitted much more effectively in a visible or nonverbal form than it could ever be by spoken words. Furthermore, the child's intellectual grasp of the meaning of what has happened, his understanding of the transaction that has taken place, has very little, if anything, to do with the reality and effectiveness of the message conveyed. *Let us remember this when we discuss infant baptism later on!*

E. OPERATIVE SYMBOLS

The meaning of religious symbolism was discussed in chapter 2, and the suggestion was made that *symbol* might be a more comprehensive and meaningful term than *sign* for a contemporary understanding of sacraments. In the language of the Reformation and later Protestantism, "sign" usually referred mainly to the material element (bread, wine, or water). But a "symbol," as Tillich has pointed out, participates in the reality it represents. Another way of saying this, looking at it from the other end, so to speak, is that symbols *do* something.

When we speak of sacraments as symbols, we imply that the sacraments accomplish something; they perform some work; they "operate"—albeit not apart from faith, Protestants would insist on affirming. Thus Christian theology, for the most part, has understood sacraments as "operative symbols." Let us look at the "operation" the sacraments perform.

To call sacraments operative symbols is to affirm not only that they *proclaim* a truth but that through them God *performs* an act of grace corresponding to that truth. Their "work" is to convey grace to the person who receives the sacraments in faith. This does not mean—we must be careful to remember—that grace is some quasi-physical substance channeled to us by way of the sacraments. Rather it is grace in a *relational* sense. It is God's offer of His unmerited favor to the one who comes to baptism or to the Lord's table to appropriate by faith the divinely given "means" of grace.

As operative symbols, the sacraments are more than mere indications of something that has been done apart from and without the sacraments, as if the sacraments were a "take it or leave it" option. Perhaps the illustration of marriage will make this clearer.[49] The rite of matrimony involves certain symbolic acts, words, and material things. Among these are the spoken wedding vows, the giving and receiving of a ring, the signature of the officiant on a piece of paper, and the recording of that paper at the county courthouse or wherever legal records are kept. Now at first glance it might appear that all those things are merely *outward signs* of the marriage and that the marriage itself

---

49. For this illustration I am indebted to Lawson, 164.

is something inward, or spiritual, or invisible, that takes place in the hearts of the bride and groom. But in human society this is not the case at all. The vows, the ring, the signature on a paper, and the filing of that document in an official depository of records—*these things are what actually marry the couple!* Of course, they are also vivid expressions by which the bride and groom declare their love to each other. But at the same time, they perform a work, and convey a status, corresponding to the love that is symbolized. They are operative symbols. Incurable romantics like to believe the old saying that "marriages are made in heaven." We can hope that they are, but that is not the whole truth. For the protection of society, as understood by the consensus of human history, marriages are also made at the county courthouse!

Now if one wishes to argue against this, and keeps insisting that those things and actions and words are mere unnecessary and dispensable outward indicators of something that is really inner, spiritual, invisible, and heavenly, then that person cannot argue against the modern practice of living together without marriage. Many couples who choose the latter life-style will ask, "What is a mere piece of paper?" They will insist that it is only love that counts, that the promises they make to each other in private are all that matters, that they do not need public or legal trappings to make their marriage authentic. Translated into theological language, they have a low view of sacraments; they are trafficking in cheap grace![50] Marriage is not merely an individual matter, or an agreement between *two* individuals; it is a *community* affair. In Christian marriage, the marriage is brought inside the church, and grace is operative for the community as well as for the individuals being married.

Of course the illustration of marriage does not *prove* anything about the sacraments of baptism and the Lord's Supper. It only illustrates something. But the sacramentalist would argue

---

50. Of course, it must be granted, this may be an argument for making marriage a sacrament. One may wonder if by doing so, Protestantism might have been more resistant to the pressures of secular culture in yielding to easy divorce. Maybe not, for Roman Catholicism has been slowly yielding to the same pressures. But when the Christian society, the believing community (the church), is involved in the marriage union, there can be more help in maintaining the relationship than when it is treated as a merely private arrangement. Cf. James F. White, *Christian Worship*, 160.

that what is illustrated is abundantly true with regard to sacraments. Not only do they *say* something, but they actually *do* something. It must be remembered, however, that neither the outward signs of a marriage nor the outward signs of a sacrament perform their work *ex opere operato* ("by the work performed"). Without inner love and commitment, the marriage ceremony would only be a farce, a parody of the true meaning of marriage. Likewise, without faith the sacraments are merely outward forms accomplishing nothing. But *with* love and commitment, the marriage ceremony actually brings a true marriage into being. And *with* faith, the sacraments accomplish what they were designed to do—impart to the believer the grace of God. The "outward sign" and the "inward grace" working together— these are what make a sacrament.

In discussing sacraments as operative symbols, John Lawson shows how the Eucharist falls into that category:

> The Holy Communion is much more than a solemn dramatization of the truths seen in the Cross, as a visual alternative to a spoken sermon on the same subject, though among other things it is this. To celebrate the sacrament is the way by which the Church makes herself one with the Lord as He offers His atoning sacrifice, and by which she receives her share of what Christ accomplished in His death and resurrection. Thus the Holy Communion is not only a visual and acted symbol of Christ's sacrifice of obedience. It is an *operative* symbol of His sacrifice. God has pledged Himself to use it to bring to the Church, and to reverent and believing communicants, a due share of the merits of Christ's death and resurrection.[51]

Among the means of grace, therefore, sacraments are unique. God has ordained them, and Christ has commanded our participation in them, and when received in faith, they convey to us a special status before God and unlimited access to His grace.

F. GUARDIANS OF BIBLICAL FAITH

There is still one more important answer to the question,

---

51. Lawson, 164.

What *are* sacraments? In a profound way, the Christian sacraments are the Church's way of safeguarding biblical faith against heretical points of view that arise from nonbiblical sources but that have from time to time in Christian history made inroads into Christian thought. Against such viewpoints, the sacraments of baptism and Eucharist stand as sentinels with flaming swords, like the cherubim at Eden's gate, guarding the entrance to the garden of biblical truth. In this role, the sacraments perform three important functions:

1. *The Sacraments Safeguard the Biblical Doctrine of Creation.* Against all forms of *dualism,* the biblical faith asserts the essential goodness of the created world. Dualism is the theory that there are two ultimate realities, both of which have existed from all eternity. The two are mutually opposed and completely different. These two realities (or "substances") are variously designated, for example, as spirit and matter, mind and matter, mind and body, soul and body, good and evil, or God and Satan.[52] There have been many forms of dualism, such as Zoroastrianism and Manichaeism in ancient Persia, Taoism in China, most Eastern mystical religions, much of Greek thought (especially Platonism), and the Gnosticism of the early Christian centuries.

Gnosticism became the first great heresy to pose a threat to early Christianity. It reached its peak of development in the second century. It takes its name from *gnōsis,* the Greek word for knowledge, but it was not a merely intellectual kind of knowledge that the Gnostics sought, but a mystical illumination that only the spiritually elite could attain. One of its basic tenets was dualism, the belief that all matter, including the human body, is evil. "Salvation" to the Gnostic was the release of the human spirit from the bondage of the physical world and its return to the realm of pure spirit. Such dualistic explanations often seem to give a plausible account of what is so obvious in the world around us, the presence of good and evil, order and disorder.

---

52. Although there is a biblical doctrine of Satan, such a being is not eternal, i.e., he once was not (having been first, according to some traditions, a fallen angel), and, in the Book of Revelation, he is destined to be eventually destroyed. This is a type of dualism, but not an *ultimate* dualism.

"Dualism requires one to shut one's eyes to neither side of the picture."[53] But faith in the one God who is Creator and Lord rules out any absolute dualism in the Bible.

Of course, the contrast between sin and forgiveness, misery and salvation, or evil and good was clearly recognized by Israel, and she refused easy answers—easy attempts to reconcile such troublesome opposites, attempts that would blur the distinction between good and evil. The same realism is continued in the New Testament. Paul speaks of an antithesis between law and gospel, works and faith, flesh and spirit, and the inner and the outer man. John speaks of the opposition between light and darkness, life and death, truth and falsehood. Nevertheless, these practical biblical descriptions do not amount to an *ultimate* dualism, since the Bible understands that God is Lord of all nature and all history.[54]

Dualism puts soul and body in opposition, destroying the unity of the human being, and making the senses useless or even harmful for spiritual life. Plato considered the body to be the soul's prison, blocking the way to its contemplation of Beauty. If, then, the soul would contemplate, it must escape from the body. For Plato, the religious life demands that human beings become wholly immaterial. One's religious life cannot be perfected, even if it can exist at all, unless the body is left behind.

Against all worldviews that see reality in terms of ultimate dualism, the sacraments stand as safeguards. How? The sacramentalist vision discerns a meeting point between the earthly and the heavenly. Sheer dualism is rejected, if by this we understand that the universe is forever divided between the spiritual and the material, the eternal and the temporal, or the visible and the invisible, realms. Sacramental theology rejects the popular Platonic notion that reality is located totally in the spiritual realm, and that the material realm is only a shadow. It also rejects many of the popular teachings of various Eastern religions

53. Geddes MacGregor, *Introduction to Religious Philosophy* (Boston: Houghton Mifflin Co., 1959), 71.

54. Cf. Rob L. Staples, "Dualism," in *Beacon Dictionary of Theology,* ed. Richard S. Taylor (Kansas City: Beacon Hill Press of Kansas City, 1983), 176.

whose idea of salvation is escape from the visible world into some spiritual reality.

Sacramental theology is world-affirming, not world-renouncing. It is unhappy with references to "visible" and "invisible" realms as if they were two different worlds. Of course, it recognizes that such a distinction may be helpful for many of our human patterns of thought. But at the heart of sacramentalist vision lies the robust affirmation that the created order, from aardvarks to zebras, from angels to zygotes, are all cut from one good piece of the fabric of creation. There are not two entirely distinct worlds, one visible, the other invisible. God is Maker of heaven and earth in one great creative act. "He made spirits and he made stones, and they all inhabit one huge world."[55]

In biblical faith, sin and evil brought about the distinction. It is after the Fall that we get a distinction between incorruptible and corruptible realms, and it must be remembered that corruption applies as much to the spiritual realm as to the material. Devil, demons, and damned souls in hell are spirits in a state of corruption. Paul's catalog of the "works of the flesh" in Gal. 5:19 is mostly a list of "spiritual" sins. Howard suggests that

> although there is not a syllable explaining this in the Bible, and certainly no scientific research will ever be able to uncover any data on the point, it may be imagined that a film, as it were, was imposed on our very eyeballs at the Fall, so that we lost the ability to perceive the one whole fabric in which angels and ourselves inhabit a continuous realm. We can no longer *see* very much. We had sown a disjuncture into things by our action (this is ours, and that is God's), and we reaped the harvest in our very eyeballs. We had now to perceive things as divided. Who knows?[56]

A fanciful desciption, for sure, but the point is well-taken. A world divided into two eternally opposed realms is not the world of the Bible. Philosophical theologians would say the world is "existentially" fallen but "essentially" good. In simple terms, that means that the world as God made it is good; we messed it up; He seeks to redeem it, because it is valuable. Fur-

55. Thomas Howard, "IRM," 11.
56. Ibid., 12.

thermore, His Son, the Lord Christ, bequeathed to His Church a way to keep proclaiming this basic goodness of creation and to guard against all dualistic threats. How? Through sacraments.

Whenever we submit to being baptized with water (matter), or each time we approach the Lord's table and eat a piece of bread (matter) and drink the fruit of the vine (matter), we are affirming something about our *redemption*. But in addition to that—and admittedly secondary to it—we are saying something about the *creation*. We are striking a blow against all forms of dualism. We are saying: This water, or this bread, or this wine is a vehicle, a residency, a "means" of divine grace; it is therefore good!

Historic Christianity is essentially sacramental in character because through the Incarnation matter has been shown to be, not evil or alien to divine indwelling, but capable of being the expression of divine truth and grace (John 1:14). This is the point we made in the first section of chapter 3, that the same principle that made Incarnation possible also makes sacraments possible. But this idea has been a difficult one for some Christians to grasp. One of the long-standing objections to sacraments is that there is something unspiritual about the use of such material aids to worship, and that a truly spiritual religion would not need them.

What is involved here is one's understanding of spirituality. For biblical faith, it cannot mean an escape from the material world. Nor can it mean a sort of grudging putting up with the material world while we shut it out as much as possible so that we may cultivate the spiritual life. Spirituality is formed in personal and interpersonal ways, through living together in a material world. This means living together in a most material sense— sharing the same house, the same room, the same table, the same meals. For animals, a meal is a meal—a necessity for survival. But for persons, it is also a means of fellowship. In all ages the breaking of bread together, and the sharing of a common cup, have had profound spiritual significance, as a means and expression of community.

The same can be said of our personal relationship with God. "God is Spirit," we read in John 4:24 (Phillips), but we human beings are *both* spiritual *and* physical beings, and neither aspect is to be considered inferior to the other. When God wanted to reveal himself to us fully, He sent His Son, born of a woman. The Word became flesh! In talking or thinking about God, it is therefore impossible for Christians to dispense with metaphors and symbols drawn from the natural world, for that is the world into which God came to reveal himself to us. He does not ask us to rise above our natural world in order to worship Him in some world-renouncing "spiritual" way. No, He came down to us in the Incarnation, and again He comes down to us in the bread and the cup! We cannot easily engage in the public worship of God without words and music and gestures and standing and kneeling and holding hymnals and reading scriptures. We need to hear something and also to do something and to see something—some "thing." So we need not only the Word but also the sacraments—the "visible word." The water and the bread and the wine are perceived by our bodily senses. There is nothing unspiritual about that. The body is not evil. God made it and said it was good. We may prostitute or pervert or defile or abuse what God has made. But when He redeems it, it is still a body. Even in the final resurrection we will be spiritual bodies rather than disembodied spirits (1 Cor. 15:44). For such profound truths as this, the sacraments are a safeguard.

Because the sacraments safeguard the biblical understanding of creation, the consistent sacramentalist will be an environmentalist concerned about ecology. It would be presumptuous for a book on sacraments to dogmatize about specific ways of implementing this concern. The fields of science, technology, law, and politics, as well as religion and ethics, all converge upon that problem. But a proper view of sacraments will give the Christian some general guidelines for forming a personal theology of ecology and will give him or her a basic perspective toward creation. The sacramentalist will not carelessly and needlessly contribute to the waste of natural resources, the depletion of the ozone layer, the production of acid rain, or the pollution of rivers, oceans, and atmosphere. The sacramentalist vision enables one to sing with profound conviction,

> This is my Father's world,
> And to my listening ears
> All nature sings, and round me rings
> The music of the spheres.

This is my Father's world;
I rest me in the thought
Of rocks and trees, of skies and seas—
His hand the wonders wrought.

This is my Father's world.
The birds their carols raise;
The morning light, the lily white
Declare their Maker's praise.
This is my Father's world.
He shines in all that's fair;
In the rustling grass I hear Him pass;
He speaks to me everywhere.
                          —MALTBIE D. BABCOCK

The sacramentalist knows that everything we are and have on this pilgrimage from womb to tomb belongs to God. We are but stewards of whatever portion of planet earth's crust has been entrusted to us. Idolatry is not something that only the ancient Canaanites practiced; we engage in it whenever we forget that everything we have is a gift. One function of sacraments is to help us remember. In short, baptism and the Eucharist, when all their remarkable nuances are appropriated by the religious imagination, stand as sentinels guarding the priceless treasure of the created world whose essential goodness was declared by the Creator himself in the very beginning.

2. *The Sacraments Safeguard the Historicity of Biblical Faith.* For the earliest Christians, with their background in Judaism, the sacraments were less a bridging of the gulf between spirit and matter than a conquest of the temporal tension between the present age and the age to come, which Christ had ushered in. In the above discussion, as we considered the relation between spirit and matter, and between the living Christ and the elements of bread and wine, the problem was posed more in terms of *space* than of *time.* Important as the spatial dimension of the problem is, it is more of a Hellenistic way of getting at the problem than a biblical one. Time and history, more than nature, are the categories of biblical thought.

In both nature and history, God makes himself known. As for nature, biblical faith has said, "The heavens declare the glory of God; the skies proclaim the work of his hands" (Ps. 19:1). But God is not seen in nature unambiguously. Many phenomena in nature "impress upon us the meaninglessness and cold insensitivity of existence" and "imply a testing rather than a support of faith."[57]

God's revelation in *history* is even more decisive than that found in nature. History is in a special sense the locus of God's revelation, for it is in history that His mighty acts of salvation were accomplished. But with history, as well as with nature, the revelation of God is not without ambiguity. "If nature contains much that is mysterious and meaningless, this is true in still greater measure of history."[58]

What is decisive in history for faith is the appearance of Jesus Christ in the midst of history as the One who incarnates and reveals God. Christianity is a historical faith. Its formative events were played out on the stage of history. To forget this is to slip into a false intellectualism that fails to understand the way the biblical God accomplishes His purposes. Early Christian theologians appropriated Plato's idea of the "Form of the Good" or the "Form of Forms" and used the concept to describe the Christian God. In so doing, they opened up the unfortunate possibility of conceiving God as utterly transcendent and beyond history, unlike the God of the Bible. This amounts to a dualism between eternity and time, similar to the dualism between spirit and matter that we considered previously.

In neither kind of dualism could God possibly establish sacraments. He could not act in the world. But the biblical God does act. He acts not only in establishing sacraments but in imparting His grace to the recipient, through faith, whenever the sacraments are administered. The sacraments therefore constitute not merely a human word whereby we give testimony to our faith, but a divine action in which grace is given. It is a divine action in the world, in history, and in the present. This concept of a God who acts is safeguarded whenever we receive the sacraments. In baptism, and at the table of the Lord when we receive the bread and the cup, we become the beneficiaries of

---

57. Aulén, 27.
58. Ibid., 28.

the action of God who imparts His grace to us here and now.

3. *The Sacraments Safeguard the Idea of the Transcendence of God.* Opposite to the spatial and temporal kinds of dualism we have been discussing is the error known as pantheism. This is the view that identifies God and nature as if they were the same. "God is All and All is God" is a popular pantheistic slogan. Pantheism was present as a religious concept in Greek and Roman thought, and in Hindu and other Eastern religions. From time to time it has appeared in Western thought in varying degrees and has influenced some forms of Christian thought. It is currently found in the thought of the so-called New Age movement. Pantheism is more subtle and less explicitly a system than dualism. Its tendency is to obliterate the boundaries between spirit and matter, between God and the world.

Pantheism may be conceptualized in different ways, or according to different models. First, and the most simple, is the view that God and nature (or God and the world) are merely two names for the same thing. Most pantheism, however, is not quite that simple. A second model depicts God as the "soul" of the world, but "soul" is not exactly spiritual but a sort of highly refined matter that permeates the world and constitutes its unity. A third model pictures the world as "erupting" out of the being of God, much like lava erupts from a volcano or water issues from a spring.

In each of these models the line of demarcation between God and the world is difficult to detect, if it exists at all. In none of these models is the world the result of the free creative act of God, as it is in biblical thought. The basic error of pantheism, from the standpoint of biblical faith, is its erasing, or at least blurring, the distinction between the Creator and the creation. In each of these models (and others that could be constructed), the emphasis is on God's *immanence,* which is the exact opposite of transcendence.

How do the sacraments safeguard biblical faith against this error? The answer lies in the significance of symbolism. If God and the world are the same, or if the boundaries between them are blurred, then there can be no creation of symbols, and no communication through them, no art, no rites, no actions that point us beyond the world. Thus to eat bread in the Eucharist would be to eat a piece of God! Even more absurdly, since we humans are part of the world also, and thus a part of God, in the Eucharist God would be eating a piece of himself![59] There would be no symbolism in that, and no necessity for symbolism. But we have already seen how dependent Christian faith is on symbolism. We have noted that symbols participate in the reality to which they point, but are *not identical to the reality they symbolize.*[60] As Tillich says, "The ultimate transcends all levels of reality, it is the ground of reality itself."[61] In order to express the ultimate ground of reality (i.e., God), we must use religious symbols that are taken from the material of our daily experiences—natural, personal, and historical. Religious symbols participate in the holiness of that to which they point, that is, to the holy itself, but the symbol is not itself the holy. There would be no need of symbolism to bridge the gap between God and the world if there were no gap to be bridged.

Sacraments stand as a sentinel against pantheism and guard the idea of the transcendence of God. In the sacramentalist vision, a sacrament betokens God, bespeaks God, constitutes a communication between God and human being; but it is not the same as God. This is true even in the Roman Catholic view of the Eucharist, where the bread and wine are changed into the body and blood of Christ during the celebration of the mass. This is known as "transubstantiation" and will be discussed in chapter 7. Here it need only be noted that, although Protestants reject the theory, transubstantiation is not pantheistic. In the theory of transubstantiation, bread *becomes* the "body of Christ"; it is not already a part of God.

*   *   *

In this chapter we have considered the question, What *are* sacraments? Applying the Protestant criteria, we agreed with the

59. Another view of God and the world is known as *panentheism*, sometimes called dipolar theism, which holds that although God is not identical with the world, the world is *in* God, and that the world is, in a sense, God's "body." Although this view softens somewhat the objections raised against pantheism, it does not dispose of them completely. Traditional Christianity has held that although God creates and maintains a relation with the world, He is nevertheless *other than* the world.

60. See the discussion of symbolism in chapter 2, section C.

61. Paul Tillich, "Theology and Symbolism," in *Religious Symbolism*, ed. F. Earnest Johnson (Port Washington, N.Y.: Kennikat Press, 1955), 109.

Chapter Five

BAPTISM: SACRAMENT OF INITIATION

God's Word is spoken in nature and in history, in creation and in redemption, in preaching and in sacraments. The supreme and final Word of God is Jesus Christ, the Word made flesh. If Jesus Christ is the Word of God, and if the Word is to speak to the whole person, Christian faith dare not lose the word that comes through sacrament, because human beings are not disembodied spirits but beings of both body and spirit. We live by symbol and sacrament, as well as by the spoken word, and we need "*every* word that comes from the mouth of God" (Matt. 4:4, italics mine).

For many Christians, especially Protestants, and more especially those in the Wesleyan/holiness tradition, sacramental practice seems meaningless and irrelevant. To some extent, this is the case with regard to the Lord's Supper, but it is even more the case with baptism. In Communion services, the sermon often attempts to interpret the meaning of the Lord's Supper, but one seldom hears sermons on the meaning of baptism, despite the fact that in the New Testament there are more allusions to baptism than to the Eucharist. This near-silence from the Wesleyan/holiness pulpit regarding baptism is ironic in view of the emphasis the same pulpit places on the Great Commission and on the event of Pentecost, in each of which baptism is highly significant.

Baptism, as it is known in the New Testament and practiced in the Church, is the first of the two sacraments recognized by Protestants. It is administered only once, at the point of initiation into the Christian community. The forms and modes of administration vary greatly among Protestant denominations, but the essential action and the accompanying words are quite uniform and consistent where Christian baptism is practiced.

It is not our purpose here to trace the history of the beginnings of this sacrament. A brief summary will have to suffice. Washings and lustrations of various kinds have been practiced in many religions, including the religion of the Old Testament (for example, in much of Leviticus and Numbers). Ezek. 36:24-26 has full New Testament ramifications. The message of Jeremiah and others was that the old covenant was to be replaced by a new covenant. This produced in later times various attempts to actualize the new covenant. The best-known example is the group connected with the Dead Sea Scrolls who regarded themselves as the Community of the New Covenant. Entry into such groups seems to have been by a form of baptismal ablution. The importance of washing in water was emphasized by the sects of later Judaism, such as the Pharisees, whose many washings we read about in the Gospels. These are not direct antecedents of baptism, except that they illustrate the importance the people of God placed upon ceremonial washings and cleansings.

The exact origin of baptismal practice is not completely clear and has been a subject of considerable debate. It has been generally understood that an immediate antecedent of Christian baptism was the rite of Jewish proselyte baptism, which came to take the place of circumcision for those Gentiles who were converted to Judaism. But it is uncertain exactly when proselyte baptism began and whether it preceded the ministry of John the Baptist.[1]

The most immediate antecedent of Christian baptism was Johannine baptism (the baptism practiced by John the Baptist), in which those who were Jews by birth were treated as prose-

---

1. For a discussion of this issue and others concerning Jewish proselyte baptism, see G. R. Beasley-Murray, *Baptism in the New Testament* (Grand Rapids: Wm. B. Eerdmans Publishing Co., 1962), 18-31.

lytes and called to repentance (Matt. 3:8-9). Jesus identified himself with the Baptist's work and was baptized at the hands of John (Matt. 3:13 ff.; Mark 1:9-11; Luke 3:21-22; John 1:29 ff.). He then took up the theme of baptism, and His disciples took up its practice. According to John's Gospel, the disciples practiced baptism even during Jesus' earthly ministry,[2] and Matthew gives us the direct command of the risen Lord that His apostles should baptize as well as preach and teach (Matt. 28:19). Finally, baptism was urged and practiced on the Day of Pentecost, the birthday of the Christian Church (Acts 2:38-41), and from that time forward in the Church's history.

Christian baptism, then, had its real beginning at Pentecost. John the Baptist had explained the difference between his baptism and that of Christ. The distinctive element of the latter would be the gift of the Holy Spirit, which is imparted neither by Jewish proselyte baptism nor by John's baptism (Matt. 3:11; Luke 3:16; cf. Acts 19:2). Thus Christian baptism is only possible after the Pentecostal outpouring of the Spirit. Thereafter in the Book of Acts, faith in Christ was accompanied by baptism (Acts 2:38, 41; 8:12-13, 36, 38; 9:18; etc.). This is substantiated by Paul in his Epistles. He implies that baptism was already generally practiced by the time he wrote First Corinthians (12:13), and he presupposes that those in the Church at Rome—of which he had no firsthand knowledge—had been baptized (Rom. 6:3). The Church had been baptizing new converts for approximately two decades before the first documents about baptism were written, such as the Acts of the Apostles and Paul's Epistles. A generation of Christians had grown up familiar with baptism. By the time written New Testament documents came into existence, baptism was already a common practice in the Church.

As the documents began to appear, however, what we see are not technical theological explanations of why Christians baptize. Instead, we find metaphors and images in which baptism is compared to something already well-known. These images are strikingly natural in their form. They are not cast in ra-

---

2. John 4:1-2. Verse 2 seems to be a clarification of 3:22, where John states that Jesus also baptized. If He did, it was apparently during the earliest stages of His ministry. Cf. Oscar Cullmann, *Baptism in the New Testament*, trans. J. K. S. Reid (London: SCM Press, 1950), 9 n. 1.

tional categories but in experiences from everyday life, such as birth, washing, putting on clothes, death, and burial. They are not abstractions but daily events. They are images with an amazing richness and variety.

In the New Testament, Christian baptism always carries the meaning of *initiation* into Christian faith and life. Wesley calls it "the initiatory sacrament, which enters us into covenant with God."[3] As such, it has five interrelated but distinguishable meanings: (1) It is the mark of our inclusion in the new covenant that Christ established. (2) It is the symbol of our identification with the death of Christ. (3) It is the symbol of our participation in the resurrected life of Christ. (4) It is the symbol of our reception of the Holy Spirit, which is the Spirit of Christ. (5) It is the action through which we are made part of Christ's Body, the Church. There is much overlapping between these different aspects of baptism, and seldom does the New Testament discuss one aspect in complete isolation from the others. But there are instructive theological nuances in each of them that can easily be missed if one does not consider them separately. We will now give attention to each.

A. BEARING THE MARK OF CHRIST

From the beginning, God has "marked" His people. Very early in the biblical story, when Cain, the firstborn of Adam and Eve, brought to God an unacceptable sacrifice and subsequently murdered his brother, he was sentenced to be a restless wanderer on the earth. Such punishment was deserved. But the God of judgment is also the God of mercy. This merciful God "put a mark on Cain." This mark was not so much one of judgment as it was of grace. God put His mark on Cain, not to condemn him but to protect him from the violence of retaliatory justice (Gen. 4:15). The exact nature of the mark remains a mystery, but the story teaches us that God does not easily let go of sinful and fallen human beings, that He does not lightly abandon us to the hell of our own making (estrangement, loneliness, and fear), but that God's mercy, as well as His judgment, follows us wherever we go.

---

3. *Works* 10:188.

Where can I go from your Spirit?
Where can I flee from your presence?
If I go up to the heavens, you are there;
If I make my bed in the depths, you are there.
(Ps. 139:7-8)

Still, the story of Cain remains a tragedy. In spite of the divine mercy, Cain fears the blood of his slain brother more than he trusts the Lord of Life. He "went out from the Lord's presence" and remained a fugitive and a wanderer, alienated from God (Gen. 4:16).

Of course, the New Testament does not build upon the story of Cain in its treatment of baptism. Yet the parallel is instructive. In His grace, God finds us where He found Cain— lonely, fearful, guilty, and estranged from the community by our own waywardness. In baptism, He puts His mark on us. To be baptized is to recognize the need for redeeming grace. In baptism we confess that alone we are lost and helpless. We acknowledge that we belong with the community of God, and that we are our brother's keeper. Yet, like the mark of Cain, the mark of baptism is no harsh, vindictive judgment, but the offer of God's grace, which is extended to us even when we have been disobedient and hidden ourselves from His presence.[4] Baptism is God's mark of ownership.

We do not know what Cain's mark was. Was it physical? Was it visible? Was it an indelible scar like Hester Prynne's scarlet letter in Hawthorne's masterpiece? We do not know. But this we know: *The mark of baptism leaves no scar.* How marvelous are the methods of grace! Baptism is a "washing" that points to the reality that we are "washed in the blood of the Lamb." We do not need to bear the deeper scars of that mark, for the scars are Christ's. He bore the burden of sin and estrangement to give us His fellowship. "He was pierced for our transgressions . . . and by his wounds we are healed" (Isa. 53:5). The mark of Christ is seen in the Cross. The Cross is the proclamation of a redeemed community of God, and baptism is His mark that welcomes us into that community.[5]

---

4. Cf. John Frederick Jansen, *The Meaning of Baptism* (Philadelphia: Westminster Press, 1958), 21 ff.
5. Ibid., 24.

The story of Cain is found in the Book of Genesis. At the other end of the biblical revelation, we encounter again the truth that God has marked His people. In that strange and mysterious vision that is the Book of Revelation, the seer of Patmos expresses a tremendous truth. Years before, Jesus had taught that "no one can serve two masters" (Matt. 6:24), but for John this truth takes on cosmic proportions as he foresees the ultimate destiny of all humanity. On one hand he sees a vast host following the Beast who forces everyone to receive a mark on the right hand or on the forehead, so that no one can buy or sell unless he has the mark. But on the other hand John looks and sees on Mount Zion 144,000 who have the name of the Lamb and of the Father written on their foreheads (Rev. 7:1-8; 13:11-17; 14:1). At other times in John's vision the company of the redeemed swells to "a great multitude that no one could count, from every nation, tribe, people and language, standing before the throne and in front of the Lamb" (7:9). The Lamb does not stand alone, for His people bear His name on their foreheads.

The meaning for us is clear. Every man is a marked man. Every woman is a marked woman. Every child is a marked child. In the conflict of loyalties there is no middle way. We cannot serve two masters. Every person bears either the mark of the Beast or the mark of the Lamb.

From Genesis to Revelation, and everywhere in between, God marked His people. Under the old covenant, God ordained a sign by which to mark His chosen people. He told Abraham, the father of the faithful, to circumcise himself and all the male descendants that would be born in his house. "You are to undergo circumcision, and it will be the sign of the covenant between me and you" (Gen. 17:11). All uncircumcised males were breakers of God's covenant and were to be cut off from their people (v. 14).

Here is established a pattern of salvation from which God never wavers. He takes the initiative in making a covenant with Abraham and approaches him in sheer grace. God's grace is met by Abraham's faith, and he is put right with God (Gen. 15:6; Rom. 4:3). Circumcision was proof of the validity of God's covenant, but its efficacy was not automatic. Others (such as Ishmael and Esau) were circumcised, but it did them no good, for their hearts were not right in the sight of God. The outward sign did not correspond with the inner reality.

Baptism is the mark of initiation into the new covenant, just as circumcision was initiation into the old. Paul brings these two sacramental symbols together and links them with the death and resurrection of Christ. He tells the Colossians: "In him also you were circumcised with a circumcision made without hands, by putting off the body of flesh in the circumcision of Christ; and you were buried with him in baptism, in which you were also raised with him through faith in the working of God, who raised him from the dead" (2:11-12, RSV). Baptism, then, like circumcision under the old covenant, is a mark of the agreement between God's grace and our response. Not of His grace alone, but "through faith." Not of our response alone, but "the working of God." It is the seal stamped both on His initiative and our response.[6]

Circumcision was not the only covenant sign in the Old Testament that is used by New Testament writers to illuminate the meaning of baptism. For the apostle Peter, the flood in the time of Noah throws light on the sacrament. He writes about the days when

> God waited patiently in the days of Noah while the ark was being built. In it only a few people, eight in all, were saved through water, and this water symbolizes baptism that now saves you also—not the removal of dirt from the body but the pledge of a good conscience toward God. It saves you by the resurrection of Jesus Christ *(1 Pet. 3:20-21).*

Here it is clear that, for Peter, baptism is salvific, but not automatically so; it does not save *ex opere operato* ("by the work performed"). An inward response ("the pledge of a good conscience") to the divine initiative is necessary. This word "pledge" (Greek *eperōtēma*, which may be translated "request," "appeal" [RSV, etc.], or "response," as well as "pledge" as in the NIV) is used, in this form, only here in the New Testament.[7] It has a

---

6. Cf. Michael Green, *Baptism: Its Purpose, Practice, and Power* (Downers Grove, Ill.: InterVarsity Press, 1987), 25.
7. The verb form is used often and is translated as "ask." Cf. W. F. Arndt and F. W.

meaning similar to the Latin *sacramentum*.[8] On the authority of "many good interpreters," Wesley translates *eperōtēma* as "stipulation, contract, or covenant."[9] Just as God marked off Noah's family, setting them apart from the rest of sinful humanity, and saved them through water, the apostle says He now saves us through an outward symbol (water) that requires an inward response.

Water is a powerful symbol. It helps to create life, but it can destroy it. It nourishes life, yet it can drown it. It can be healing, but it can be destructive. The biblical writers knew this. They knew that though water can cover the entire earth and close over all humanity, it cannot close over God whose Spirit in the beginning "was hovering over the waters" (Gen. 1:2). During the Flood, God remembers Noah and brings the ark to safety. The waters recede, and God sets a rainbow in the sky and remembers His covenant. "And God said, 'This is the sign of the covenant I am making between me and you . . . a covenant for all generations to come: I have set my rainbow in the clouds, and it will be the sign of the covenant between me and the earth'" (9:12-13). Thus the story of the Flood, which is the story of destruction, becomes in an even greater measure the story of salvation. Because of this, Peter sees an analogy between the Flood and baptism.

> The water of Baptism, like the water of the Flood, symbolizes for the writer the end of an old life, for it sweeps an old aeon into oblivion. The old life, as the old world, must die if a new life and a new world are to be born. He points out that Baptism means much more than the cleansing judgment of God. The same Spirit who moved over the face of the deep to create light and life moved over the sign of the baptismal water. The same God who saved Noah through the Flood is still calling and gathering his people today.[10]

Peter's words in the scripture passage under discussion, 1 Pet. 3:20-21, are paraphrased by J. B. Phillips as follows:

Gingrich, *A Greek-English Lexicon of the New Testament and Other Early Christian Literature* (Chicago: University of Chicago Press, 1957), 284-85.

8. See the discussion at the beginning of chapter 4. Cf. Green, 27.
9. *Works* 10:191.
10. Jansen, 67.

That water was a kind of prophetic parable of the water of baptism which now saves you. Baptism does not merely mean the washing of a dirty body; it is the appeal of a clear conscience towards God—a thing made possible by the power of Christ's resurrection.

God still remembers His covenant. The covenant with Noah was written in nature by the symbol of a rainbow in the sky. The new covenant is written in history by a symbol greater than a rainbow. It is a Cross on a hill, where the floods of the deep closed over God's Son but were rolled away by the power that raised Him from the dead. In baptism, we become identified with Christ's death on the Cross and raised with Him to a new life (Rom. 6:3-4).

Another old covenant sign is used by the New Testament to throw light on the meaning of baptism. In the time of Moses, God once again marked His people. As the Israelites were preparing to flee Egypt, their houses were marked with blood on the doorframes, to save from destruction those who were within. "The blood will be a sign for you on the houses where you are; and when I see the blood, I will pass over you" (Exod. 12:13). In the New Testament, Paul picks up the story at the point of the Exodus, to illuminate the meaning of baptism and the salvation it signifies. In 1 Cor. 10:1-11, he shows that the Israelites had their counterpart to baptism—the experience of going through the waters of the Red Sea.[11] Paul's point is that baptism and Communion, like the escape through the Red Sea and the manna given to them, are no certain protection from apostasy. The covenant demands obedience. Paul also suggests that the real sustainer of the Israelites in the desert was Christ, the Rock from which they drank. The passage reminds us also that salvation, in the Old Testament and in the New, is the work of God's grace. Baptism graphically proclaims this. "The very passivity of being baptized symbolizes the fact that God has done all that is necessary to put us in the right with him."[12]

Behind each of these Old Testament allusions by New Tes-

---

11. They also had their counterpart to the Eucharist in the manna that came from heaven, but that is not our concern here.

12. Green, 30.

tament writers lies the idea that God is a covenant-making God. He binds himself to His people by a physical token. The token to Moses was the Passover (Exodus 12). The token to Noah was the rainbow (Gen. 9:8-17). And the token to Abraham was circumcision—the supreme mark that has continued for centuries among Jews, and to which Christian theology has most often connected the sacrament of baptism. To be circumcised was, for the Jewish male, the unmistakable sign that he was one of God's chosen people. "Circumcised on the eighth day," declared the apostle Paul, in an assertion of his Hebrew heritage (Phil. 3:5). Baptism is precisely such a sign in the covenant of grace. Martin Luther often became so despondent that he could virtually sense Satan slithering to his side and sorely tempting him to doubt his salvation. In such times, he could cause the devil to slink away by declaring emphatically, "I am baptized!" All his inward distress, emotional states, and subjective feelings to the contrary notwithstanding, Luther knew he bore Christ's mark!

The connection between circumcision and baptism has not been without its disputants. The majority of scholars who reject it are from the Anabaptist or Baptist traditions, and a main reason for their opposing the idea is because of their rejection of infant baptism, which is much easier to reject if its kinship with circumcision is denied.[13] But theologians from those traditions are not alone in opposing the relation between circumcision and baptism. The great Karl Barth threw his weight against infant baptism and consequently played down the importance of circumcision as the Old Testament counterpart to baptism in the New Testament. He is followed in this by the influential contemporary German theologian, Jürgen Moltmann.[14] And the American evangelical scholar George Eldon Ladd expresses doubt that Paul understood baptism as the Christian counterpart of circumcision.[15]

On the other side, Oscar Cullmann, longtime colleague of

---

13. Cf. Beasley-Murray; also Paul K. Jewett, *Infant Baptism and the Covenant of Grace* (Grand Rapids: William B. Eerdmans Publishing Co., 1978).

14. Jürgen Moltmann, *The Church in the Power of the Spirit*, trans. Margaret Kohl (London: SCM Press, 1977), 226-42.

15. George Eldon Ladd, *A Theology of the New Testament* (Grand Rapids: Wm. B. Eerdmans Publishing Co., 1974), 548.

Barth at Basel, takes sharp issue with Barth's position, calling it the weakest point in Barth's doctrine of baptism. In his careful study of baptism, Cullmann insists that there is "a fundamental kinship between circumcision and Christian Baptism."[16] He holds that "the doctrine and practice of circumcision, and of proselyte baptism that is closely bound up with it, are presuppositions for the whole complicated question of New Testament baptismal doctrine and its consequent practice."[17] Christian baptism, Cullmann claims, is a fulfillment, and thus a repeal, of Jewish circumcision. He cites Col. 2:11-12 as establishing this explicitly, and finds it implied in Rom. 2:25 ff., 4:1 ff., Gal. 3:6 ff., and Eph. 2:11.[18]

John Wesley certainly sees baptism as the fulfillment and replacement of circumcision, and the Wesleyan/holiness tradition has generally followed him in this. Wesley asserts it in the very beginning of his "Treatise on Baptism." Baptism was designed by Christ, he says, "to remain always in his Church. . . . It is the initiatory sacrament, which enters us into covenant with God . . . perpetually obligatory on all Christians . . . instituted *in the room of circumcision*."[19] He insists that just as circumcision was the way of entering into the covenant God made with Abraham, so baptism is now the way of entering into the new covenant.[20]

The apostle Paul said: "I bear on my body the marks of Jesus" (Gal. 6:17). Of course, Paul is not in that verse speaking directly of baptism. Rather he is speaking of the cross of Christ, and this suggests the only way the owner's mark can be worn. "I have been crucified with Christ and I no longer live, but Christ lives in me" (2:20). That is to say, the old life has been put aside, and I now share the Owner's concerns and live in His Spirit. Baptism is the solemn symbol that the Lord of our life is the

---

16. Cullmann, *Baptism*, 56-57.
17. Ibid., 56.
18. Ibid.
19. *Works* 10:188, italics mine. The word "room" should be read as "place."
20. Ibid., 191. In this view, Wesley is joined by all the early Methodist theologians such as Richard Watson, Adam Clarke, and William Burt Pope, as well as by 20th-century thinkers in the Wesleyan/holiness tradition such as A. M. Hills and H. Orton Wiley, and by contemporary Wesleyan/holiness theologian H. Ray Dunning.

Savior whose own baptism was of blood. That is why in some rituals of baptism the owner's mark is graphically portrayed by the minister's making the sign of the Cross on the baptizand's forehead with his finger that has been dipped in the baptismal water. Baptism declares me to be owned. Most gladly therefore will I bear on my body the mark of my Owner!

There is still another facet of truth in the idea of bearing the mark of Christ. To bear the mark of Christ means to bear His *name*. In the vision of Revelation, as we noted above, the "mark" on the forehead of the redeemed was the "name" of the Lamb. When the gospel began to spread from Jerusalem and reached Antioch, the early disciples of Jesus began to be called "Christians" (Acts 11:26). "Christians!" "Followers of Christ." "Little christs!" Incarnations of God's love in the world! Persons marked with Christ's name!

The earliest baptisms, according to the Book of Acts, were "in the name of Jesus Christ" (2:38). This should not be seen as conflicting with the Lord's command that His disciples baptize "in the name of the Father and of the Son and of the Holy Spirit" (Matt. 28:19). Where there is no mention of the Father and the Spirit, they may be inferred from the context (Acts 2:38-39). The New Testament evidence suggests that baptism into the name of Christ, and baptism into the name of the Father, Son, and Holy Spirit, are different ways of referring to the same event. Moreover, Christ's command to baptize would inevitably reflect His own baptism by John the Baptist, where the Spirit descended upon Him and the Father addressed Jesus as His Son. Baptism in the name of Christ involves the coming of the Spirit from the Father in the name of the Son.

Christian theology has found significant theological content in the Gospel accounts of our Lord's baptism. G. W. Bromiley notes that, for Bible scholars at the time of the Reformation, a clue to the meaning of baptism was found in the baptism of Jesus at the hands of John. He says:

> The Father speaks the word of election from heaven, acknowledging Jesus as the elected Son. Baptism is thus a sacrament of the covenant of election. The Son is the One baptized, accepting the baptism of repentance, and thus entering the way of identification with sinners which was to reach

its climax in His obedient self-offering on the cross. Baptism is thus a sacrament of the fulfillment of the covenant in the substitutionary death and resurrection of the Incarnate Son. The Holy Spirit is the One who descends upon the Son, empowering Him for the ministry upon which He enters. Baptism is thus a sacrament of the outpouring of the Holy Ghost.[21]

In the light of all the New Testament evidence, it can be safely said that the Trinitarian baptismal formula, as given in the Great Commission, is not something different from baptism "in the name of Jesus," although probably a later development. The doctrine of the Trinity enshrined in the baptismal formula is that view of God made necessary by what we believe about Jesus Christ. In Jesus Christ the name of God becomes fully known. We know the name of the Father and the Spirit because we know the Son. In baptism, therefore, we declare, with St. Patrick:

> I bind unto myself today
> The strong name of the Trinity![22]

It is well known that among the ancient Hebrews the *name* of a person denoted that person's character, nature, or authority. Because so much is in a name, particular attention was given to choosing the right name for children. The Bible often describes the transformation of a person's character through a change of the person's name. In the Old Testament, Jacob, the usurper, becomes Israel, the friend and servant of God. The classic New Testament example is Simon who becomes Peter, the Rock. Like Jacob, Simon was an unlikely prospect for sainthood, but the good news of grace is that Christ sees more in us than we can see in ourselves. "Blessed are you, Simon . . . I tell you that you are Peter, and on this rock I will build my church" (Matt. 16:17-18). Of course, the new name does not mean the end of struggle. Even after the name change, Peter forgot his Lord. But the Lord did not forget Simon. "Simon, Simon, Satan has asked to

---

21. G. W. Bromiley, *Sacramental Teaching and Practice in the Reformation Churches* (Grand Rapids: Wm. B. Eerdmans Publishing Co., 1957), 21.

22. Cf. the translation by Ludwig Bieler in *Ancient Christian Writers*, ed. Johannes Quasten and Joseph C. Plumpe (Westminster, Md.: Newman Press, 1953), 17:69.

sift you as wheat. But I have prayed for you, Simon, that your faith may not fail" (Luke 22:31-32).

This suggests that we need a name stronger than our own. Whose name? In the Roman Catholic tradition the name of a patron saint was added in baptism, so that the baptized person might claim the saint's protection. In itself, there is nothing wrong in linking oneself with the faithful who have gone before us and won the battle. Many a Protestant parent has given to a baby boy the name David or Peter or Paul or Luther or Wesley; or to a baby girl the name Sarah or Rebecca or Mary or Lydia. Yet only one name can be our Protector. We need more than patron saints. The one name in heaven and earth that can save us is the name of Jesus. No other is needed. This, baptism declares.

As we have seen, "the name" is a common Old Testament phrase that represents a person's character, nature, or authority. Therefore to invoke upon a person, place, or thing the sacred name of God meant that God had claimed it for His own, placed it under His authority and protection. Baptism in the name of Jesus (or in the name of Father, Son, and Holy Spirit) means that Christ has claimed me, placed me under His authority, and extended me His protection.

Of course, the sacrament of baptism leaves many questions unanswered. When and how does it happen? Do I receive my new name when I am baptized, or am I baptized because I have been given the new name? Or does the promise of baptism wait for some future confirmation? On such questions Christians through the centuries have widely disagreed.

But do we need to know? Interestingly, the Gospels do not make it clear when Simon received his new name. The Gospel of John suggests that he received it when he first met Jesus (1:42). Luke suggests that the name was received when he was chosen to be one of the Twelve (6:13-14). Matthew suggests that he received the name when he made his great confession of faith (16:17-18). Apparently the Early Church felt a similar uncertainty about baptism. In Acts, the transforming Spirit is sometimes described as coming to people prior to their baptism, sometimes at the time of baptism, and sometimes after baptism. This is a wholesome reminder that we cannot stereotype or structure or channel or corral the Holy Spirit. John Wesley was correct when he said: "There is an irreconcilable variability in the operation of the Holy Spirit upon the souls of men."[23] The Spirit is like the wind, said Jesus, and it "blows wherever it pleases" and we "cannot tell where it comes from or where it is going" (John 3:8).

But we know this: God marks His covenant people, and Christ gives them a new name that corresponds to His own (they were called "Christians"). Through the power of His name, we who bear that name are given God's protection. Jesus prayed for His followers

> that they may know you, the only true God, and Jesus Christ, whom you have sent. . . . Holy Father, protect them by the power of your name—the name you gave me—so that they may be one as we are one. While I was with them, I protected them and kept them safe by that name you gave me. . . . I have made you known to them, and will continue to make you known in order that the love you have for me may be in them and that I myself may be in them *(John 17:3, 11-12, 26)*.

The written Word of God tells me that by His grace I may receive a new name. Shall not the enacted "visible word" of baptism tell me the same thing? The sacrament of baptism declares that God has marked me with Christ's name, so that I may be kept by His grace and may come to know even as also I am known.

B. Dying the Death of Christ

"What shall we say, then?" asks the apostle Paul. "Shall we go on sinning so that grace may increase? By no means! We died to sin; how can we live in it any longer? Or don't you know that all of us who were baptized into Christ Jesus were baptized into his death?" (Rom. 6:1-3). This passage, along with the verses following it, is resplendent with theological truth regarding baptism. To be baptized is to become *identified with Christ in His death.* But what does this mean?

Before we can understand what it means to be "baptized into Christ's death," we must first understand the significance of

---

23. *Letters* 7:298.

Christ's own death. Before considering Paul's statement, let us leave it for a moment and turn to a statement of John's that can help us. Writing many years after the Synoptics and Paul's Epistles were written, John has had much time to meditate on the meaning of the Lord's death. The significance of baptism is obliquely but vividly portrayed in a description of Christ's death recorded in the Fourth Gospel. John reports that "one of the soldiers pierced Jesus' side with a spear, bringing a sudden flow of blood and water" (19:34). This description of Christ's crucifixion is a meaningful sacramental sign, given, says the apostle, "so that you also may believe" (v. 35). He sees the whole drama of redemption expressed in the event of the Cross. He sees the Cross not only as a *past* event but also as the event that shapes the present and the future. He sees that it is through the atoning death of the Son of God that we have true life, and that His blood cleanses us from all sin.

We have seen that Roman Catholicism affirmed seven sacraments that link the various stages of human growth to the grace of God. Protestants, reflecting Luther's influence, have generally rejected this schema, holding that only baptism and the Eucharist bring us directly to the event of the Cross.[24] We must let the water and the Blood bind us to Calvary. Failure to remember that water as well as blood flowed from His wounded side has, for many people, made baptism a less-meaningful symbol than the Lord's Supper. When the water of baptism is separated from the blood of the Cross, baptism loses its significance for many Christians, and the focus of attention wanders from Christ to the skill of the minister, or the structure of the baptistry, or the wet clothing after immersion, or, in the case of infant baptism, the beauty (or the crying!) of the baby, or the religiosity of the parents. Such "missing of the mark" is nothing short of tragic. Paul must have seen a similar tragedy in the Corinthians' attitude toward baptism when he asked, "Was Paul crucified for you? Were you baptized into the name of Paul?" Certainly not, he insisted! "We preach Christ crucified" (1 Cor. 1:13, 23).

---

24. But see Eph. 5:25-26, which could be seen as an exception to this, relating marriage to the death of Christ.

Let the water and the blood,
From Thy wounded side which flowed,
Be of sin the double cure,
Save from wrath and make me pure.
                              —AUGUSTUS M. TOPLADY

When Jesus began His ministry by being baptized in the Jordan, the Baptist protested, saying, "I need to be baptized by you" (Matt. 3:14). Imagine it! The Son of God baptized as if He were a sinner! But He chose to be baptized. At His baptism the nature of His mission was clarified. He saw the heavens opened and heard a Voice saying, "You are my Son, whom I love; with you I am well pleased" (Mark 1:11). Those words combine portions of Ps. 2:7 and Isa. 42:1. The first underscores the so-called messianic consciousness of Jesus—He knew who He was! The second is a reference from the Servant Songs of Isaiah and shows that in His baptism Jesus knew that the Messiah must become a Servant, "numbered with the transgressors," suffering vicariously for His people. Other Jews came to the Jordan to be baptized by John for their *own* sins. But Jesus, at the moment of His baptism, hears a voice that in essence declares: *You* are baptized not for *Your own* sins but for those of the whole world. This means that Jesus is baptized in view of His death, which effects forgiveness of sins for everyone. For this reason Jesus must unite himself in solidarity with all His people and be baptized "to fulfill all righteousness" (Matt. 3:15). Cullmann thinks the word "all" should be emphasized here. Thus he can say:

> It is clear in view of the voice from heaven why Jesus must conduct himself like other people. He is distinguished from the mass of other baptised people, who are baptised for their own sins, as the One called to the office of the Servant of God who suffers *for all others.*[25]

His own baptism in the Jordan was therefore of decisive importance to Jesus. This was His baptism of water, which pointed Him toward His baptism of blood. It pointed Him forward to that death in which Christian baptism finds both its foundation and its fulfillment. This once-for-all death of Jesus is what Cullmann calls Christ's "general baptism."

---

25. *Baptism,* 18-19.

> *It belongs to the essence of this general Baptism effected by*
> *Jesus, that it is offered in entire independence of the decision of*
> *faith and understanding of those who benefit from it.* Baptismal
> grace has its foundation here, and it is in the strictest sense
> "prevenient grace."[26]

Jesus told His disciples, "I have a baptism to undergo, and how
distressed I am until it is completed!" (Luke 12:50). It is completed only when from the Cross He cries, "It is finished" (John
19:30). *What* is finished? The redemptive act, the atoning deed,
the triumph of God's love over the power of sin.

> *Amazing love! How can it be*
> *That Thou, my God, shouldst die for me?*
> —CHARLES WESLEY

This is the baptism of blood. "This," says John, "is the one who
came by water and blood—Jesus Christ. He did not come by
water only, but by water and blood" (1 John 5:6). The baptismal
death of Jesus completed once for all on the Cross becomes the
foundation of Christian baptism. "Christian baptism is rooted in
the once-for-all event which now becomes the event-for-me."[27]
Baptism witnesses to the truth that what Christ has done *for* me
He now wills to do *in* me. The act of being baptized does not of
itself forgive and cleanse me. But the One who was baptized for
me by the death of the Cross, and in whose name I am baptized
—*He* forgives me from the guilt of sin and delivers me from its
power. And so, in his Gospel, the apostle John says: "One of the
soldiers pierced Jesus' side with a spear, bringing a sudden flow
of blood and water. The man who saw it has given testimony,
and his testimony is true. He knows that he tells the truth, and
he testifies so that you also may believe" (19:34-35). In the sacrament of baptism we say, "I do believe."

   In his First Epistle, John says: "Everyone who believes that
Jesus is the Christ is born of God" (5:1). What it means to be a
Christian could scarcely be said more clearly. Nevertheless, John
tries to make it even clearer by the use of sacramental language:
"Jesus Christ himself is the one who came by water and by
blood—not by the water only, but by the water and the blood"

---

26. Ibid., 20.
27. Jansen, 55.

(v. 6, Phillips). He came by water, being baptized in the Jordan to fulfill all righteousness and identify himself with us in our need. He came by blood—the blood of Calvary, shed for the remission of our sins. The Word of God declares that everyone who believes that Jesus is the Christ is a child of God. But lest God's Word be obscured by our own words, the sacramental symbol declares anew:

> The Church's one Foundation
> Is Jesus Christ, her Lord.
> She is His new creation
> By water and the word.
> From heav'n He came and sought her
> To be His holy bride;
> With His own blood He bought her,
> And for her life He died.
> —SAMUEL J. STONE

With the significance of Christ's own death in mind, we are better able to understand what it means to be "baptized into his death." Let us now return to the Pauline passage quoted at the beginning of this section, Rom. 6:1-3.

> What shall we say, then? Shall we go on sinning so that grace may increase? By no means! We died to sin; how can we live in it any longer? Or don't you know that all of us who were baptized into Christ Jesus were baptized into his death?

G. R. Beasley-Murray calls this passage "the most extensive exposition of baptism Paul has given."[28] Our chief concern here is to ascertain what Paul means by *dying* to sin and being baptized into Christ's *death.* What is the connection between baptism and the death of Christ? Beasley-Murray describes the three main answers to this question that have been put forward by New Testament scholars.[29] (1) The first view is that *in baptism the believer suffers a death like Christ's.* He experiences a death to sin *at the time of his baptism.* This view, says Beasley-Murray, is characteristic of British scholarship, although some Continental exegetes hold to it also. It holds that we died to sin when we be-

---

28. Beasley-Murray, 126.
29. Cf. ibid., 131-32.

came Christians and submitted to baptism. Baptism is thus a re-enactment for the believer of Christ's own baptism. What happened to Christ in His death has happened to us in our baptism. (2) The second view holds that *the death of the baptized is the death of Christ on the Cross.* That is, *the believer died to sin precisely at the time Christ died.* It has been the Continental theologians, mostly German, who have promoted this view. The believer is not asked to die to sin when he is baptized but to believe that he has already died with Christ and to seize this reality as an accomplished fact. Such a view is not always easy for the popular mind to grasp, but it is not too different from the sentiment expressed in the old spiritual that asks, "Were you there when they crucified my Lord?" The answer implied in the song is, "Yes, we were all there; it was our sins that nailed Him to the tree." In a similar way, according to this theory, we died to sin when Jesus died on the Cross. (3) A third view opposes both the above interpretations and stresses the *ethical* nature of baptism as *a dying to sinful passions and conduct by the renunciation of self.* The purpose of baptism is that we should not follow the sinful will and that we should enter upon a new moral way of life.

Beasley-Murray, a Baptist scholar, believes that each of the three views has some essential truth and that none of them is complete in isolation from the others. He says:

> If we take into account Paul's theology generally . . . it can be shown that his interpretation of baptism in relation to the redemptive event of Christ has a threefold reference: first, it relates the baptized to the death and resurrection of Christ, involving him in the actual dying and rising of Christ Himself; secondly, it involves a corresponding event in the life of the baptized believer, whereby an end is put to his old God-estranged life and a new one begins in Christ and His Kingdom and His Spirit; thirdly, it demands a corresponding "crucifixion" of the flesh and a new life in the power of the Spirit that accords with the grace received, which "dying" and "rising" begins in the baptismal event.[30]

---

30. Ibid., 132. In this attempt to synthesize the three views, Beasley-Murray reverses

Richard E. Howard, writing from within the Wesleyan/holiness tradition, also understands that there are different senses in which we die with Christ. He says:

> When we, through faith, enter into Christ we enter into His death. This means that the believer appropriates by faith the death that Christ died *for* him. He participates or shares in Christ's death. He dies along with Christ. All men died *provisionally* with Christ when He died on the Cross, but only those who by faith accept that death die *experientially* with Christ.[31]

However, Howard takes exception to the purely *ethical* view (Beasley-Murray's third position) if the new ethical life is understood merely as something we are to do in our human strength. He says: "Dying to sin does not mean to simply stop sinning!" We cannot die to sin merely by cutting ourselves off from it. "Death to sin . . . is always related to our identification with Christ's death—by faith. Similarly, crucifixion is *never* used by Paul as a metaphor of self-denial, but *always* relates to Christ's death and our sharing in it."[32]

Regardless of how the intricacies of Paul's teaching about dying with Christ in baptism are to be understood, we know that, for him, the purpose of it all is that "we too may live a new life" (Rom. 6:4), or, as the King James Version states it, that "even so we also should walk in newness of life." William H. Willimon writes:

> When Paul described the Christian life, he seems not to know whether to call what happened to him "birth" or "death." It felt like both at the same time. Whether birth or death, Paul knew firsthand that conversion meant change. . . . Baptism is clearly the demarcation between the old world and the new, between death and life.[33]

As Beasley-Murray says, "Whatever else lies buried deep in the

---

the order of the first and second positions. He does not explain why, but it is probably a chronological rearrangement according to the *ordo salutis*.

31. Richard E. Howard, *Newness of Life: A Study in the Thought of Paul* (Kansas City Beacon Hill Press of Kansas City, 1975), 101.

32. Ibid., 101-2.

33. William H. Willimon, *The Service of God* (Nashville: Abingdon Press, 1983), 101.

theology of Rom. 6:1ff, this lies on the surface. For it cannot be too firmly emphasized that Paul's concern in this passage was not to give a theological excursus on the nature of Christian baptism but to oppose the heretical appeal, 'Let us carry on in sin that grace may abound!'"[34] Our "dying the death of Christ" must be followed by our "living the life of Christ."

C. LIVING THE LIFE OF CHRIST

In its relation to baptism, and to the salvation baptism signifies, Christ's death cannot be separated from His resurrection. Actually, Christ's death and resurrection are two inseparable aspects of God's one great redemptive act. Since this is the case, there is also an inseparable relation between our baptism into Christ's death and our resurrection with Him to a new life. Paul, who tells us that we were baptized into Christ's death, also declares the glorious implication of that fact:

> We were therefore buried with him through baptism into death in order that, just as Christ was raised from the dead through the glory of the Father, we too may live a new life. If we have been united with him like this in his death, we will certainly also be united with him in his resurrection. . . . Now if we died with Christ, we believe that we will also live with him *(Rom. 6:4-5, 8)*.

It is significant that in Romans Paul speaks of our resurrection in the future tense, whereas in Colossians he uses the aorist tense, which denotes past action: "You have been raised with Christ" (3:1). The same aorist tense is used in Eph. 2:6: "God raised us up with Christ." It is necessary for Paul to speak in this double manner of our resurrection as something that in one sense has already happened, and in another sense is to happen in the future.[35] On the one hand, Christ has been raised, and since we participate in this we are raised with Him. But on the other hand He will come again to consummate His work, and until that consummation there can be no final resurrection; the com-

---

34. Beasley-Murray, 143.
35. In Paul's language, the "inner man" has already been raised, while resurrection of the "outer man" is still in the future.

pleted transfer from the old creation to the new awaits His coming again.

Just as Christ's death and resurrection are not totally separated in Paul's thought, neither are Christ's resurrection and His ascension to the right hand of God. Thus the new life of the baptized is described as an ascended life, in which we set our hearts and minds on things above (Col. 3:1-4). The whole series of divine acts accomplished in the death, resurrection, and ascension of Jesus is spiritually reenacted in the life of the Church. Christians therefore must see that this happens visibly in their everyday behavior. Paul's indicatives are followed by imperatives (cf. vv. 1-17). The "dying to sin" we experienced in baptism (Rom. 6:2-3) is to be followed by a "putting to death" of whatever belongs to our earthly nature (Col. 3:5).

The "putting off" of the old means a "putting on" of the new. Paul writes to the Galatians: "You are all sons of God through faith in Christ Jesus." He continues: "All of you who were baptized into Christ have clothed yourselves with Christ" (3:26-27). Some have thought that this imagery of a garment is borrowed from the Greek mystery religions, but "the figure of changing clothes to represent an inward and spiritual change was so common to Hebrew-Christian tradition as to make a direct borrowing from such a source unlikely."[36] The language is probably taken from the Jewish liturgy of investment and consecration to the priesthood. The Church seems to have carried this into the rite of baptism. As the candidates emerged from the water, stripped of their old life, they put on white robes as a symbol of their putting on Christ. Christians are baptized into a royal priesthood and a holy people (1 Pet. 2:5 ff.).

This pattern of putting off and putting on, of descent and ascent, of death and resurrection, not only is the pattern of Christ's redemptive action on behalf of the world but also is the pattern of all Christian behavior. This is brought sharply into focus for us Christians at our baptism, to which we look back for encouragement and renewal in times of need (just as Luther

---

36. Beasley-Murray, 148.

did) and from which we are always looking forward to the final
resurrection when God will be "all in all" (1 Cor. 15:28). Christians are constantly seeking to reproduce this double pattern in
their lives. We have stripped off an old life and put on a new
one.

Baptism signifies the death of the person I once was—
unforgiven and alienated from God. Baptism says farewell to all
that.

> Death *means* death. At times it will be devastating: death
> to your hopes, dreams and ambitions. It may mean death to
> a work you have built up and seen flourish. It will mean
> death, all along the line, to self-will. That is what it really
> means to say, "I have been baptized". Therefore I must expect
> these "grave" experiences. Life will not be a bed of roses. And
> when they come, I can cope with them in his power, because
> I know they are not the end: it is through death that resurrec-
> tion comes.[37]

Baptism means that the Christian life is in essence a dying
and rising life. The entire life of the Christian, in time and in
eternity, is graphically portrayed in baptism.

> Baptism is rather like a drop of rain in a meadow on a
> day when the sun has just come out. It is only a single globule
> of water, but it refracts all the colours of the spectrum. And in
> baptism I catch reflected all the blessings of God made avail-
> able for me in Christ. I catch, too, the command, "Come, fol-
> low me." In this sacrament God confronts me with total de-
> mand, and total succour.[38]

The new resurrection life, made possible by Christ's own
death and resurrection, and signified by baptism, includes the
forgiveness of sins. Peter concluded his Pentecost sermon with
the appeal: "Repent and be baptized, every one of you, in the
name of Jesus Christ for the forgiveness of your sins" (Acts
2:38). And Paul was told by Ananias, "Get up, be baptized and
wash your sins away, calling on his name" (22:16). Later, Paul
could write of Christians as those who "were washed" (1 Cor.
6:11). The writer of Hebrews says we are to "draw near to God

---

37. Green, 49-50.
38. Ibid., 50.

with a sincere heart in full assurance of faith, having our hearts sprinkled to cleanse us from a guilty conscience and having our bodies washed with pure water" (10:22).

In the New Testament, to say the least, the road into the Christian life is wet! Not that the mere ritual of "getting wet," by itself, saves a person—the New Testament does not teach that. Salvation is by God's grace through faith (Eph. 2:8). But if we are to follow the New Testament pattern, our inward response of faith will be accompanied by the outward symbol of baptism, which is the covenant symbol of God's prior grace. Baptism makes visible our faith response, but this is only secondary to its primary function of making visible God's action toward us. The New Testament knows nothing of "unbaptized Christians."[39] Such a term would be as contradictory as the term "square circle." There is nothing in the New Testament that treats baptism as an optional extra. George Eldon Ladd writes that "in the early church saving faith and baptism were practically synonymous."[40]

But synonymous in this case does not mean "interchangeable." It is always faith that is the condition of salvation. Faith is not faith, however, apart from obedience. Baptism is commanded, therefore required as our faith response, unless it is an impossibility due to circumstances beyond human control. That it may sometimes be an impossibility is evident. For this reason, Wesley often called baptism the "ordinary" means of receiving salvation, thereby granting exceptions to the rule. "Indeed, where it cannot be had, the case is different," he said, "but extraordinary cases do not make void a standing rule."[41]

Furthermore, if we take the New Testament as our pattern, we will not allow baptism to be postponed indefinitely. In the Book of Acts, no significant interval of time elapsed between believing in Christ and being baptized. When they believed, they were baptized as soon as possible. This is evident from the baptisms of Pentecost (2:41), the Samaritans (8:12), the Ethiopian

---

39. This assumes Cullmann's claim that Christian baptism began at Pentecost. Thus the repentant thief on the Cross was saved without baptism, but this is hardly a pattern for Christians in the age of the Spirit.
40. Ladd, 548.
41. *Works* 10:193.

eunuch (8:36-37), Saul (9:18), and the households of Cornelius (10:47-48), Lydia (16:14-15), and the Philippian jailer (16:33). Nor is baptism in the New Testament something simply "tacked on" *after* their conversion. Rather, it seems to be presented as the proper *conclusion* or *climax* of conversion itself.[42]

In the New Testament Church, believers experienced baptism as a "means of grace" through which, by faith, their sins were washed away and they were united to Christ with a clear conscience. In theology, this is called *justification.* The past is put behind us, and we, members of a fallen race, are given hope through God's gracious gift of forgiveness. Our identification with Christ's death and resurrection in baptism means that by God's action we are forgiven and reconciled to Him. "Therefore, if anyone is in Christ, he is a new creation; the old has gone, the new has come! All this is from God, who reconciled us to himself through Christ" (2 Cor. 5:17-18).

The new life that we experience in Christ is known also as the *new birth,* or *regeneration.* It is a fitting metaphor. Birth is always a gift; we can never give birth to ourselves. Through our identification with Christ, God knows us as new creatures. The transformation we experience in the new birth is not our own doing but something done for us by another. For this reason, baptism is primarily the sign of *grace* and only secondarily the sign of our *faith.* Paul tells Titus that Christ "saved us through the washing of rebirth and renewal by the Holy Spirit" (3:5). Baptism marks the beginning of our existence as new creations.

Interestingly, new birth is the most *feminine* of the biblical metaphors of salvation. In the human realm, giving birth is always the act of a woman, regardless of the gender of the child that is birthed. This image shows us a feminine side of God. In the new birth, divine life is given to us by grace. We cannot enter into new life by our own effort but are completely dependent on the divine love and nurture.[43]

---

42. But during the third century, according to the *Apostolic Tradition* of Hippolytus, written early in that century, a period of preparation, which could last as long as three years, was to precede baptism. Still, the *beginning* of such preparation was not to be indefinitely postponed. Cf. Gregory Dix, ed., *The Treatise on the Apostolic Tradition of St. Hippolytus of Rome* (London: SPCK, 1937).

43. Such dependence on the divine initiative is also underscored by the New Testament metaphor of "adoption."

Paul's words in Titus 3:5 are paralleled by the words of Jesus in John 3:5, where Nicodemus is told that "no one can enter the kingdom of God unless he is born of water and the Spirit." New birth, or regeneration, is John's favorite metaphor for the new life. The conjunction of "water" and "Spirit" in relation to the new birth is most interesting. Some Christians (primarily those who tend to minimize the importance of baptism) have interpreted "born of water" to mean *human* birth. In other words: You must be born both naturally and spiritually in order to enter the Kingdom. Thus to be born of water means to be delivered from the mother's womb where the fetus lives in a watery environment. Such an interpretation has very little to commend it. Against it is John's own declaration in 1:13 that birth from God has nothing to do with human birth. More importantly, in 3:3 Jesus tells Nicodemus that "no one can see the kingdom of God unless he is born again" (or "born from above," as the Greek phrase may best be translated). After Nicodemus' expression of incredulity, Jesus explains the meaning of this by using the phrase "born of water and the Spirit" in verse 5. Thus "born from above" (or "born again") is the equivalent of "born of water and the Spirit." The expression in verse 5 defines that of verse 3. The *whole* expression "of water and the Spirit" defines the manner in which one is born from above.

It should be remembered that John's writings are generally believed to be the last in the New Testament to be written. Therefore baptism would be widely practiced by the time John wrote his Gospel. If by "born of water" Jesus meant natural birth, then He was telling Nicodemus that he could not see the kingdom of God unless he were born naturally! That one cannot enter the Kingdom unless he or she exists as a human being is obvious; to make a point of it would be ludicrous, and it strains one's imagination to think Jesus would have made such a fatuous statement. Nowhere else does the New Testament describe natural birth by the phrase "born of water."[44] If John had meant

---

44. But some have pointed out that among the Jews anything damp, such as water, dew, or rain, was a euphemism for male semen. If Jesus' words are understood in this sense, "born of water" would refer to natural birth. Cf. Leon Morris, *Jesus Is the Christ: Studies in the Theology of John* (Grand Rapids: Wm. B. Eerdmans Publishing Co., 1989), 151. But the interpretation of "water" as "semen" in John 3:5 seems strained.

natural birth, he likely would have used the expression "born
. . . of blood" (or "bloods" in Greek), which is his term for natural birth in 1:13, KJV. The NIV translates it "born of natural descent."

Wesley interprets the words "except a man be born of water
and the Spirit" in John 3:5 (cf. KJV) to mean: "Except he experience that great inward change by the Spirit, and be baptized,
(wherever baptism can be had,) as the outward sign and means
of it."[45] The late Nazarene theologian H. Orton Wiley also understood "born of water" to mean baptism. Speaking of John 3:5,
he says: "Here, evidently, the sign is the outward baptism with
water, and the thing signified is the inner work of the Spirit."[46]
All arguments to the contrary notwithstanding, we believe it difficult to take seriously the suggestion that the words "born of
water" refer to something other than baptism.

One key to John 3:5 is the declaration of the Baptist that he
baptized only with *water,* but Christ would baptize with the
Holy Spirit (1:33). Nicodemus, although not familiar with Christian baptism, which did not have its beginning until the Day of
Pentecost, was undoubtedly familiar with Jewish proselyte baptism, probably also with the baptism of the disciples of Jesus
(mentioned soon afterward, in John 3:22 and 4:2), and certainly
with John the Baptist's baptism for repentance. As Nicodemus
heard the words of Jesus, *water* carried with it a reference to
John's baptism; the *Spirit,* on the other hand, marked that inward power John placed in contrast with his own baptism.[47]

Jesus can thus be understood as telling Nicodemus: To enter
the Kingdom, you must accept the divinely sanctioned rite (1:33)

45. *Explanatory Notes upon the New Testament,* 2 vols. (London: Wesleyan Methodist
Book Room, n.d.; reprint, Kansas City: Beacon Hill Press of Kansas City, 1981, hereafter
cited as *NT Notes*).

46. H. Orton Wiley, *Christian Theology,* 3 vols. (Kansas City: Beacon Hill Press, 1940-
43), 3:175.

47. The "sacramental" interpretation of John 3:5 that is espoused here is sometimes
opposed on the grounds that it is a form-critical approach, which reads back into the *sitz
im leben* of Nicodemus, a point of view developed much later (at the time the Fourth
Gospel was written). Thus it is held that Nicodemus would not have associated "born of
water" with baptism. But the "sacramental" understanding of the verse is not dependent
on the form-critical method, for the reasons here noted.

that is the seal of repentance and of forgiveness, and following on this the new life, which is the work of the Holy Spirit.[48]

> In the proclamation of John these two things were separated as a prophecy and a hope of fulfilment, since the baptizer in water was one and the baptizer in Spirit another. On the lips of Jesus they come closer, as a promise "in sure and certain hope" of fulfilment, for the baptism is from Him who shall baptize with Spirit.[49]

The "outward sign" and the "inward grace" are not the same, but they are not to be separated. Since Nicodemus knows about the preaching as well as the baptizing of John, it is noteworthy that he accepts Jesus' words about the Holy Spirit without the slightest hesitation. Thus this reference of Jesus to baptism is not understood by Nicodemus in an *ex opere operato* sense, as if entrance to the Kingdom were a mere mechanical matter, but as being vitally connected with repentance and the inward working of the Holy Spirit.

The conjunction of birth, Spirit, and Kingdom in Jesus' words carry a further implication. Beasley-Murray insists that "it hints of the eschatological background presumed in the idea of being born from above."[50] Ezekiel prophesied that God's Spirit would be poured out in the last days, enabling His people to keep His laws and to experience resurrection from the dead (Ezek. 36:26 ff.; 37:9 ff.). This foreshadows the ritual use of water in connection with the gift of the Spirit. At Pentecost this was fulfilled: "Repent and be baptized . . . And you will receive the gift of the Holy Spirit" (Acts 2:38).

The above prophecies of Ezekiel were among John Wesley's favorite Old Testament texts. The images of water, sprinkling, cleansing, heart of flesh, and new Spirit all figure prominently in Wesley's teaching of the holy life that is possible under the new covenant. Also the conjunction of "born of water" and "born of the Spirit" in the Fourth Gospel is reflected in John Wesley's definition of a sacrament as an "outward sign of inward

---

48. Cf. B. F. Westcott, *The Gospel According to St. John* (London: John Murray, Albemarle Street, 1889), 49-50.

49. Beasley-Murray, 230.

50. Ibid., 228.

grace." "Born of water" is the outward sign. "Born of the Spirit" is the inward grace.

It must be kept carefully in mind that the new life we receive in baptism, which may be called *regeneration*, does not mean "baptismal regeneration," in the sense that the act of baptism, in and of itself, brings salvation. Contrary to popular opinion, few have actually taught such a mechanical view of baptism, although the Roman Catholic concept of *ex opere operato* has been understood along such lines. At any rate, Protestantism seeks to make clear that baptism is ineffectual apart from faith, and, as we shall see, this applies in the case of infant, as well as adult, baptism. For the Wesleyan/holiness tradition, the danger lies in the other direction—an unbiblical disregard of baptism.

The new life that we experience in Christ, which we enter through the gate of baptism, involves us in Christ's *work*. At His baptism, Jesus heard His Father's call to be a Suffering Servant. His work centered in His death and resurrection. In our baptism, we become united with Christ in all that He does. We become God's servants. In baptism, we make the work of Christ our work. His work involves suffering and servanthood. That is what it means to live the life of Christ.

D. RECEIVING THE SPIRIT OF CHRIST

It is impossible to "live the life of Christ" without His Spirit dwelling within. If, as was noted above, Christian baptism in its beginnings was largely formed with Jesus' own baptism in mind, the relation between the giving of the Holy Spirit and baptism is obvious. All three Synoptic accounts of the Lord's baptism at the Jordan state that the Holy Spirit came upon Jesus at that time. "At that moment heaven was opened, and he saw the Spirit of God descending like a dove and lighting on him" (Matt. 3:16). Although the Fourth Gospel does not record the actual baptism of Jesus, it makes the same point by reporting the Baptist's testimony that he saw the Spirit descend on Jesus (John 1:32).

Of course, even before His baptism Jesus was no stranger to the Holy Spirit. It was by the Holy Spirit that He had been conceived, and it was by the power of the Spirit that He grew in wisdom and stature and in favor with God and men. But now at the beginning of His public ministry the Spirit comes upon Him to equip and empower Him for His Servant role as the Savior of humanity. In this, the prophecy of Isaiah was being fulfilled: "The Spirit of the Lord will rest on him" (11:2). As Michael Green comments,

> The evangelists saw great significance in this "resting". The Holy Spirit could be withdrawn in Old Testament days. A Saul, a Samson, might do great exploits in the power of the Spirit, and then the Spirit might be withdrawn because of disobedience. It would be a marvelous thing if the Spirit came *to rest* on someone.[51]

Such a "resting" of the Spirit took place with Jesus. The Spirit comes upon Him to make manifest who He is, and from that time on Jesus would be seen as the Bearer of the Spirit, the One in whom the Spirit dwells and who defines the Spirit for us, and who thus defines what it means for us to live the life of the Spirit. It was to be a permanent endowment. The Spirit had come and would not be taken away. This is one of the glorious aspects of *our* baptism as well. Baptism is the sacrament in which the permanent presence of the Spirit is offered to us.

> We may, like Jesus, have had dealings with him before. Subsequently, we may go through barren periods of life when we are deaf to his gentle voice, and other times when we are vitally aware of his power. But baptism is the rite in which his permanent presence in our lives is pledged by God Almighty, just as it was with Jesus.[52]

This is not to say that we cannot withdraw ourselves from the Spirit's presence by disobedience, and it is certain that "if anyone does not have the Spirit of Christ, he does not belong to Christ" (Rom. 8:9). Wesleyan theology believes it possible for the baptized Christian to forsake his or her baptismal vows and fall out of relationship with God.[53] But our doing so does not nullify

---

51. Green, 40.
52. Ibid.
53. The advocates of "eternal security" or the "perseverance of the saints" often claim that one can lose *fellowship* but cannot lose *relationship* with God. There is not a word in the Bible to support such a distinction. Such a view sees "relationship" as something external, mechanical, and necessary, whereas true relationship in the personal realm is always characterized by inwardness, mutuality, and freedom. The very essence of relationship with God is *fellowship* with Him.

the promise of baptism. God does not go back on *His* pledge. Baptism stands as the reminder to us of what we have forsaken, and when we return to God by way of confession and repentance, it is a return to our baptism. We were the ones who moved—not God.

Jesus was the "only begotten" Son of God. But because we have been *adopted* into God's family, we are His children—"heirs of God and coheirs with Christ." Because we are children of God, "God sent the Spirit of his Son into our hearts," enabling us to call God our "Abba" (Rom. 8:15-17; Gal. 4:1-7). The Holy Spirit is none other than the Spirit of Christ. Paul has difficulty distinguishing between the experience of the Holy Spirit living in us and the risen Christ living in us. In the Paraclete passages in John, Jesus himself makes the point that the Holy Spirit will come, not to replace an absent Christ but to complete the presence of Christ.[54]

What has this to do with baptism? The message of John the Baptist was that although he baptized with water for repentance, there was One coming after him who would baptize with the Holy Spirit (Matt. 3:11). On the surface, John's proclamation might seem to imply that once baptism with the Holy Spirit became a possibility, water baptism would be superseded. Such a severing of the bestowal of the Spirit from baptism was clearly not the case, however, as we can see from the account of the outpouring of the Spirit in Acts, where the Baptist's prophecy was fulfilled. On the Day of Pentecost, Peter admonished his listeners: "Repent and be baptized, every one of you, in the name of Jesus Christ for the forgiveness of your sins. And you will receive the gift of the Holy Spirit" (2:38).[55] In those words of Peter, baptism, forgiveness of sins, and the reception of the Holy Spirit are all intertwined. To be more specific, baptism, as God's

---

54. Cf. John 14:15-18, 26; 15:26; 16:12-15.

55. Wesleyan/holiness preaching has sometimes attempted to interpret this as if it said, "Repent and be baptized *now* for the forgiveness of sins, and *sometime in the future* you will receive the gift of the Holy Spirit." This attempt is made by some who identify the outpouring of the Spirit at Pentecost exclusively with entire sanctification and who are concerned to safeguard the "secondness" of the latter. Such a procedure is misguided, the exegesis is strained, and those who follow it actually do their cause a disservice. In classical Wesleyanism, the secondness of entire sanctification does not depend on such an interpretation.

new covenant sign and as an expression of our repentance, brings about a dual effect—forgiveness of sins and the gift of the Holy Spirit.

The other accounts in Acts also show how closely connected are water baptism and the reception of the Holy Spirit. However, the exact nature of the connection is not spelled out. In fact, as James F. White remarks, "Sometimes the Holy Spirit's timing seems a bit off."[56] At the house of Cornelius, the Spirit is poured out "even on the Gentiles" before Peter finishes his sermon, and it is only afterward that they are baptized (10:44-48). In Samaria the order is reversed; those who had been baptized into the name of the Lord Jesus had not yet received the Spirit. The Spirit was not given to them until Peter and John came and laid their hands on them (8:17). At Ephesus, the situation is similar, except that the disciples Paul found there had received only the baptism of John the Baptist. When under Paul's ministry they were baptized in the name of Jesus, and after Paul had laid his hands on them, they received the Holy Spirit (19:3-7).

The "laying on of hands" at Samaria and Ephesus is another rite that might, at first glance, appear to be a further separation between baptism and the reception of the Spirit. The case of Samaria might seem to set up this pattern: baptism with water for the forgiveness of sins and the laying on of hands for the imparting of the Holy Spirit. Just as with baptism, however, there is no consistent pattern regarding the laying on of hands. It is used in close conjunction with baptism in Ephesus, but in Samaria its use by Peter and John could be viewed as a rite separate from baptism. At Pentecost, and at the "Gentile Pentecost" in the house of Cornelius, it does not occur at all. The solution seems to be that laying on of hands became a part of the baptismal rite, although it is impossible to know the exact time at which the two became conjoined. It was probably added to the baptismal rite to underscore the reality of the gift of the Spirit in baptism. But it was added, not to convey something that could not be associated with baptism as such, but to strengthen this element (the giving of the Spirit) that is already associated with baptism itself.[57] Alan Richardson is surely correct in saying that

---

56. *Sacraments*, 39.
57. Cf. Beasley-Murray's discussion of the "laying on of hands," 122-25.

"in the New Testament the whole baptismal action is a unity which cannot be analyzed into its component parts, and it is in the whole action that the Spirit is bestowed."[58]

The difficulty in finding a consistent pattern in Acts regarding the time of the bestowal of the Spirit in relation to baptism and the laying on of hands should not cause undue consternation. In late medieval Catholicism there was a tendency to clock the exact moment of God's activity in the sacraments. Regrettably, Wesleyan/holiness theology has had a similar tendency to hold a stopwatch to the actions of grace and to chart meticulously the order of salvation. With regard to baptism and its relation to the bestowal of the Spirit, such attempts seek to know more than the New Testament will tell us. Although baptism and the reception of the Holy Spirit stood in close relation in the New Testament Church, allowance must always be made for the freedom of God in bestowing His Spirit. The important element in baptism is not the exact manner in which the rite is carried out but that to which the rite points—the work of the Spirit in the person who acknowledges the claim of the crucified and risen Christ over his or her life. When we are baptized in the name of the Lord Jesus, the name of the Lord is called over us, declaring us to be His.

> Baptism in Acts is repentance and faith coming to expression in an act that anticipates the turning and renewal of the whole course of life; *by it the purely inward experience steps into the open and so comes to completion;* consequently the act was the occasion for the bestowal of the Spirit.[59]

The truly important matter was the outpouring of the Spirit, and water baptism was the "outward sign" of the greater gift. Baptism bestows neither forgiveness nor the Spirit apart from faith. James Dunn is correct in his amusing remark that "Luke was no 'early Catholic.'"[60] But in the Book of Acts, the giving of the

---

58. Alan Richardson, *An Introduction to the Theology of the New Testament* (New York: Harper and Brothers, 1958), 355.

59. Beasley-Murray, 121, italics mine, citing F. Büchsel in *Geist Gottes im Neuen Testament.*

60. James D. G. Dunn, *Baptism in the Holy Spirit* (Naperville, Ill.: Alec R. Allenson, 1970), 102.

Holy Spirit becomes apparent, often with great intensity, in those who, in repentance and faith, were baptized. Paul wrote a whole chapter about the manifestations of gifts of the Spirit (1 Corinthians 12), where he discusses the "varieties of gifts" found in those who were "made to drink" of the Spirit through baptism (vv. 4, 13, RSV).

One issue has not yet been discussed, namely, the baptism with the Holy Spirit in the Book of Acts and its relation to water baptism. In the American holiness movement of the 19th century, and in many present-day groups originating in that movement, "baptism with the Holy Spirit" came to be associated with entire sanctification as a second work of grace subsequent to the new birth. As is widely recognized among Wesley scholars, such an association departs somewhat from the teaching of John Wesley. It is not our purpose here to explore this issue. It has already been debated intensely among Wesleyan theologians and Bible scholars.[61] Only one point needs to be considered.

John Wesley did not distinguish between "receiving the Holy Spirit" and being "baptized with the Holy Spirit" as the holiness movement has tended to do. It was his friend John Fletcher who first began to identify Spirit baptism with entire sanctification, and Wesley resisted the idea. In referring to the "second change" of entire sanctification or Christian perfection, he says: "If they like to call this 'receiving the Holy Ghost,' they may: only the phrase in that sense is not scriptural and not quite proper; for they all 'received the Holy Ghost' when they were justified."[62] After Fletcher's suggestion of identifying the bestowal of the Spirit on the disciples at Pentecost with the experience of entire sanctification, the idea seems to have virtually disappeared in early Methodism. None of the standard Methodist theologians after Wesley made such an identification.[63] But the

---

61. The bulk of the literature on the debate can be found in upwards of 20 articles by various Wesleyan scholars published in the *Wesleyan Theological Journal* between 1973 and 1980.

62. *Letters* 5:215.

63. The list includes such respected Methodist scholars as Adam Clarke, Richard Watson, William Burt Pope, Miner Raymond, Olin A. Curtis, and Thomas N. Ralston—all of whom taught, with varying emphases and varying degrees of dependence on Wesley, the doctrine of entire sanctification. Included in the list also, according to Herbert McGonigle, are 41 of the first Methodist preachers. Cf. McGonigle's article, "Pneumatological Nomenclature in Early Methodism," *Wesleyan Theological Journal*, Spring 1973, 68.

idea arose again in the 19th-century American holiness movement, through the impetus of Charles G. Finney, Asa Mahan, Phoebe Palmer, and others.[64] Some in the Wesleyan/holiness churches today believe this idea to be an improvement over Wesley. Whether it is or not, it is a *change* from Wesley. Wesley's doctrine of entire sanctification, and his views on Christian perfection, were based on entirely different biblical grounds.

The main point for our discussion is that John Wesley believed that to become a Christian is to receive the Holy Spirit, which is the promise of the new covenant (Ezek. 36:25; Gal. 3:14). In this sense, he viewed the disciples as becoming Christians at Pentecost, when by faith they entered the new covenant and received the Spirit.[65] Wesley would have agreed with Oscar Cullmann that *Christian* baptism began at Pentecost. The 3,000 who were converted on the Day of Pentecost and received the Spirit were baptized as the outward sign of their entry into the new covenant, just as Jews were circumcised as the sign of their entry into the old covenant. Wesley certainly agreed with Paul that without the indwelling Holy Spirit one is not a Christian.[66] And he doubtless would have agreed with James Dunn's comment on Rom. 8:9, that Paul "rules out the possibility both of a *non*-Christian possessing the Spirit and of a Christian *not* possessing the Spirit: only the reception and consequent possession of the Spirit makes a man a Christian."[67]

As noted above, there are examples in the New Testament of persons receiving the Holy Spirit without or before baptism. This might lead some to reason that, since God bestowed His Spirit without baptism, the use of water is not needed at all. Wesley sees in such ideas the danger of enthusiasm (fanaticism), and of what today we would call subjectivism, and refutes it in his commentary on Acts 10:47:

---

64. Cf. J. Kenneth Grider, *Entire Sanctification: The Distinctive Doctrine of Wesleyanism* (Kansas City: Beacon Hill Press of Kansas City, 1980), 65-76, for a brief discussion of the views of these persons.

65. He would consider the disciples to be "saved" previous to Pentecost, under the terms of the old covenant.

66. Wesley comments on Rom. 8:9 as follows: *"If any man have not the Spirit of Christ*—Dwelling and governing in him. *He is none of his*—He is not a member of Christ; not a Christian; not in a state of salvation." *NT Notes.*

67. Dunn, 95.

> *Can any man forbid water, that these should not be baptized,*
> *who have received the Holy Ghost*—He does not say, They
> have the baptism of the Spirit; therefore they do not need
> baptism with water: but just the contrary; If they have re-
> ceived the Spirit, then baptize them with water.
>
> How easily is this question decided, if we will take the
> word of God for our judge! Either men have received the
> Holy Ghost, or not. If they have not, "Repent," saith God,
> "and be baptized, and ye shall receive the gift of the Holy
> Ghost." If they have, if they are already baptized with the
> Holy Ghost, then, *who can forbid water?*[68]

Wiley agrees with Wesley. He says:

> Some have argued that because Christ baptizes with the
> Holy Ghost, water baptism is no longer necessary. That it su-
> perseded John's baptism, is doubtless true; but . . . there is a
> wide distinction between John's baptism with water as a
> preparatory rite, and Christ's baptism with water as a sign
> and seal of an inward work of grace.[69]

The two go together. One must be born of water *and* of the
Spirit. To receive, in true repentance and faith, God's outward
sign of baptism is to receive the inward grace of the gift of the
Holy Spirit.

E. BECOMING THE BODY OF CHRIST

If the possession of the Spirit makes a person a Christian,
being a Christian is more than a merely *individual* affair. "Christianity is essentially a social religion," said Wesley, "and . . . to
turn it into a solitary religion, is indeed to destroy it."[70] Pentecost
was a *corporate* affair. When the disciples were assembled in the
Upper Room, the Holy Spirit "came to rest on each of them," but
it was only when "they were all together in one place" (Acts
2:1-3). The Spirit was experienced by every person individually,
but only as they were knit together in a common quest and a
common obedience (Luke 24:49). At the close of his Pentecost
sermon, Peter states that the same Spirit will be bestowed on

---

68. *NT Notes.*
69. Wiley 3:174.
70. *Works* 5:296.

those who repent and are baptized. Baptism, as God's covenant sign, marks the bestowal of the Spirit, and it is the Spirit who thus creates and constitutes the Church. Those who accepted Peter's message were baptized, and about 3,000 were added to their number that day (Acts 2:41). Thus the Church had its beginnings.

One of the most vivid metaphors of the Church in the New Testament is Paul's reference to the Church as the Body of Christ. When this metaphor is coupled with the correlative image of Christ as the Head of the Body (Col. 1:18), a striking picture of the Church emerges. Each individual Christian is a part ("member") of Christ's Body, living in harmony with the other parts, and under the control of the Head!

We have been trying to suggest the ways in which Christian baptism expresses Christian faith. Heretofore in this chapter we have discussed baptism as bearing Christ's mark, dying Christ's death, living Christ's life, and receiving Christ's Spirit. These all come together and find their meaning in the living fellowship of the Church into which we are initiated by baptism. Wesley said: "By baptism we are admitted into the Church, and consequently made members of Christ, its Head."[71]

The Nicene-Constantinopolitan Creed (A.D. 381), which is cherished by Catholics and Protestants alike, declares that baptism is no mere appendage but an integral element of our Christian faith. It says in part:

"I believe in one holy, catholic, and apostolic Church.
I acknowledge one baptism for the remission of sins."

The gospel is not a system of timeless ideas but is rooted in the soil of a particular history where the Word was made flesh. Therefore our appropriation of the gospel is not an abstract, inward, invisible acceptance, but is ever expressed in a given, historical, visible outward sign so that the Word may become flesh in our own experience. That sign is baptism. To dispense with the sign, the creed seems to tell us, would be to scorn the thing signified. The inward grace may exist without the outward sign (as the Society of Friends and the Salvation Army bear laudable

---

71. Ibid. 10:191.

witness), but it is the central conviction of the Wesleyan/holiness tradition, along with Roman Catholicism and most branches of Protestantism, that the inward grace is best propagated when the outward sign is given its proper place.

In its affirmation of "one baptism," the Nicene Creed is faithful to the New Testament, especially to the Epistle to the Ephesians, that eloquent and exultant description of the majesty of our Christian faith. In a beautiful passage there, the apostle Paul sums up the whole magnitude of Christian experience. He has already shown how God's gracious love has bridged the chasm of sin and overcome deep divisions among human beings to create a redemptive order of fellowship in Christ. Now he exhorts his readers to maintain the unity of the Spirit that God's love has created. Then he gives the reason such unity is to be kept—unity is at the very heart of Christian reality: "There is one body and one Spirit—just as you were called to one hope when you were called—one Lord, one faith, one baptism; one God and Father of all, who is over all and through all and in all" (4:4-6).

In this great catalog of seven Christian realities, Paul gives baptism a place without any apology. In a listing of realities that are mostly spiritual, or invisible, Paul includes a physical, visible sacramental sign. This seems even more remarkable when it is noted that Paul does not even include the Lord's Supper here, or Scripture, or other means of grace. If baptism were not important, it would be difficult to understand why Paul gives it such prominence.

There is one body. "I believe in one holy, catholic, and apostolic Church." The unity of the Church is often obscured by the fragmentation of a divided Christendom. Yet the Church remains one. The communion of saints is not something that can be built by ecclesiastical structures. Nor does unity mean uniformity. There are many members, but one body, and "to each one of us grace has been given as Christ apportioned it" (Eph. 4:7). There is one body. The Church that is Christ's Body is not to be built out of the denominational structures, but *into* them! Baptism expresses our initiation into this one Body. As divergent as our several theological and denominational traditions may be, it is a tremendous truth that one baptismal formula gathers us all together as one body under one name—"in the name of the Father and of the Son and of the Holy Spirit" (Matt. 28:19).

There is one Spirit. This is the reason there is only one body. A body without spirit is merely a corpse. And a body with many "spirits" is a schizophrenic demoniac. Both are as true of a church as of an individual. The Church is called "the church of the living God" (1 Tim. 3:15) because it has His Spirit. At Pentecost, the Spirit reversed the conflicting voices of Babel and created a new community, enabling the gospel to be spoken in every person's own language. Through His Spirit, Christ still lives in the Church, doing His work, speaking His words, and continuing His redemptive mission. And the Church sings:

> Come, Holy Spirit, heav'nly Dove,
> With all Thy quick'ning pow'rs;
> Come, shed abroad a Saviour's love,
> And that shall kindle ours.
> —ISAAC WATTS

The Greek word *pneuma* means both "spirit" and "breath." Unless breath be in the body, the body is dead. The vitalizing breath of the Church is the Holy Spirit.

There is one hope. Paul says, "You were called to one hope when you were called" (Eph. 4:4). We were called, and therefore we are *His*, and therefore we have hope. The same hope is expressed by John in these words: "Dear friends, now we are children of God, and what we will be has not yet been made known. But we know that when he appears, we shall be like him, for we shall see him as he is" (1 John 3:2). This promise is portrayed in baptism, where God declares that we are His, because we bear Christ's mark and have been given His name.

There is one Lord. "The Church's one Foundation," says the hymn writer, "is Jesus Christ her Lord." One Lord! And God has given Him a "name that is above every name, that at the name of Jesus every knee should bow, in heaven and on earth and under the earth, and every tongue confess that Jesus Christ is Lord, to the glory of God the Father" (Phil. 2:9-11).

There is one faith. This is what binds us together into the one Body—faith in Jesus Christ as Savior and surrender to Him as Lord of our lives.

There is one baptism. There are differing interpretations of this phrase. It may be well to recall here our previous discussion under the topic, "Dying the Death of Christ." Jesus referred to His approaching death on the Cross, to which His baptism at the Jordan pointed, as a "baptism" that He must undergo (Luke 12:50). Is this the "one baptism"? But we have also seen that the gift of the Spirit was first made to the Church at Pentecost. This event is identified as that baptism "with the Holy Spirit and with fire" foretold by John the Baptist (Matt. 3:11; Luke 3:16). Is this the "one baptism"? We have further seen that at Pentecost Peter preached to "every one" of the people there that they should be baptized with water for the forgiveness of sins. Is this the "one baptism"? The answer is: all three. The once-for-all baptism Christ underwent on the Cross made possible the once-for-all baptism of the Spirit He bestowed on the Church at Pentecost, and both of those form the foundation for the baptism of each individual.

In regard to the last of these (individual water baptism): Whether it is by sprinkling, pouring, or immersion; whether it is administered to infants or to adult believers only; whether it takes place in the church building or in a flowing stream—there is only one baptism! If it is done in the name of the Trinitarian God, and if it truly expresses our acceptance of God's covenant through faith and repentance and a thirst for the Spirit and our desire to be a part of the Christian fellowship, then it is the proper Christian baptism. Although there is a legitimate place for differences of opinion regarding matters of mode and method (and certainly the history of biblical studies demonstrates that the New Testament is not unambiguously clear on them), the beauty of baptism is marred when such things as these become matters of first priority.

Finally, there is one body, one Spirit, one hope, one Lord, one faith, and one baptism because there is *"one God and Father of us all, who is above all and through all and in all"* (Eph. 4:6, RSV, italics mine).

In another passage dealing with the unity of Christ's Body, Paul says:

> The body is a unit, though it is made up of many parts;
> and though all its parts are many, they form one body. So it is

> with Christ. For we were all baptized by one Spirit into one
> body—whether Jews or Greeks, slave or free—and we were
> all given the one Spirit to drink *(1 Cor. 12:12-13)*.

Whether we interpret Paul here as giving a theology of the
Spirit, or a theology of the Church, or a theology of baptism,
they all amount to the same thing. "By one Spirit are we all baptized into one body" (KJV). To be a Christian is to possess the
Spirit. It is to be a baptized person. It is to become, in unity with
all fellow Christians, the Body of Christ. The one Spirit, which
John Wesley says "we received in baptism,"[72] unites us into one
Body. According to Wesley, it is God's plan, intended to last as
long as the Church lasts, that baptism bestows on us the Spirit
and admits us into the Church. "In the ordinary way, there is no
other means of entering into the Church or into heaven."[73] Just
as circumcision was "to last among the Jews as long as the law
lasted, . . . by plain parity of reason, baptism, which came in its
room, must last among Christians as long as the gospel covenant into which it admits, and whereunto it obliges, all nations."[74]

It is its possession of the Holy Spirit that marks out the
Church as the fellowship of those "on whom the fulfillment of
the ages has come" (1 Cor. 10:11) and stamps the Church as the
community of those who wait for "the glory that will be revealed" (Rom. 8:18). Unbelievers live between birth and death;
believers live between baptism and the return of Christ. Already
a part of Christ's Body, they yet wait in travail and imperfection
for the final consummation.

In this faith and in this hope the baptized live and serve—
in completeness and incompleteness, between the "already" and
the "not yet." Because they have died and risen with Christ in
baptism, the other sacrament of the Church—the Eucharist—is
possible; and because they await the final resurrection, the Eucharist is necessary.

---

72. *NT Notes,* on 1 Cor. 12:13.
73. *Works* 10:192.
74. Ibid.

Chapter Six

WHAT ABOUT INFANT BAPTISM?

In perhaps no other aspect of their sacramental practice have the churches in the Wesleyan/holiness tradition strayed from their classical Wesleyan heritage more conspicuously than in the matter of infant baptism. The causes of this are complex and varied, but the phenomenon is basically the result of the intrusion into the holiness movement of ideas whose roots lie in that wing of the Protestant Reformation variously called the "Anabaptist," or "radical," or "sectarian," or "left" wing.

A. ANABAPTIST INFLUENCE IN WESLEYANISM

In 19th-century America, many persons from non-Methodist backgrounds were brought into the holiness movement because they embraced the doctrine and experience of entire sanctification as taught by Wesley and early Methodism. This doctrine and experience was the basis on which they united. Sacramental beliefs and practices were secondary. Among these converts to the holiness movement were Quakers who did not practice sacraments at all, and persons with various Anabaptist backgrounds who believed that only adult believers should be baptized. Such an amalgamation of persons with differing sacramental views, uniting around the doctrine and experience of holiness, brought about a diminishing of the importance placed on sacraments in general and of infant baptism in particular.

There were more important truths to be propagated. This process is an earlier example of what church historian Martin E. Marty has described as the "baptistification" of American religion in recent times.[1]

Another factor contributing to the decline of infant baptism within the holiness groups was their heavy involvement in missionary activity. The same situation exists today. In non-Christian cultures, the baptism of adults into the Christian faith has a certain dramatic significance that cannot be matched by infant baptism. As converts are baptized, especially by immersion, a graphic visible witness is given to their non-Christian friends, portraying their deliberate "putting off" of the old life and "putting on" of the new.

Another objection to infant baptism is often voiced by Wesleyan/holiness missionaries in Catholic countries. They complain that it is difficult to explain to converts from Catholicism why, in baptismal practice, "we are no different from Catholics." It should go without saying that being different from members of other Christian traditions is, of itself, a poor reason for formulating doctrines and practices, but such a motivation does exist. For the above reasons, and others, the churches in the Wesleyan/holiness tradition have, in sacramental practice if not in theory, moved a great distance from their classical Wesleyan origins.

In most churches within the Wesleyan/holiness tradition, infant baptism, as well as adult baptism, is embodied in the official statements of faith, and a ritual for the baptism of infants is provided. This is true of both the Church of the Nazarene and the Free Methodist church. In The Wesleyan Church, the Articles of Religion do not mention infant baptism. The statement that water baptism is "administered to believers" could be interpreted as an Anabaptist position that would exclude infants.[2] In seeming conflict with its own Article on Baptism, The Wesleyan Church's *Discipline* contains a ritual that may be used for either infant baptism or infant dedication. It states that the ritual may be used by parents or guardians who desire either to dedicate

---

1. Martin E. Marty, "Baptistification Takes Over," *Christianity Today,* September 2, 1983.
2. Although, from Martin Luther's perspective, as we shall presently see, infants may be "believers" too.

their child *without* the sacrament of baptism or to dedicate him or her *through* the sacrament of baptism. These are stated as two types of dedication. Baptism is thus subsumed under dedication. The care taken not to give baptism the "top billing" is probably due to the Quaker influence within the Pilgrim Holiness church, which merged with the Wesleyan Methodist church in 1968 to form the present denomination known as The Wesleyan Church. In the current issues of both the *Manual* of the Church of the Nazarene and the *Discipline* of the Free Methodist church, separate rituals are provided for the *baptism* of infants and the *dedication* of infants, and parents may choose between them. Thus these churches make a greater distinction between infant baptism and dedication than does The Wesleyan Church, although the distinction is clearer in theory than it sometimes is in practice.

No reliable statistics are available to show the proportion of infant baptisms to infant dedications in the Wesleyan/holiness denominations, but it is widely perceived that dedications are far more numerous. Often pastors are responsible for this, particularly when they fail to inform parents that infant baptism is a valid option in their denomination. Trusting the church and its leadership, laypersons often perceive that the choice is between dedication and nothing, rather than between infant baptism and infant dedication. Of course, when dedication is an informed and deliberate choice, those who choose it generally do so because they share the Anabaptist conviction that baptism should be administered only to adults who are capable of making a conscious decision and exercising personal faith. This represents a great difference between the practice prevailing within the present-day Wesleyan/holiness churches and that of early Methodism and is a significant departure from the theology of John Wesley himself.

Powerful arguments have been raised against the doctrine and practice of infant baptism. To many, it seems a scandal because it makes people think they are Christians when they may be nothing of the kind. It thus inoculates people against the true gospel. Countless biblical and theological arguments are made against it. But when we strip away all the verbiage, the arguments against the baptism of infants reduce basically to this:

Since as Protestants we believe that salvation is by faith, baptism should be the personal response of our faith to God's grace. Since little children are not old enough to understand the call of God, or to make a conscious choice to respond, they should not be baptized. Adults are baptized because they are capable of making such a decision and exercising saving faith. This is commonly called "believer's baptism," although that is a misnomer, because it assumes that faith is only possible in an adult. This was one of the assumptions of the Anabaptists that was challenged by Martin Luther.

Brief note was taken earlier of the dispute between Luther and the Anabaptists over baptism as it related to the role of experience in Christian faith and life.[3] Since most subsequent disputes about infant baptism reflect, in some measure, the classic debate on the subject at the time of the Reformation, it is important to understand the two points of view developed at that time.

In pressing for the right of infant baptism against the Anabaptists, Luther relies heavily on the common Christian tradition and argues on the basis of his theology of history: Infant baptism has been practiced since the beginning of the Church, and "God will not permit something wrong to continue so long from the beginning to the present day."[4] Of course, he recognizes that the argument from tradition is valid only if the institution under discussion is not contrary to Scripture.[5] He admits that infant baptism is not *explicitly* commanded in Scripture. But since it is obviously not contrary to Scripture (since God has preserved it for so long), no one can in good conscience reject it.[6] Building on this basic conviction, Luther cites the instances in the Gospels where Christ allows children to come to Him and says that the kingdom of God belongs to them. He cites the Lord's command to baptize, in which children are not excluded. He also cites the instances in the Book of Acts where entire "households" were baptized, upon the conversion of the head of

---

3. See the last section of chapter 1.
4. Althaus, 359.
5. He opposed many of Rome's other institutions for this very reason: They were contrary to Scripture.
6. Althaus, 361.

the household.[7] He insists that "children are surely a good part of the household."[8]

> This undifferentiated universality of the command to baptize, which apparently corresponded to the apostolic practice of baptism, is only an expression of the universalism of the gospel. And this is the decisive point for Luther. Luther ultimately bases the right and necessity of infant baptism on the basic meaning of the Gospel.[9]

As far as Scripture is concerned, Luther's argument for the validity of infant baptism is largely an argument from silence. He believed that (1) Scripture does not oppose it, (2) Scripture does not expressly exclude children from baptism, and (3) Scripture does not command that only adults be baptized.

The Anabaptists argued that the sacraments are efficacious only when they are received in faith. Certainly Luther did not oppose this, for it was also his argument against the *ex opere operato* doctrine of Roman Catholicism! To the objection that infants cannot have faith, he teaches a concept of "infant faith." In essence, he raises the question: Just how old does a child have to be before it can have faith? This was a question the Anabaptists could not really answer. To insist that faith is impossible below a certain chronological age was, for Luther, confusing faith with understanding or intellectual capacity. Salvation would therefore be not by faith but by knowledge or reason. To the objection that children below the age of reason cannot have faith, Luther replies that the opposite is generally true—reason stands in the way of faith. Children are "more fitted for faith than older and more rational people who always trip over their reason and do not wish to push their swelled heads through the narrow gate."[10]

In spite of these points Luther makes to refute the Ana-

---

7. Cf. Acts 16:15; 18:8; 1 Cor. 1:16. In those verses, the Greek word *oikos* is usually translated "household." In Acts 16:33, *oikos* does not appear, but the phrase meaning "all his" is rendered as "all his household" in NASB, "all his family" in NIV and RSV, and "his whole family" in NEB.

8. *Luther's Works* 40:245.

9. Althaus, 362.

10. *D. Martin Luthers Werke,* Kritische Gesamtausgabe (Weimar: H. Böhlau, 1883—), quoted in Althaus, 366.

baptist claim that a child cannot have faith, he does not finally base the validity of infant baptism on the presence of faith in the child. Instead, his argument aims in the opposite direction. He maintains that because infant baptism is valid, and scriptural, and according to the will of God, children can have faith. Since faith must accompany baptism, and since infant baptism has divine approval, we know it is possible for infants to have faith!

But this is still not the decisive point. We cannot know whether or not a particular child has faith. The same is true in the case of adults; we cannot know if they truly believe. Everything depends on God's word and commandment. *Faith does not constitute baptism but receives it.* Baptism summons us to faith. Even adults who come to baptism in faith cannot rest on the fact that they believe, but must rest on the fact that it is God's commandment. The same is true of infant baptism. "We bring the child to be baptized because we think and hope that it will believe, and we pray that God will give it faith; we do not baptize it because of this, however, but only because God has commanded it."[11]

Not only did Luther defend infant baptism against the Anabaptist attacks, but also he attacked *their* baptismal practice, which he held to be impossible on the basis of the gospel. He raised two objections: First, as already mentioned, making baptism dependent on the faith of the person baptized always leaves us uncertain about any particular baptism, for we can never know for sure whether the person really believes.[12] Second, depending on faith in this way actually turns it into a "work," and a new works-righteousness is the result. Saving faith becomes "faith in faith." Faith is corrupted and destroyed when it becomes its own object. Our faith must be put in God and not in our own faith.

Since the Reformation in the 16th century, the debate over infant baptism has continued, with neither side having much success in convincing the other. The issue was a live one for John Wesley in the 18th century. With an uncharacteristic lack of

---

11. Althaus, 369.
12. *Luther's Works* 40:239-40.

restraint, Wesley refers to the Anabaptists as "some not very holy men in Germany" who "were far from being of the best Characters."[13] In one edition of his *Treatise on Baptism*, he rejects the baptism of the Anabaptists as not having apostolic authority behind it. He says: "The baptism—I ought to call it the 'dipping'—of the Anabaptists, as much stress as ever they lay upon it, is no baptism at all."[14]

B. WESLEY ON INFANT BAPTISM

"The baptism of young children is to be retained in the Church," Wesley wrote in the Twenty-five Articles of Methodism. In his *Treatise on Baptism*,[15] he argues that infants are proper subjects of baptism, and he proposes to "lay down the grounds of infant baptism, taken from Scripture, reason, and primitive, universal practice" and to "answer the objections against it."[16] In numerous other places in his writings the same points are made, sometimes in a less structured way and sometimes in the context of other discussions.

In order to understand Wesley's view of infant baptism, it is necessary, of course, to set it in the context of his doctrine of baptism in general and to see it in relation to his ideas on adult baptism. In the *Treatise on Baptism*, Wesley declares that the first benefit of baptism is the washing away of the guilt of original sin by the application of the merits of Christ's death.[17] This in-

---

13. Borgen, 145, incl. n. 98.
14. Cf. Outler, 318.
15. This treatise was an abridgment of a confirmation manual published by his father three years before John Wesley's birth, and called *The Pious Communicant*. It was a summary of Anglican sacramental theology. Cf. Outler, 317.
16. *Works* 10:193.
17. In theology, the *guilt* of original sin is distinguished from original sin itself. The latter most often refers to the depraved nature that Adam passed on to his descendants, with its accompanying tendency toward sinning, whereas the former means that all persons actually participated in Adam's transgression (being already "in Adam's loins" when he sinned) and thus share his guilt and need forgiveness for their action. In commenting on Rom. 5:12, in his *NT Notes*, Wesley says: "These words assign the reason why death came upon *all men;* infants themselves not excepted, *in that all sinned.*" On verse 19, he says: "*As by the disobedience of one man many* (that is, all men) *were constituted sinners*— Being then in the loins of their first parent, the common head and representative of them all." Thus many followers of Wesley hold that the *guilt* of original sin may be taken away even as the depraved *nature* remains. The question of when in the *ordo salutis* (the "order of salvation") Wesley believed these two are dealt with will be discussed below in the section on "Baptismal Regeneration?"

cludes infants, for they too have sinned, not by "actual sin" but by "original" sin, since "in Adam *all* died." Being "in Adam's loins" when he sinned, all infants participated in Adam's transgression and are thus guilty of it. By baptism we enter into covenant with God, are admitted into the church, and are made the children of God. "By water then, as a means, the water of baptism, we are regenerated or born again."[18] To be sure, it is not the mere *outward washing* but the *inward grace* added thereto that makes it a sacrament, but "in all ages, the outward baptism is a means of the inward; as outward circumcision was of the circumcision of the heart."[19] "Herein a principle of grace is infused, which will not be wholly taken away, unless we quench the Holy Spirit of God by long-continued wickedness."[20]

By contrast, the sermon "The New Birth" places the emphasis more heavily on regeneration as a conscious inward experience, and a distinction is drawn between the new birth and baptism, even though they are not totally severed from one another. The two are differentiated just as the two parts of a sacrament are differentiated.

> "The parts of a sacrament are two: The one an outward and sensible sign; the other, an inward and spiritual grace, thereby signified. . . . Baptism is a sacrament, wherein Christ hath ordained the washing with water, to be a sign and seal of regeneration by his Spirit." Here it is manifest, baptism, the sign, is spoken of as distinct from regeneration, the thing signified.[21]

He goes on to say that "as the new birth is not the same thing with baptism, so it does not always accompany baptism. . . . There may sometimes be the outward sign, where there is not the inward grace."[22] Whereas Wesley believes (in the case of adults) that the new birth does not *necessarily* accompany baptism, he never considers it acceptable that baptism not accompany the new birth, unless baptism is an impossibility in a given situation. But lest he be misunderstood with reference to the baptism of infants, he explains:

---

18. *Works* 10:192.
19. Ibid.
20. Ibid.
21. Ibid. 6:73.
22. Ibid., 74.

> I do not now speak with regard to infants: It is certain our Church supposes that all who are baptized in their infancy are at the same time born again; . . . But whatever be the case with infants, it is sure all of riper years who are baptized are not at the same time born again.[23]

With this understanding of the relation between adult baptism and infant baptism, we may now examine more closely his views on the latter. In defending infant baptism in the *Treatise*, Wesley argues on five levels. First, infants are proper subjects of baptism because of the sin of Adam in which all persons participated. "God does not look upon infants as innocent, but as involved in the guilt of Adam's sin."[24] Since they are "guilty of original sin," they are "proper subjects of baptism; seeing, in the ordinary way, they cannot be saved, unless this be washed away by baptism."[25] Christ has provided a remedy for "the disease which came upon all by the offence of the first," but the benefit of this remedy is to be received "through the means which he hath appointed; through baptism in particular, which is the ordinary means he hath appointed for that purpose; and to which God hath tied us, though he may not have tied himself."[26]

Second (and this is the argument to which Wesley seems to give the most weight), baptism is proper for children because of the continuity of the covenant of grace God made with Abraham. This covenant is "everlasting," and all who believe are heirs of Abraham. In continuity with the new covenant established by Christ, the covenant with Abraham was a "gospel covenant" with the same condition (faith) and the same benefits ("I will be thy God"). Furthermore, it was established by the same Mediator (Gen. 22:18; Gal. 3:16). "But the blood of Christ being shed, all bloody ordinances are now abolished. Circumcision therefore gives way to baptism."[27] Baptism is now the "circumcision of Christ" (Col. 2:11-12). Infants, therefore, are capable of entering into covenant with God, just as they always were, and

---

23. Ibid.
24. Ibid. 9:316.
25. Ibid. 10:193.
26. Ibid.
27. John Wesley, *Explanatory Notes upon the Old Testament*, reprint from the 1765 edition (Salem, Ohio: Schmul Publishers, 1975), Gen. 17:10 (hereafter cited as *OT Notes*).

are thus entitled to baptism. As circumcision was the seal of the covenant with Abraham, baptism is the seal of the covenant established by Christ. When the old seal was set aside, baptism was added in its place, "our Lord appointing one positive institution to succeed another."[28] "A new seal was set to Abraham's covenant; the seals differed, but the deed was the same."[29] For Wesley, the fact that baptism differs in some respects from circumcision is no proof that it did not take its place, any more than one can prove the Lord's Supper did not succeed the Passover because it differs from it in some respects.[30] Infants may enter into covenant with God and may be put under obligation "by compacts made by others in their name, and receive advantage by them."[31] Citing Deut. 29:10-12, where the "little ones" are included in the covenant, Wesley says:

> Now, God would never have made a covenant with little ones, if they had not been capable of it. It is not said children only, but little children, the Hebrew word properly signifying infants. And these may be still, as they were of old, obliged to perform, in aftertime, what they are not capable of performing at the time of their entering into that obligation.[32]

Third, on the basis of Matt. 19:13-14 and Luke 18:15, Wesley argues that small children should be brought to Christ, and that therefore they are capable of coming to Him and being admitted into the church. He believes admittance into the church to be through baptism. Borgen says, "Wesley understands this aspect of Baptism to include the parents' willingness to give their child to God by bringing him to be baptized, as well as their taking a two-fold vow: in behalf of the child they promise to take up the obligations as well as the privileges of the covenant; and on their own behalf they promise to teach the child the ways of the Lord."[33]

---

28. *Works* 10:194.

29. Ibid., 194-95.

30. Ibid., 195. For example, whereas infant girls, as well as boys, are baptized, only males could be circumcised. This reflects the patriarchial society of the Hebrews and their concept of corporate personality, and for Wesley, would not prove that baptism did not take the place of circumcision.

31. Ibid., 193.

32. Ibid., 194.

33. Borgen, 142-43.

Fourth, Wesley appeals to the practice of the apostles; if they baptized infants, then infants are proper subjects of baptism. Like Luther, he knows the New Testament does not *explicitly* tell of infants being baptized, although he believes it to be a valid inference. He argues on the basis of probability. The Jews baptized all infant proselytes; it is therefore likely that the apostles did the same, since the Lord did not forbid it when He commanded the apostles to disciple all nations by baptizing them. Again sounding a little like Luther, he argues from the mention of entire households being baptized in Acts.

> If it be objected, "There is no express mention in Scripture of any infants whom the Apostles baptized," I would ask, Suppose no mention had been made in the Acts of those two women baptized by the Apostles, yet might we not fairly conclude, that when so many thousands, so many entire households, were baptized, women were not excluded? especially since it was the known custom of the Jews to baptize them? The same holds of children; nay, more strongly, on the account of circumcision.[34]

He goes on to mention the 3,000 on one day, and 5,000 on another, who were baptized by the apostles, as well as the households mentioned in Acts, and ends his argument by appealing to Peter's Pentecost sermon, which concluded with the words, "Be baptized . . . For the promise is unto you, and *to your children*" (2:38-39, KJV, italics mine).

Finally, appealing to the authority of tradition, Wesley finds support for infant baptism in the practice of the church "in all ages and in all places." He cites Augustine, Origen, and Cyprian, and says if there were need he could cite also Athanasius, Chrysostom, and "a cloud of witnesses." "Nor is there one instance to be found in all antiquity, of any orthodox Christian who denied baptism to children when brought to be baptized."[35] Since infant baptism has been the general practice of the Christian church in all places and in all ages, and has continued without interruption for the many centuries, Wesley concludes that

34. *Works* 10:196-97.
35. Ibid., 197.

"it was handed down from the Apostles, who best knew the mind of Christ."[36]

C. Is Baptism a Human or Divine Act?

The decision regarding infant baptism ultimately must rest on theological grounds. Of course the church, in the development of its theology, must constantly be driven back to its beginnings and thus to a study of the Scriptures and of the practice of the Church in the New Testament. In regard to infant baptism, then, the question is: Was infant baptism taught and practiced in the New Testament Church? Although much research has been devoted to that issue, biblical scholarship has failed to provide definite and unambiguous answers to the question. Some highly competent modern scholars find New Testament authority for infant baptism (Oscar Cullmann and Joachim Jeremias, for instance) while others (such as Kurt Aland and G. R. Beasley-Murray) deny it.[37] One point of ambiguity is the so-called *oikos* formula (from the Greek word for "house" or "household") used in Acts to state that whole households, or families, were baptized. It seems very likely that at least some of these households included children, but it cannot be said with absolute certainty that they did. On whether or not the New Testament Church baptized infants, scholars argue both ways, and we cannot here list all the arguments. To borrow a Johannine hyperbole, if every one of them were written down, the whole world would not have room for the books that would be written (John 21:25)! Because exegetical study of the issue has been inconclusive, it has only penultimate importance in coming to a decision regarding infant baptism. Ultimately, the decision must be a *theological* one.[38]

---

36. Ibid., 198.

37. Aland does not, however, consider it improper for churches to baptize infants. But he finds the basis for it not in the New Testament texts but in the meaning of the gospel, i.e., on doctrinal grounds.

38. The monumental work of Joachim Jeremias, *Infant Baptism in the First Four Centuries*, trans. David Cairns (London: SCM Press, 1960), defended infant baptism and concluded that only two theologians in the first four centuries (Tertullian and Gregory of Nazianzus) advocated the postponement of baptism beyond the years of infancy, and that neither did it on theological grounds. Jeremias' work was challenged by Kurt Aland, in *Did the Early Church Baptize Infants?* trans. G. R. Beasley-Murray (Philadelphia: West-

That it must be a theological decision is in keeping with Wesleyan theology and its view of Scripture. Fundamentalism tends to need proof texts for its positions, because its view of biblical authority rests on a particular concept of verbal inerrancy. Inerrancy as taught in Fundamentalist theology may be called "epistemological inerrancy." That is, it believes the basic question in theology to be: *What is truth?*[39] Only after the source of truth has been established as reliable can we go on to discuss other matters such as salvation. Since the Bible is epistemologically inerrant (i.e., everything it says must be true), we can trust its message of salvation; it could not be trusted otherwise.

But Wesleyan theology works differently.[40] For Wesleyanism, the basic theological question is: *What must I do to be saved?* "I want to know one thing," said Wesley, "the way to heaven; how to land safe on that happy shore."[41] The Wesleyan concept of scriptural inerrancy is one of "soteriological inerrancy." Salva-

---

minster Press, 1963), an equally thorough book. Jeremias answered Aland in yet another book titled *The Origins of Infant Baptism*, trans. Dorothea M. Barton (Naperville, Ill.: Alec R. Allenson, 1963), in which he further defends his initial conclusions, stating that under no circumstances could Paul and Luke have said that "a household" was baptized if they had wished to say that only adults had been baptized. On Aland's side in the controversy is the already-mentioned work of G. R. Beasley-Murray titled *Baptism in the New Testament* (1962). These works, and many others dealing with the same issue, amply demonstrate that the evidence for either position is ambiguous. Conclusions reached in biblical studies on this topic are greatly influenced by the prior theological commitments of the authors. Of course, that is a bad thing only if the theological commitments are out of harmony with the whole gospel.

39. This was made abundantly clear in the writings of Harold Lindsell during the 1970s, which exemplify the typical Fundamentalist argument. In his book *The Battle for the Bible* (Grand Rapids: Zondervan Publishing House, 1976), he says: "Of all doctrines connected with the Christian faith, none is more important than the one that has to do with the basis of our religious *knowledge*. For anyone who professes the Christian faith the root question is: From where do I get my *knowledge* on which my faith is based?" (17, italics mine). Later he poses what to him is the fundamental question: "Is the Bible a reliable guide to religious *knowledge?*" In a sequel to this book, published three years later, to reply to critics of his first book, Lindsell lists the two fundamental questions of theology as "(1) What is the source of our religious *knowledge* . . . ? (2) Is the source from which I get answers to my basic questions reliable—i.e., does the source tell me the *truth?*" *The Bible in the Balance* (Grand Rapids: Zondervan Publishing House, 1979), 11, italics mine.

40. Although some individual members of the Wesleyan/holiness churches see themselves as Fundamentalists, such a position is not compatible with the basic principles of Wesleyan theology. Cf. Paul M. Bassett, "The Fundamentalist Leavening of the Holiness Movement: 1914-1940," *Wesleyan Theological Journal*, Spring 1978, 65-91; and R. Larry Shelton, "John Wesley's Approach to Scripture in Historical Perspective," *Wesleyan Theological Journal*, Spring 1981, 23-50.

41. *Works* 5:3.

tion *is* the truth. Truth is determined and defined by what salvation is, not the other way around. The Scriptures are *sufficient* for salvation.[42] The Bible cannot fail to lead us to God and to salvation if we obey its precepts; that is what it means to say it is inerrant. In Fundamentalism, truth is the foundation and salvation is the superstructure. In Wesleyanism, the opposite is the case—salvation is the foundation and truth is the superstructure. When we know the source and way of salvation, we know what truth is. This means that truth is Christological, for Jesus said, "I am the Truth" (cf. John 14:6).

Although John Wesley was continually quoting Scripture to make his points, his view of biblical authority was broader than a mere proof-text approach. Using Albert Outler's term, many Wesley scholars have discussed "the Wesleyan Quadrilateral" of Scripture, tradition, reason, and experience, which were all authoritative theological sources for Wesley. The four were not equal partners for Wesley, however, for Scripture had priority. In reality the final religious authority for Wesley was the *gospel*. But it was the gospel as revealed to us in *Scripture,* mediated to us through the historic Christian *tradition,* explicated and made understandable through *reason,* and authenticated in *experience*. In the final analysis, then, the gospel is Jesus Christ. He is the Word of God incarnate. Such a concept of religious authority gives Wesleyanism a robust confidence that transcends any anxiety that might be created by the lack of absolute proof-texts on questions such as that of infant baptism, which apparently cannot be settled by biblical exegesis alone. Wesleyanism is comfortable in knowing that the question must ultimately rest on a theological decision.

Such a theological decision, of course, must be true to the Scriptures *in principle*. The New Testament does not tell us conclusively of the *practice* of the Earliest Church with regard to the baptizing of infants, but infant baptism is within the *principle* of the gospel. Christianity began as a mission, and as P. T. Forsyth has reminded us,

---

42. Wesley spoke much more about the "sufficiency" of Scripture than about its "inerrancy" or "infallibility" or even its "authority."

The New Testament Church *practice* . . . is that of a missionary Church. But its *principles* are those of a universal, settled, and triumphant Church. And when, early in its history, the practice of the Church changed to infant Baptism, it was not departing from New Testament principles. It was applying them in a changed way to changed conditions— especially such a principle as the sanctity of the children of the children of the saved (I Cor. 7:14).[43]

The crucial theological principle concerns the nature of the gospel. Specifically, with regard to infant baptism, the question is this: In baptism, *who* does *what?* Is baptism merely a human action, a visible human word in which the person baptized gives testimony to his or her faith and acceptance of the benefits and obligations of the covenant of grace? Or is baptism something more than that? Is baptism, in some way, the visible action (and word) *of God?* These questions apply equally to adult and infant baptism, but the answer given to them will determine the validity of the latter.

When a baby is baptized "as a sign and seal of the new covenant," does that make any difference to the child? Some claim it cannot possibly be more than an act of dedication on the part of the parents and the church. Therefore rituals of dedication have been formulated by those churches that take this position and therefore desire to postpone baptism until the child can choose it personally. Dedication is something of a modern invention for those who do not believe in infant baptism but who nevertheless wish to do something "religious" in regard to the children. In Wesleyan/holiness circles, its widespread acceptance is the result of the "baptistification" of the holiness movement that was mentioned earlier. It is, of course, consistent with Anabaptist or Baptist principles, for dedication is mainly a human action and a testimony on the part of the parents and the church, and it does not imply any action or transaction on God's part. Those who believe this should not practice infant baptism.

But classical Wesleyan theology believes in the validity of

---

43. P. T. Forsyth, *The Church and Sacraments* (London: Independent Press, 1917), 180.

infant baptism and insists that baptism (both infant and adult) is primarily an act on God's part.

Then does baptism make the child's salvation automatic? Certainly not. The child, along with all of us, must eventually come to his or her own personal decision of faith. Neither parent, nor minister, nor church can make that choice for the child. Baptism is not a magic rite. Does baptism then merely express a fond parental hope? Surely not! Baptism expresses God's will, not just the will of parents and congregation. How can this be? If baptism is neither magical nor meaningless, how shall we understand it? It is a legitimate question, but failure to understand how God can do what He does is not a valid objection against any of His works. In defending infant baptism as a divine work, Wesley says: "Nor is it an objection of any weight against this, that we cannot comprehend how this work can be wrought in infants. For neither can we comprehend how it is wrought in a person of riper years."[44]

How can we say that baptism is an act of God? Surely it is obvious that in baptism, whether adult or infant, *human* agency and action are quite centrally involved. The adult comes to baptism, the parents or guardians bring the child to baptism, and the minister sprinkles or pours the water or immerses the candidate under it. These are all human actions.

But wait! Is not Jesus Christ the Incarnation of God? And is Christ not the Head of the Church? And is not the Church the Body of Christ? And did not the Head command the Body to baptize? If all this is true (and who will say it is not?), then when the Church, in obedience to its Head, baptizes a person, *God is then and there performing an action in His world!*

> *Christ has no hands but our hands*
> *To do His work today.*
>   —ANNIE JOHNSON FLINT

In a sermon on infant baptism, that eloquent preacher Arthur John Gossip said:

> Always, in every sacrament, God is the Central Figure,
> and it is what He does that is of supreme moment. So here,

---

44. *Works* 6:74.

it is not the baby nor the parents upon whom we ought to keep our eyes, but upon the Lord God Himself, most surely in our midst—taking this little one into His arms, pledging Himself to stand—towards him—to every word of grace that He has ever spoken, erasing the general terms out of the promises, and writing in his very name instead, so that it runs, no longer, God so loved the world, but God so loved this little soul—that He gave His only begotten Son for very him, if he will have, and take, and use that wonderful gift. Meantime here is the personal pledge to very him, that God intends it, and has planned it all for him.[45]

When Wesley calls baptism an "outward sign," he means that it is a sign that *God makes*, not merely a human sign. It is the covenant sign of God's grace. Baptism is God's act, whether of adults or infants. Of course it is a human act also. The candidate and the minister *do* something. And in the case of infant baptism, the parents or guardians also *do* something. The question is: Whose doing comes first? Who takes the initiative? To whom belongs the "prevenience"?

D. INFANT BAPTISM AND PREVENIENT GRACE

The doctrine of prevenient grace has major importance in Wesleyan theology. It played a crucial role in John Wesley's own thought. It was the means whereby he was able to avoid a Calvinistic doctrine of unconditional election on one hand and a Roman Catholic (and Pelagian) concept of works-righteousness on the other.[46]

The word "prevenient" or "preventing" means "going before" or, more correctly, "coming before" (from the Latin *prae*, before, and *venire*, to come). Prevenient, then, means "preceding." Prevenient grace therefore is the grace of God that "goes before" (or "comes before") human action. It is the grace that precedes the human response of faith. Wesley rejected

---

45. Arthur John Gossip, *Experience Worketh Hope* (New York: Charles Scribner's Sons, 1945), 169.

46. For an excellent explanation of this, see Cushman, 103-15. Cf. Robert E. Chiles, *Theological Transition in American Methodism: 1790-1935* (Nashville: Abingdon Press, 1965), 144-83.

universalism—the doctrine that everyone will be saved. He also rejected unconditional election as taught by Calvinists—the doctrine that those will be saved whom God has elected to be saved, and all others will be damned. By contrast to both, he taught that all persons are given some measure of grace and will be saved if they respond to the grace they have been given.[47]

In his sermon on "Free Grace," Wesley says: "The grace or love of God, whence cometh our salvation, is FREE IN ALL, and FREE FOR ALL."[48] It is *free in all* to whom it is given. It does not depend on any human merit, or good works, or good purpose or intention. And it is *free for all.* Everyone has been given a measure of prevenient grace. Only the person who has "quenched the Spirit" and resisted and stifled the promptings of prevenient grace can be said to be without grace. "No man sins because he has not grace, but because he does not use the grace which he hath."[49] Prevenient grace restores a measure of freedom lacking in the bondage of original sin.[50] It has performed its ultimate function when it brings us to Christ for justification.[51]

Now it might appear quite natural for Wesley to advocate infant baptism as the sacrament that bestows prevenient grace upon a child. Since in his definition of "means of grace" he affirms that they are "ordinary channels whereby he might convey to men, *preventing,* justifying, or sanctifying grace,"[52] it would seem logical that prevenient grace should be given in infant baptism as well. But Wesley does not take this approach. He believed that it was the universal atonement of Christ, rather than baptism, that places every human being into that preliminary state of grace where the guilt of Adam's sin has been canceled. No infant (whether baptized or not) "ever was or ever will be 'sent to hell for the guilt of Adam's sin,' seeing it is cancelled by the righteousness of Christ as soon as they are sent into the world."[53]

To be sure, Wesley is not a Pelagian; he does not believe

---

47. *Works* 10:229-30.
48. Ibid. 7:373. The small capital letters are Wesley's.
49. Ibid. 6:512.
50. Ibid. 10:229-30; 9:273, 275, 294; 8:52.
51. Ibid. 8:373.
52. Ibid. 5:187, italics mine.
53. *Letters* 6:239-40.

children are born guiltless. They sinned when Adam sinned.[54] But their guilt is altogether mitigated, or canceled out, by prevenient grace. In Wesley's understanding of salvation, therefore, there is little reason to include prevenient grace in the grace that is conveyed in baptism. Students of Wesley have sometimes wondered why he did not utilize his doctrine of prevenient grace in expounding his views on infant baptism. But in his understanding of the gospel, baptism was not necessary to convey salvation to a newborn child; this was already conveyed by the Atonement.

What, then, is the connection, if any, between prevenient grace and infant baptism? Wesley himself spoke little of any direct connection. But on the basis of Wesley's theology as a whole, and in particular his view of prevenient grace, at least this much can be said: Prevenient grace is not conveyed by infant baptism, but it is *proclaimed* by it. Infant baptism, in the words of J. S. Whale, "proclaims that Christ has done something for me, without ever consulting me or waiting for my approval; before ever I was born or thought of he died to redeem me."[55]

Sometimes the issue is clouded by the question whether or not a person should be committed to a way of life without his or her consent. Were Christianity merely a matter of intellectual opinion, involving a clear choice between obvious alternatives, one could say that children should be allowed to decide for themselves. But Christianity is not an opinion. It is a life, and one learns it only by living it. Other important matters of the home—eating, table manners, wearing clothes, early education—are not left solely to the infant's choice. At least this is true of parents who love their children. Neither should the most important matter of all—bringing the child up "in the training and instruction of the Lord" (Eph. 6:4)—be left to the choice of the child.

As a sacrament, baptism is not a purely personal matter between an individual and God. It is a sacrament of the Church.

---

54. In his *NT Notes* on Rom. 5:12, Wesley says: "*All sinned*—In Adam. These words assign the reason why death came upon *all men;* infants themselves not excepted, *in that all sinned.*"

55. J. S. Whale, *Christian Doctrine* (Cambridge: Cambridge University Press, 1942), 164.

This means that the baptized person belongs to a fellowship. Christ came to overcome human isolation (1 John 1:3), and Christian life can be meaningful only in the fellowship of others. In baptizing infants, the Church is saying that the child is included in the fellowship, is a part of the Body, is under the covenant. From the moment of baptism, as the baptized child grows and develops toward maturity, the parents and the Church are under solemn obligation to use every means available to communicate to the young person this Good News: "When you were too young to walk, we carried you in our arms. Likewise when you were too young to choose to be a part of the Body of Christ, we chose for you. We brought you into the fellowship, and you were incorporated into the Body. Now you will need to decide whether you will choose for yourself that which was chosen for you. We pray that you will choose it and not reject it." This would seem to be more sound psychologically, as well as theologically more so, than saying, in effect, to the young person, what the Anabaptist position seems to say: "You were not included in the Body until you could decide for yourself whether to come in, but we hope you will come in."

It is not primarily *our faith* but *God's grace* that saves us. Our faith is but the response to God's prior grace. First and foremost, baptism shows God's initiative toward us. It is only secondarily and consequentially that baptism shows our active response to God. Baptism is a *sign* (symbol) of the promise of the gospel, but it is also a *seal* confirming the sign, much like one's signature on a contract or circumcision in the Old Testament. There is nothing in the Bible that says children have a separate status in relation to the covenant of God. They are not outside it. The Old Testament understanding of the covenant did not admit of distinctions based on age. Children were brought into the covenant by virtue of the fact that God's promises were given to Noah's family and their descendants, to Abraham and Sarah and their descendants, to the Hebrew slaves delivered from Egypt and their descendants unto every generation. Nor does the New Testament divide humans into three groups— believers, unbelievers, and children! No, there are only two groups—believers and unbelievers. And children are nowhere in the New Testament classified as unbelievers! Peter's proclamation at Pentecost can be understood as teaching that the children of believers are included in the new covenant ushered in by the outpouring of the Spirit. "The promise is for you and your children" (Acts 2:39). If by "your children" he refers to future generations yet unborn, as the words are often interpreted, he does not qualify his statement to include only children who had attained a certain chronological age. Nor did he indicate that these future children would have to mature to a certain age before the promise would apply to them.

But the assumption that the church is only for adults is strange indeed. This participation of children in covenants made by others is true in other domains of life, such as, for instance, a life insurance policy in which an infant is the beneficiary. Early Christian thinking followed Jewish thinking in regard to family unity. The idea of *solidarity* is behind the "household" baptisms in Acts. Just when is a child a part of the family of God? Both Jewish and early Christian thought held that there is not a time when the child is *not* a part of God's family, until in responsible maturity he or she turns away by personal rejection. It is important that we understand that it is God's prevenient grace that saves us. Long before a child can understand or believe—even before the child exists—God initiated that child's salvation. But isn't this true of adults also? Certainly it is. And in a sense, *all* baptisms are really "infant" baptisms. "Anyone who will not receive the kingdom of God like a little child will never enter it" (Mark 10:15). None of us is ever old enough or knowledgeable enough to fully understand the mystery of salvation. No one comes to baptism complete. It is only a beginning point—in adults as well as children. So baptism celebrates "the grace that goes before."

Baptism is a sign of our repentance and faith, but this is not its primary significance. Primarily, it is a sign of divine grace— not a sign of anything *we do* at all. It is a covenant sign, and therefore a sign of the work of God on our behalf that precedes and makes possible our own response. When infants are baptized, it is right and necessary that when they come to maturity, they make their own confession of faith. But they do so with the clear witness that it is not their confession alone that saves them, but the work of God already done for them long before they ever believed. Their own confession of faith is their personal acceptance of what God has already offered. It is possible they will fail to make such a confession. But this cannot be avoided by denying them baptism. Rather, if they are granted baptism, and carefully taught and nurtured as to its meaning and significance as they grow older, the probability of their making a confession of their own would seem to be greater than if baptism is denied them. It becomes, then, the responsibility of the church and the parents to nurture them, and teach them, and guide them toward that eventual confession of personal faith.

E. BAPTISMAL REGENERATION?

The last paragraph raises a question concerning the time when one is born again. Where infant baptism is practiced, does the new birth occur at the time of baptism or at the time when, having sufficiently matured, the person makes a personal confession?

Members of the Wesleyan/holiness churches almost unanimously opt for the latter. Good reasons can be given for this. But John Wesley believed that the new birth occurred in infants at their baptism. In fact, he believed that baptism was a "converting ordinance" for adults also.[56] When the adult unbeliever submits to baptism, in repentance and faith, he or she is born again.

> By baptism, we who were "by nature children of wrath" are made the children of God. And this regeneration which our Church in so many places ascribes to baptism is more than barely being admitted into the Church, though commonly connected therewith; . . . By water then, as a means, the water of baptism, we are regenerated or born again.[57]

He goes on to say that "in the ordinary way, there is no other means of entering into the Church or into heaven."[58] These statements of Wesley's apply to infants as well as adults.

---

56. He also believed the Eucharist to be a "converting ordinance," as we shall see later.
57. *Works* 10:191-92.
58. Ibid., 192.

It is inevitable that in Christianity some equation should be made between baptism and regeneration. The New Testament makes an explicit connection between the two. In John 3:5 we are told that one must be born of water and of the Spirit in order to enter the kingdom of God.[59] In Titus 3:5 we read that we are saved "through the washing of rebirth and renewal by the Holy Spirit." In theology, this equation is made most strongly by the phrase *baptismal regeneration*. Within the context of the whole gospel, the phrase is not completely objectionable, as long as Wesley's stipulation is kept in view, namely, that baptism and the new birth are not the same thing, and that there may sometimes be the outward sign where there is not the inward grace. It is when such a stipulation is absent that baptismal regeneration becomes an unfortunate term. Medieval theology had a tendency to make the inward grace an automatic accompaniment of the outward sign, at least to the popular mind. This Wesley rejected.

Nevertheless, much confusion has prevailed among students of Wesley in the attempt to understand his view of the relationship between baptism and the new birth. Some have concluded that he strongly believed in baptismal regeneration; some insist that he rejected it, even though he tolerated the Anglican tradition that affirmed it; and some hold that his teachings on the subject were confused and contradictory.[60] In seeking for clarity, we offer the following as a summary of Wesley's views on baptism as it relates to regeneration and as it applies to infants.[61]

---

59. See the previous discussion of this passage in section D of chapter 5.

60. Examples of the first position are Borgen, 144 ff.; Harald Lindström, *Wesley and Sanctification* (London: Epworth Press, 1950), 107; and David Ingersoll Naglee, *From Font to Faith: John Wesley on Infant Baptism and the Nurture of Children* (New York: Peter Lang, 1987), 122 ff. The second position is found in William Ragsdale Cannon, *The Theology of John Wesley* (New York: Abingdon-Cokesbury Press, 1946), 126 ff. The third position is put forth in Lycurgus M. Starkey, Jr., *The Work of the Holy Spirit: A Study in Wesleyan Theology* (New York: Abingdon Press, 1962), 91-92. Starkey attempts to explain the contradictions by making Wesley a High Churchman before his Aldersgate experience and an evangelical afterward, his views on baptism being changed by the experience.

61. After years of trying to understand Wesley on this issue, this writer believes that Wesley's view has been correctly grasped by the Scandinavian Methodist scholar Ole Borgen, in his book *John Wesley on the Sacraments*, mentioned earlier. The discussion in this section is heavily indebted to Borgen. He believes Wesley's views to be self-consistent and not at all contradictory as some interpreters have portrayed them. Some well-known

At the outset, it is important to recognize that Wesley distinguished between baptism and the new birth.

> Baptism is not the new birth: They are not one and the same thing. . . . For what can be more plain, than that the one is an external, the other an internal, work; that the one is a visible, the other an invisible thing, and therefore wholly different from each other?—the one being an act of man, purifying the body; the other a change wrought by God in the soul: So that the former is just as distinguishable from the latter, as the soul from the body, or water from the Holy Ghost.[62]

He continues the argument, recognizing the possibility that the two parts of the sacrament may be torn apart:

> The new birth . . . does not always accompany baptism: They do not constantly go together. A man may possibly be "born of water," and yet not be "born of the Spirit." There may sometimes be the outward sign, where there is not the inward grace.[63]

He is careful to make it clear, however, that he is here speaking only of *adult* baptism.

> I do not now speak with regard to infants. . . . all who are baptized in their infancy are at the same time born again. . . . But whatever be the case with infants, it is sure all of riper years who are baptized are not at the same time born again. "The tree is known by its fruits."[64]

Although Wesley did *distinguish* between baptism and the new birth (the sign and the thing signified), he also insisted on their *unity* as well. They could be distinguished but were not to be separated. The new birth, "by the free mercy of God," is "ordinarily annexed to baptism."[65] Infants are born again in baptism. It is possible for them to subsequently fall from grace when they grow older, so that they cannot rest their entire hope

---

Wesley scholars who have misunderstood Wesley on this point are William Cannon, Robert E. Cushman, David Naglee, John R. Parris, Paul S. Sanders, and Lycurgus Starkey, Jr. As for Albert Outler's claim that Wesley held to two different ideas on regeneration, see the previous discussion in chapter 1, section C.

62. *Works* 6:73-74.
63. Ibid., 74.
64. Ibid.
65. Ibid. 5:212. Cf. ibid. 10:191-93, 198.

on the fact that they were once baptized. But restoration is possible: "Those who were made the children of God by baptism, but are now the children of the devil, may yet again receive 'power to become the sons of God;' that they may receive again what they have lost."[66] This proves that Wesley believed they were *once* born again in baptism.

Adults also are born again through baptism. His assertion, quoted above—that the new birth does not *always* accompany baptism, that they do not *constantly* go together, and that there may *sometimes* be the outward sign, where there is not the inward grace—implies that they *do* go together *some, perhaps even most, though not all, of the time*. He contends that the sign and the thing signified (*signum* and *res*) must be neither separated nor fused together. To fuse (or confuse) them would be to fall into the *ex opere operato* doctrine, which he clearly opposes. To separate them would be to put asunder what God has joined together. The new birth is the same in infants and adults. In neither is it a merely "objective" thing, in the sense of being impersonal and formal only. To be baptized is to "put on Christ," to be "mystically united to Christ, and made one with him." It is a "spiritual, vital union with him."[67] The same work is wrought in adults and infants. Everything is the same in each case except the age, abilities, and circumstances of the subject. Borgen says:

> In discussions about the new birth in adults, it is too often (and very conveniently) forgotten that Wesley firmly believes in adults' being "born again" through the means of Baptism. He only adds, with the Church of England, two conditions: ". . . if they repent and believe the gospel," and *"Be baptized and wash away thy sins*—Baptism, administered to *real penitents,* is both a means and a seal of pardon. Nor did God ordinarily in the primitive Church bestow this on any, unless through this means."[68]

Finally, Wesley held that the new birth is not given through the means of baptism alone. It may be given through other means as well. "To say, then, that ye cannot be born again, that there is no new birth but in baptism, is to seal you all under

---

66. Ibid. 5:222-23.
67. Ibid. 10:191.
68. Borgen, 159.

damnation."[69] Wesley's acknowledgment that baptism is not the only means of the new birth does not represent a denigration of baptism on his part, but arises out of his resistance to an *ex opere operato* view on one hand and to a Calvinist doctrine of perseverance on the other.

A highly significant point, and one widely overlooked or even ignored, is Wesley's use of the word *ordinary* in discussing baptism. It is "the *ordinary* instrument of our justification." "In the *ordinary* way, there is no other means of entering into the Church or into heaven." It is the "*ordinary* means he hath appointed" through which we are to receive the remedy for sin. Baptism is "generally, in an *ordinary* way, necessary to salvation." The privilege of being a child of God is "*ordinarily* annexed to baptism."[70] In other words, ordinarily baptism is necessary to salvation, but not absolutely so. There may be *extraordinary* or unusual means whereby the same benefits may be received. But the mistake made by many of Wesley's followers has been to generalize Wesley's allowance for the extraordinary cases, making them the norm.[71] This distorts the place the means of grace have in Wesley's understanding of salvation; they are the *ordinary* channels by which God bestows His grace.

It now remains for us to summarize Wesley's doctrine of infant baptism as it relates to the new birth, and to correlate this with his doctrine of prevenient grace, which was discussed in the preceding section. These salient points constitute a short digest of his position:

1. *All infants are guilty of Adam's sin, but this guilt is canceled by prevenient grace as soon as they are born.* Again it is important to remember that Wesley was not a Pelagian. Children are not born "innocent." They are guilty because they were "in Adam's loins" and sinned along with Adam when he sinned in the garden.[72] Prevenient grace applies Christ's atonement to newborn

---

69. *Works* 5:222.

70. *Works* 10:191, 192, 193, 198; 5:212, italics mine.

71. I cannot find where Wesley spells out such extraordinary cases. Presumably he would include situations where sickness or infirmity makes baptism impossible, or the absence of one qualified to administer sacraments, or the absence of water, although the latter would be a significant factor only where immersion is the mode.

72. *Works* 10:190, 193; cf. 6:240; 8:277-78.

children, giving them provisional salvation. Since this is the case, what is the need for infant baptism? Can it add anything to what already prevails? Yes, says Wesley:

2. *In infant baptism, one is born again.* The gift of the new birth includes the same benefits that adults receive when they are born again. The only difference lies in age, ability, and circumstance, which in the case of adults necessitate deliberate repentance and conscious faith. Also, depending on the circumstance, adult baptism functions in two ways. The adult who is already born again (i.e., "born of the Spirit")[73] should be baptized (i.e., "born of water") to conclude his or her conversion. The one who is not born again should repent and be baptized that the new birth may be received through that means.[74]

3. *The infant who is baptized must be continuously taught and nurtured as to the meaning of baptism.* If this is done carefully and diligently by the church and by the parents, it is possible for the child to develop a life of obedience to the Heavenly Father, and, after the example of another Child, increase in wisdom and in stature and in favor with God and man. Of course, repentance is necessary in this development all along the way, for Wesley preached that repentance is necessary not only "when we are setting out in the way to the kingdom" but also at "every subsequent stage of our Christian course."[75]

> The work begun in Baptism must therefore issue forth in subsequent repentance, faith and obedience, which are demands binding on all who have received God's grace, by whatever means, according to their state, abilities and circumstances. As the child is taught and achieves the understanding of reason and uses the grace he has received, he will steadily grow in grace and holiness and consciously and willingly embrace a life of holiness when he is able.[76]

According to Borgen, "This conscious embracing of the life of faith with the inward witness of the Spirit ('assurance') evidently

---

73. Such a person may represent, for Wesley, one of the "extraordinary" cases mentioned above, and in note 71.
74. *NT Notes,* Acts 10:47; Heb. 6:1-2.
75. *Works* 5:156, 157.
76. Borgen, 170.

takes the place of confirmation for Wesley."[77] Wesley never developed a doctrine of confirmation for the Methodists. He says that confirmation cannot be proved by Scripture to be a proper sacrament and calls the ceremonies attached to it "an abuse."[78] The personal appropriation of faith (an "evangelical conversion") on the part of the child who was baptized as an infant, accompanied by the inward witness of the Spirit ("assurance"), constitutes, for Wesley, a confirmation that is not merely formal but actual.[79]

4. *Both the provisional salvation made possible for the child by prevenient grace and the new birth given to a child in baptism may be lost.* It is always possible, although never necessary, to lose the relationship to God that grace makes available.[80] Then what advantage does the baptized infant have over the unbaptized one, since prevenient grace has been extended to both of them? When all of Wesley's teachings on infant baptism and the new birth are given careful consideration, the following conclusion seems inescapable: He believed it possible for the baptized infant, throughout life, never to know a significant time-gap when he or she is outside the fold of salvation. Of course, this is true only if the child is taught and nurtured properly and responds obediently to the Spirit. If the child's response to the Spirit becomes one of disobedience and rebellion, a backslidden condition exists, in which case, as a comprehending young person or adult, he or she must heed the Lord's command: "You must be born again."[81] Wesley thus offers backsliders of all kinds a way for remedial action, a second chance, which replaces the Roman Catholic sacrament of penance.[82] But there are some differences:

> The Roman Catholic position is, in general, that the baptismal grace, which is given, inescapably, *ex opere operato* in

---

77. Ibid., n. 204.

78. *Works* 10:117, cf. 135-36, 150-51.

79. Cf. Borgen, 170 n. 204.

80. The possibility is demanded by Wesley's Arminianism, in opposition to both the Catholic *ex opere operato* doctrine and the Calvinist doctrine of perseverance, both of which he abhorred. Borgen says: "Wesley's allowance that baptismal grace may be and is lost does not issue from a down-grading of Baptism and baptismal grace, but from his basic Arminian position." P. 171.

81. But in that case rebaptism is not necessary, as we will see in the next section.

82. Cf. John M. Todd, *John Wesley and the Catholic Church* (London: Catholic Book Club, 1958), 110-11.

Baptism, remains efficacious through a person's life. For Wesley . . . there is no such thing as "continued Baptism." . . . For him, the task of Baptism is completed when the new life of faith is initiated. The growth and future development of this life are maintained through other means of grace. He never questions the *validity* of a Baptism properly administered, but allows of its efficacy only to the extent a person is actually, inwardly and outwardly, a child of God. . . . In Wesley's "remedy" the emphasis is upon the actualization of living faith and holiness in a person's life, while the formal aspects become incidental.[83]

But the principle of grace that was infused in baptism, the presence of the Holy Spirit dwelling within, "will not be wholly taken away, unless we *quench* the Holy Spirit of God by long-continued wickedness."[84] One does not fall out of grace by simply grieving the Spirit (Eph. 4:30), but by living in continued willful sin to the point that the Spirit departs, that is, is quenched (1 Thess. 5:19, KJV). Wesley, being characteristically more severe on himself than on others, says of his own experience, "I believe, till I was about ten years old I had not sinned away that 'washing of the Holy Ghost' which was given me in baptism."[85] If it could be shown, from an empirical standpoint, that everyone baptized in infancy "sins away" what they received in baptism, it would not, from Wesley's theological standpoint, obviate the possibility of *not* doing so. Sin is never necessary.[86]

By contrast, in the case of the provisional salvation by which the unbaptized child is covered by prevenient grace, there comes a time when such provisionality runs out. This happens when, having come to sufficient maturity, the person fails to respond positively to the promptings of prevenient grace.[87] In

---

83. Borgen, 176-77.
84. *Works* 10:192, italics mine.
85. Ibid. 1:98.
86. This point cannot be stressed too strongly. If sin were necessary, it would not be a *moral* reality, but only a natural aspect of our creatureliness, much like the color of our eyes or the size of our feet. In that case God would be the author of sin. This was one of the arguments James Arminius made against Calvinism—that calling sin a necessity ultimately makes God the author of sin.
87. This has sometimes been called "the age of accountability," although that is not a biblical term.

such cases, repentance, faith, and baptism (now as a young person or adult) become imperative. Thus the time-gap mentioned above, which the person baptized in infancy may *possibly* (even if not *probably*, and certainly not *automatically*) avoid, is virtually inevitable in the case of the unbaptized.

But one might ask, "Is it not likely, or at least possible, that the baptized person also, upon coming to sufficient maturity, may 'sin away' the grace given in baptism?" The answer, of course, is yes. Then the difference between the two cases may seem so small as to be insignificant. On the surface it may *seem* small. But to consider it so, and leave it at that, *is to overlook the tremendous emphasis the New Testament and the historical Church have placed on baptism!* The issue comes down, then, to whether or not we Wesleyans who proclaim our belief in the authority of Scripture will allow our sacramental theology, liturgy, and practice to be shaped by the gospel as that gospel is revealed in Scripture and mediated by the historic Christian tradition. Nothing else is worthy of being called "Wesleyan."

The four points enumerated and elaborated above, if they constitute a valid summary of Wesley's view of infant baptism, show that he was more consistent than some scholars have supposed in his understanding of baptism as it relates to regeneration. To the question, Did Wesley teach baptismal regeneration? the answer is: yes and no. *Yes,* in the case of infants, if it means that the new birth is given in baptism. This assumes, for Wesley, that the church and the believing parents come in faith and obedience to the Lord's command to baptize, promising to give the child the proper Christian nurture and guidance. *Yes,* also, in the case of adults who come to baptism in sincere repentance and faith. Although regeneration (or the new birth) is, in Wesley, *distinguished* from baptism, the two are not to be kept *separate* from one another. In the New Testament they form a *unity.* They go together in the case of such a penitent and believing person. Did Wesley teach baptismal regeneration? *No,* if by the term one means that baptism has some magical or automatic efficacy. Regeneration does not happen just because the rite is performed *(ex opere operato). No,* also, if it means that the outward sign (baptism) and the inward grace (the new birth) have been fused together so that the distinction between them is lost and it is held that the two always go together. For Wesley one might receive the former without the latter. "Born of water" does not automatically translate into "born of the Spirit." To Nicodemus, Jesus commanded both. The problem of baptismal regeneration in Wesley is largely a problem of semantics and definition.

To this writer, it seems that Wesley's most serious lack of clarity in his treatment of infant baptism is not any so-called inconsistency regarding the relationship between baptism and regeneration, but rather that he allows some confusion to creep into his language with reference to the child's participation in Adam's sin. He says infants are "guilty of original sin" and therefore "proper subjects of baptism."[88] When he is speaking of baptism, he does not incisively distinguish between original sin as *guilt* and original sin as *defilement* or *pollution*. But when discussing prevenient grace, as we noted in section D of this chapter, he says that the "guilt" of Adam's sin, with which every child is born, is canceled by the provisions of the Atonement as soon as the child comes into the world. It might seem that Wesley gives conflicting answers to the question of *when* the child is freed from this participation in Adam's transgression. Is it at the point of *natural* birth, or at the point of the *new* birth?

A careful study of Wesley's language offers a clue. When speaking of the aspect of original sin that is canceled at birth by prevenient grace, his language is predominantly legal or forensic. Adam's guilt is imputed to his offspring. This is canceled by prevenient grace. But when speaking of the aspect of original sin that is corrected in the work of sanctification, which, for Wesley, has its beginning in the new birth, he speaks of "this original *stain*" that needs to be "*washed* away by baptism." He calls it a "*disease*" for which the Second Adam has found "a *remedy*."[89] He does not speak of cancellation, or of forgiveness, or of imputation—language that applies to *guilt*. He generally uses different metaphors, although there are exceptions. He was not as careful as he could have been in keeping these two types of language separate in his treatment of baptism. But he understands

---

88. *Works* 10:193.
89. Ibid., italics mine.

that from Adam we receive both a *guilt* and a *stain*. Guilt requires forgiveness, and forgiveness for the guilt of Adam's sin is made possible by the Atonement and given by prevenient grace from the time of natural birth. A stain requires cleansing or healing, and this begins in the new birth, which for Wesley was always instantaneous and the beginning of the process of sanctification.[90] Of course, both forgiveness and cleansing may be squandered by willful disobedience.

It is a fact that the Wesleyan/holiness tradition scarcely follows Wesley at all in the way he relates regeneration to baptism, as this relationship is outlined above, even with the qualifications he places on the relationship. For example, in the Church of the Nazarene, the ritual for "The Baptism of Infants or Young Children" begins with a preamble that pointedly rejects any semblance of baptismal regeneration:

> While we do not hold that baptism imparts the regenerating grace of God, we do believe that Christ gave this holy sacrament as a sign and seal of the new covenant. Christian baptism signifies for this young child God's gracious acceptance on the basis of His prevenient grace in Christ, and points forward to his [her] personal appropriation of the benefits of the Atonement when he [she] reaches the age of moral accountability and exercises conscious saving faith in Jesus Christ.[91]

Such qualifications as those built into the above statement are understandably included in order to avoid the appearance of any *ex opere operato* concept of infant baptism. The Wesleyan/holiness tradition does not believe that an infant is saved by any automatic or magical efficacy of baptism itself. Since the term *baptismal regeneration* connotes that to many people, the term may best be avoided, even with the strictures Wesley places upon the idea.

But one might wonder if a closer approximation of the re-

---

90. Wesley says: "At the same time that we are justified, yea, in that very moment, sanctification begins. In that instant we are born again, born from above, born of the Spirit." *Works* 6:45. Followers of Wesley have come to call this "initial sanctification," although that was not Wesley's term. Nor did he ordinarily make the kind of scholastic distinctions between regeneration and initial sanctification that his followers have made.

91. *Manual of the Church of the Nazarene* (Kansas City: Nazarene Publishing House, 1989), 242.

spect Wesley had for the validity of infant baptism might have avoided some of the problems the Wesleyan/holiness tradition has created for itself. For example, in the local church situation, the tradition has never done a very good job of harmonizing its practice of religious education and its views on evangelism. On one hand, it teaches little children that God loves them, that He watches over them day and night, and that He is a kind and forgiving God who will forgive their wrongdoings and bad attitudes if they will confess them as they occur. Then, somewhere along the line, the evangelistic impulse requires the child, or adolescent, to be told that he or she is an accountable sinner who needs to repent and come to Christ in a definite conversion experience. Such an abrupt shifting of pedagogical gears is avoided in Wesley's design.

There are also problems created by a wrong type of evangelistic preaching sometimes heard in the tradition, in which false guilt can be created and exploited as real guilt, and then alleviated by a response to the altar call that brings a quick emotional release that can be mistaken for true repentance. The effect on young people is unhealthy, resulting in much ostensible "backsliding" and an "on again, off again" religious experience. To be sure, a Wesleyan cannot finally rest on baptism in the same manner that Martin Luther did in his *baptizatus sum* ("I am baptized") declaration, because Wesleyanism knows it is possible to quench the Spirit and fall from grace. But that note has been sounded in the tradition far more loudly than another important note that would have resulted in a better harmony—the clarion note of baptism. We can recognize that quenching the Spirit is a real possibility, but this is very different from the life-style of one who fails from time to time in his or her spiritual life and thus grieves the Spirit by not living up to the chosen ideal of Christlikeness. Such a person *can* rest secure in baptism. In other words, an emphasis upon the *action of God* in baptism (divine initiative) rather than on the *human response* makes one's salvation experience much more secure. Salvation then becomes something that one must deliberately reject in order to be a backslider, not something that one can lose by falling short of the best that one knows.

It is this writer's observation, after almost three decades of teaching college and seminary students, that many persons in Wesleyan/holiness churches, having been wisely nurtured, and not having ever seriously or deliberately rebelled against their religious upbringing, have a difficult time pinpointing a climactic conversion experience that is anything more than perfunctory. And yet their lives evidence the fruit of the Spirit. Such persons are sometimes confused because their theology stresses the necessity of such an event. For such persons, Wesley's emphasis on the meaningfulness of infant baptism, if followed, could have been a basis of assurance. Rather than contriving a datable experience, one may rest on God's prior act of grace as proclaimed in baptism and thus give testimony to God's keeping power. Of course in the person baptized as a child, there will be many instances of failing to live up to the perfect ideal of Christlikeness. But this is true also of adults who waited for so-called believer's baptism. Nevertheless it is possible to live outside the parameters of full-grown sin that gives birth to death (James 1:15). Sin is full-grown when we cease to repent. Although "all have sinned" (Rom. 3:23), we do not need to allow sin to become full-grown by renouncing the path of repentance. When baptized children are later taught that they need an instantaneous climactic conversion experience before they can be true Christians, they may never get hold of the fact that they have been received into the family of God and do not ever need to leave it. This, of course, does not obviate the need for a personal confession of faith and an owning of one's baptism upon coming to sufficient maturity. But in order to own something, it is not necessary to have first thrown it away.

It is likely that some of the casualties in the Wesleyan/holiness tradition might have been avoided by a greater emphasis on infant baptism, followed by rigorous effort on the part of parents, pastors, and church, to teach the baptized person the meaning of his or her baptism. In other words, continually holding before a person the fact and meaning of the outward sign God has given that person would appear to be a more effective way of making real the inward grace than merely stressing the latter while ignoring the former. Religious experience is subjective, but it needs to be the experience of an objective reality.

Baptism, being an objective sign, bears witness to the objective reality.

One can only conjecture what difference a total commitment to infant baptism would have made in the Wesleyan/holiness churches if it had been relentlessly yoked to a diligent and careful effort to teach, nurture, and support the children, helping them to grow up to responsible Christian adulthood. Infant baptism has fallen into disfavor largely by default. Many have scorned the practice because of the superficiality that accompanies it whenever it is not taken seriously and followed up diligently. In such cases, it becomes a meaningless formality. The disregard, and even contempt, in which the doctrine and practice of infant baptism is held by many in the Wesleyan/holiness tradition may largely be the result of the tradition's failure to understand and appreciate Wesley's careful understanding of this sacrament. Such disregard has resulted in the "baptistification" of holiness practice that was mentioned earlier. But the abuse of a sacrament does not invalidate its legitimate use.

F. THE QUESTION OF REBAPTISM

What about persons who were baptized as infants, who subsequently "sinned away that 'washing of the Holy Ghost'" (to use Wesley's words), and who make a personal confession of faith in adulthood? Do they need to be rebaptized as adults? The evangelical Anglican writer, Michael Green, replies amusingly but with utter seriousness to this question.[92] His answer would surely be applauded by his fellow evangelical Anglican, John Wesley. The present writer also applauds his answer. Green comments that people want "rebaptism" for four different reasons, which will be stated here (with some of my own comments added to each):

1. For some, it is *because there was not enough faith.* Since they were too young to know what was going on, much less to believe, they wish now to have a proper believer's baptism. But on such reasoning the Jew could doubt the covenant significance of his circumcision. Or a man could doubt the validity of his marriage vows if he fell in love with someone else (a convenient

---

92. Green, 113-26.

dodge for many in today's world)! Or even a happily married couple, as the years go by and the early excitement wears off, could decide that they need to be remarried to each other because in their youth they did not fully comprehend all the responsibilities of marriage! In the New Testament, baptism is not a witness to faith, but a witness to the grace of God. Faith is not the gift, but the hands with which we grasp the gift.

2. For some, it is *because there was not enough confession.* There was no opportunity at their baptism to confess Christ as they would now wish. But this is confused thinking. There most certainly was a confessional element in their baptism as an infant. The church and the minister bore witness by administering the sacrament, and the parents bore witness by bringing the child and making public confession of the faith in which they brought him or her to be baptized. Again it must be remembered that baptism is primarily a witness, not to faith, but to the prior grace of God.

3. For some, it is *because there was not enough water.* They have been persuaded, perhaps by Baptist friends, that baptism is not valid unless it is by immersion. Or they may believe immersion best accords with the symbolism of burial and resurrection in Rom. 6:4 and Col. 2:12. But neither text mentions the mode of baptism, only its efficacy. The ideas of "burial" and "being raised" do not conjure up thoughts of water, but of a death and an empty tomb! Modes of baptism will be discussed more fully in chapter 9.

4. For some, it is *because there was not enough feeling.* This is an existential age. Subjectivism reigns. Having missed the marvelous feeling of having the waters close over their heads, and what this symbolizes, they come for a second baptism in order to really "feel" baptized.[93] Often persons in the Wesleyan/holiness tradition are very vulnerable to this temptation. Such a quest for human feelings ignores the objectivity of the gospel, making it a means for our own gratification. Of all the requests for rebaptism, this is the one to which most evangelical Protestant ministers seem to accede most readily. But even for evangelicals it is fraught with dangers. Those who have had the deepest

---

93. Cf. the discussion in section D of chapter 1, on "The Danger of Experience."

Christian experiences seem to be the ones who are most wary of relying on emotions rather than the steadfastness of God in the midst of our changing moods.[94] John Wesley tells us that immediately after his Aldersgate experience

> it was not long before the enemy suggested, "This cannot be faith; for where is thy joy?" Then was I taught that peace and victory over sin are essential to faith in the Captain of our salvation: But that, as to the transports of joy that usually attend the beginning of it, especially in those who have mourned deeply, God sometimes giveth, sometimes withholdeth them, according to the counsels of his own will.[95]

To seek rebaptism as a source of religious feeling is misguided. When such a request is made, the minister has an opportunity to counsel the person as to the true meaning of the sacrament—and of the gospel.

Those are Green's four reasons why people seek rebaptism. He goes on to say that rebaptism is basically wrong because *it cannot be done!* Baptism is universally understood as the sacrament of initiation. By definition, one cannot be initiated more than once into the same thing. H. Orton Wiley says:

> Baptism being an initiatory rite is to be administered only once. It establishes a permanent covenant and is not therefore to be repeated. The baptized one may fall away, but the gracious promise of God still stands. It cannot be made of none effect. If he falls away, he needs to repent and believe, and the Father stands ready to restore him, but he does not need to be rebaptized.[96]

A race has only one starting line, and the runner, even if he stumbles and falters in midcourse, need not return to the point of beginning. What is needed is to simply get up and start running again! A citizen does not petition again for citizenship. An adopted person does not seek to be adopted again into the same family. Baptism is effective, but not unconditionally so. The conditions are repentance and faith. When those have not been present, the person does not need baptism all over again. Such

---

94. Cf. Laurence Hull Stookey, *Baptism: Christ's Act in the Church* (Nashville: Abingdon Press, 1982), 55-56.
95. *Works* 1:103.
96. Wiley 3:174.

persons need to repent and believe! When this happens, they are simply catching up to their own baptism, by owning it for themselves. In Samaria (Acts 8), Philip had preached Christ, and the people had "been baptized into the name of the Lord Jesus" (v. 16). But for some reason it was ineffective; they had not received the Spirit. When Peter and John came and found this to be the case, they did not rebaptize them but prayed for them, and they received the Holy Spirit. At Ephesus (Acts 19), the people were baptized twice, but this is because their first baptism was not *Christian* baptism at all but merely Johannine baptism. There was no Christian rebaptism.

Rebaptism is prohibited not only by the initiatory character of baptism but also by the even more important truth explored above—that baptism is an act of God. It is God's steadfast covenant promise. Laurence Hull Stookey states the case against rebaptism in a penetrating comment:

> To rebaptize is to say, "God, you once promised your steadfast love and creative power to this person. But perhaps you didn't mean it. Promise it again. You supposedly incorporated this person into the community of the covenant; perhaps that didn't take effect. Do it again." Hence, rebaptism impugns the integrity of God. Stated bluntly, rebaptism is a form of blasphemy—or else it is a way of saying that baptism doesn't mean anything at all in terms of divine activity.[97]

To call it blasphemy may be overstating the case, but Stookey's final words are pertinent: Rebaptism plays down the significance of baptism as a divine act.

Baptism is the sacrament by which, in the words of Wesley, "we enter into covenant with God; into that everlasting covenant, which he hath commanded for ever; (Psalm cxi. 9;) that new covenant, which he promised to make with the spiritual Israel."[98] As such, it prohibits rebaptism. In other covenants that humans make to each other, the covenant, once made, does not need to be remade. In a marriage, when one partner has been unfaithful, the marriage ceremony does not need to be redone, and the marriage certificate does not need to be re-signed. What

---

97. Stookey, 51.
98. *Works* 10:191.

is required to rebuild the marriage is confession and repentance on the part of the unfaithful partner, and forgiveness on the part of the other. God has not lied. He has not failed His part of the covenant. If either infants or adults have failed their part, then *renewal* of the baptismal vow (including confession and repentance) is appropriate and necessary, but not rebaptism.

For those who were baptized as infants, and subsequently desire rebaptism as adults, there are creative instructional and liturgical ways that the church can meet their felt need without diminishing the significance of infant baptism. Also there may be cases when a person does not know whether or not he or she was baptized. Suggestions for these situations will be made in chapter 9.

G. AND WHAT ABOUT INFANT DEDICATION?

As already stated, infant dedications appear to be more numerous in Wesleyan/holiness churches than infant baptisms. Most churches in this group provide separate rituals for the two rites. Besides the omission of water in the ritual of dedication, it differs from baptism in being mainly a human act or testimony on the part of the parents as to their intentions with respect to their child. This is noble and good in itself. But it lacks the New Testament support and historical precedent that baptism has.

In Wesleyan/holiness churches, parents are usually given the choice, but there are many pastors who have reservations about infant baptism and do it only reluctantly. Some will even refuse to baptize infants. One may wonder about the ethics of a minister who refuses to administer a sacrament that is embodied in his denomination's faith and order![99] However, the motivation is usually not malice but rather a lack of understanding of the theology that undergirds the sacrament.

The viewpoint of this book is that infant baptism should be favored over infant dedication. There is no New Testament reference or ground for dedication. But infant baptism, whether or

---

99. E.g., the Church of the Nazarene recognizes an "elder" as a minister who, among other obligations, is "to administer the sacraments of baptism and the Lord's Supper." And in the denomination's Articles of Faith, infant baptism is affirmed as a sacrament. *Manual*, 1989, 36, 179.

not it was practiced in the New Testament, is one of the oldest traditions in Christendom, going back at least to the early centuries. Dedication is a comparatively new idea in the long history of Christianity. In dedication the emphasis is primarily on what the *parents* do (remember that the Anabaptist argument against infant baptism is that the child is unable to knowingly participate!).

Therefore the following weaknesses are highlighted when dedication is substituted for baptism: (1) It is a focus away from God's initiative to human activity, thus encouraging the kind of subjectivism that sacramental theology seeks to overcome. (2) It is a rationalistic rather than a supernatural view of life, faith, and sacrament, thus failing to underscore the possibilities of grace. (3) It conceives of faith as intellectual assent or understanding; one should not be baptized until old enough to know what it means. (4) It betokens a lack of trust in God's promise and power toward the helpless—in this case the helpless child. (5) It fails to understand that dedication of a child to God, as admirable as it is, is secondary to the gospel reality that God loves this child and sent His Son that he or she might be incorporated into the great company of the redeemed, becoming a member of the Body of Christ. This latter truth is the message of baptism. Under the old covenant, people dedicated children to God. It is still a worthy gesture. But far greater is the gospel truth proclaimed in baptism—that God gave *His* Child to die that our children might have newness of life!

Chapter Seven

EUCHARIST:
SACRAMENT OF
SANCTIFICATION

As the "sacrament of initiation," baptism stands at the beginning of the Christian life and is not meant to be repeated. In this chapter we turn to the other sacrament that is observed in most segments of the Wesleyan/holiness tradition, namely the Lord's Supper. We are calling it the "sacrament of sanctification." This seems appropriate in a book about the place of sacraments in Wesleyan spirituality, because it was in the doctrine of sanctification that John Wesley made one of his unique contributions to theological discussion as well as to the Christian understanding of spirituality. Consequently it has also been a central tenet in the Wesleyan/holiness tradition, and often considered to be the tradition's distinctive doctrine.

Of course, for Wesley and Wesleyans, sanctification has its beginning in the moment of justification and the new birth. "At the same time that we are justified, yea, in that very moment, sanctification begins. In that instant we are born again, born from above, born of the Spirit."[1] This beginning of the sanctifying work of the Spirit is represented sacramentally by baptism, the sacrament of initiation. Wesley's followers have often

---

1. *Works* 6:45.

referred to this beginning as "initial sanctification."[2] This is but the start of the process of sanctification, which Wesley believed should eventuate in a second work of divine grace called "entire sanctification" (see 1 Thess. 5:23, NASB) or "Christian perfection," which he defined as "love excluding sin; love filling the heart, taking up the whole capacity of the soul."[3]

But Wesley did not believe in a static state of perfection that "does not admit of a continual increase."[4] He viewed salvation as a process comprising a series of stages aiming at the perfection of the Christian.[5] He says:

> All experience, as well as Scripture, show this salvation to be both instantaneous and gradual. It begins the moment we are justified, in the holy, humble, gentle, patient love of God and man. It gradually increases from that moment . . . till, in another instant, the heart is cleansed from all sin, and filled with pure love to God and man. But even that love increases more and more, till we "grow up in all things into Him that is our Head;" till we attain "the measure of the stature of the fulness of Christ."[6]

To designate the Eucharist as the "sacrament of sanctification" is not to imply that it is *entire* sanctification as a second work of grace (the "another instant" in the above quotation from Wesley) that is alone signified by the Eucharist. Rather, we have in mind the whole progressive work of sanctification, however many "instants" the process may comprise. The Eucharist may be understood as that means of grace, instituted by Jesus Christ, to which we are invited for repentance, for self-examination, for renewal, for spiritual sustenance, for thanksgiving, for fellowship, for anticipation of the heavenly kingdom, and for celebration in our pilgrimage toward perfection in the image of Christ. All these are involved in our sanctification, and all these are

---

2. It is not a term that Wesley himself used, although it accurately depicts his view.

3. *Works* 6:46. "Entire sanctification" and "Christian perfection" are not completely synonymous in the history of Christian thought, but they are often used as such by Wesley, as in this passage.

4. Ibid., 5. Wesley continues: "So that how much soever any man has attained, or in how high a degree soever he is perfect, he hath still need to 'grow in grace,' and daily to advance in the knowledge and love of God his Saviour." Pp. 5-6.

5. Cf. Lindström, 113-25. Lindström's book is still one of the best in delineating the stages in Wesley's *ordo salutis*.

6. *Works* 6:509.

benefits available to us at the Lord's table.

Is it legitimate to associate the Eucharist with sanctification? Wesley thought so. "The Lord's Supper was ordained by God," he says, "to be a means of conveying to men either preventing, or justifying, or *sanctifying* grace, according to their several necessities."[7] In his sermon on "The Duty of Constant Communion," he says:

> As our bodies are strengthened by bread and wine, so are our souls by these tokens of the body and the blood of Christ. This is the food of our souls: This gives strength to perform our duty, *and leads us on to perfection.*[8]

William H. Willimon says of those words: "Wesley is here speaking of *Communion as a sanctifying activity.* It is our sustenance along the way."[9]

Sanctification, in its broadest meaning, is the lifelong process by which Christians become the "saints" they are called to be (1 Cor. 1:2, KJV; Eph. 1:1), "perfecting holiness out of reverence for God" (2 Cor. 7:1). It is the process of moving, by grace, toward our destiny. And what is our destiny? It is defined by the *imago Dei* (the "image of God") in which human beings were created (Gen. 1:27). In our sin we turned away from our destiny. The "image" that is our destiny is now defined by Jesus Christ, who is "the image of the invisible God" (Col. 1:15), "the radiance of God's glory and the exact representation of his being" (Heb. 1:3). Into that same image we are being transformed (2 Cor. 3:18). In short, our destiny is "to be conformed to the likeness of his Son" (Rom. 8:29). From its human side, the life of sanctification, in the Wesleyan/holiness tradition, basically means a commitment toward Christlikeness.[10] This is not a Christlikeness that can be attained by exerting human strength in the "imitation of Christ," but one that is the gift of grace and to the reception of which we are to be continually open.[11] "Now

---

7. Ibid. 1:280, italics mine.
8. Ibid. 7:148, italics mine.
9. *The Service of God,* 124. Willimon writes knowledgeably about Wesley's concept of sanctification as a process but does not acknowledge the many references in Wesley's writings to sanctification as also an instantaneous work of grace.
10. In the tradition, this commitment has most often been called "consecration."
11. Members of the Free Methodist church make the following commitment: "I commit myself to know God in his full sanctifying grace." In the Church of the Nazarene's

we are children of God, and what we will be has not yet been made known. But we know that when he appears, we shall be like him, for we shall see him as he is" (1 John 3:2)!

Sanctification, which for Wesley has its instantaneous aspects, is also "a progressive work, carried on in the soul by slow degrees, from the time of our first turning to God."[12] One important means of furthering that sanctifying work is participation in the Lord's Supper. Willimon is correct in saying:

> The Lord's Supper is a "sanctifying ordinance," a sign of the continuity, necessity, and availability of God's enabling, communal, confirming, nurturing grace. Our characters are formed, sanctified, by such instruments of continual divine activity in our lives.[13]

Persons brought up in the Wesleyan/holiness churches have generally not been well instructed as to the potential of the Eucharist as a means for the promotion of holiness. For them, the very normality, regularity, and ritualistic nature of the sacrament militates against such an understanding.[14] The invitation to the Lord's Supper is not particularly heard as a call to holiness. The preaching such persons have heard on sanctification, often in a revivalist atmosphere, has tended to emphasize it only as an instantaneous crisis experience, with an invitation for the listeners to seek entire sanctification then and there. This invitation has usually taken the form of an evangelistic altar call, which may be emotion-packed, rather than an invitation to the Lord's Supper, which is usually perceived as a more staid and formal occasion. It is easy to see how those whose concepts both of sanctification and of Eucharist are thus formed could easily miss the connection between Eucharist and sanctification. Willimon, however, states the case for the connection very clearly:

---

ritual for the Reception of Church Members, candidates for membership are asked: "Will you seek earnestly to perfect holiness of heart and life in the fear of the Lord?" In The Wesleyan Church, likewise, they are asked: "Have you the witness of the Spirit that you have been sanctified wholly? If not, will you diligently seek this grace?" Such commitments are in keeping with John Wesley's admonition: "*Thou* therefore look for it every moment!" *Works* 6:53.

    12. *Works* 6:74.

    13. *The Service of God*, 125.

    14. The reader is directed again to the discussion in the first two sections of chapter 1.

Sanctification asserts that the Christian life ought not be formed in a haphazard way. It takes constant, life-long attentiveness, habits, and care to embody this character. The normality, the constancy of the Eucharist is part of its power. This meal need not be special, nor exhilaratingly meaningful (though sometimes it is both). This is the normal food of Christians, the sustaining, nourishing stuff of our life. We return again and again to the Lord's table, to the source of our life together . . . as habitually and normally as we gather at the breakfast table.[15]

We must now examine this sacrament more specifically. Whereas baptism is the sacrament of *initiation* and consequently is not to be repeated, the sacrament of *sanctification* is to be celebrated again and again from baptism until death.[16] It goes by different names, which are generally used interchangeably, although each of them highlights a different aspect of the sacrament. The most common of these names are "the Lord's Supper" (1 Cor. 11:20), or simply "the Supper" or "the Meal" (based on John 13:4, on the various references to Jesus eating with His disciples, and on His parables of the Kingdom and sayings about eating in the kingdom of God), "Communion" or "Holy Communion" (based on 1 Cor. 10:16, KJV), "Eucharist" (derived from the Greek word for "thanksgiving" in 11:24 and a variant reading of 10:16), "the Table of the Lord" (cf. 10:21, RSV), and "the Breaking of Bread" (based on Luke's use in Luke 24:35, KJV, and Acts 2:42). In churches where this sacrament is the dominant feature of worship, it is sometimes referred to simply as "the Liturgy." Among Roman Catholics, the main term is "the Mass," a nonbiblical word derived from the Latin *missio*, which refers to the dismissal, before the Lord's Supper was celebrated, of those who were not yet full members of the church.

The term Eucharist has been used since the end of the first century and is found in the writings of the post-Apostolic Fathers. It is still widely used today among both Protestants and

---

15. *The Service of God,* 127.

16. The phrase "from baptism" assumes two presuppositions expressed elsewhere in this book, (1) that infant baptism is valid, and (2) that persons not baptized as infants should, upon confession of personal faith, be baptized without undue delay.

Catholics. Some authorities on liturgy consider it to be the most descriptive term.[17] It is used frequently in recent theological works, perhaps because, more strongly than the other terms, it emphasizes the note of celebration that should characterize our participation in the Lord's Supper and that has been a prominent theme in recent theology. For these reasons it is used in the title of this chapter, although the other terms will also be used in our discussion, especially "the Lord's Supper," which is the most widely used term in the doctrinal statements of churches in the Wesleyan/holiness tradition.

To embark on an exploration of eucharistic theology is to plunge headlong into a veritable thicket of exegetical and theological controversy. Agelong misunderstandings abound. Ironically, in the church's history, the rite that stands for unity and communion has sadly been the source of disunity and strife. Battles have been fought over the numerous questions raised by the New Testament texts. For example, what does Jesus mean by "Do this"? What is "this" that His disciples are to do? And what is the meaning of "is" in Jesus' words, "This *is* my body . . . This *is* my blood"? In most of the disputes over such questions, no clear winners emerged, the controversies usually ending only in something like an uneasy truce. Happily, there is today more mutual respect and understanding between the different traditions than perhaps at any time in many centuries.

It is not the intent of this book to explore in depth all the critical or exegetical issues involved in the study of the Eucharist. An abundance of literature on this topic already exists.[18] Our purpose here is more practical.

In the next section we will take only brief note of the main exegetical issues relating to the "institution" of the Supper by Jesus on the night of His betrayal.[19] Our main interest is in get-

---

17. E.g., James F. White, *Christian Worship*, 203.

18. Four good examples are Joachim Jeremias, *The Eucharistic Words of Jesus*, trans. Norman Perrin (London: SCM Press, 1966); I. Howard Marshall, *Last Supper and Lord's Supper* (Grand Rapids: Wm. B. Eerdmans Publishing Co., 1980); A. J. B. Higgins, *The Lord's Supper in the New Testament* (Chicago: Alec R. Allenson, 1952); Alasdair I. C. Heron, *Table and Tradition* (Philadelphia: Westminster Press, 1983).

19. "Inception" might be a better word than "institution," because it would allow for a broader New Testament base for the origins of the sacrament, but we will adhere to the traditional term.

ting a feel for the action and the mandate. The *meaning* of the Eucharist, both for the Early Church and for us, will be discussed in the third section of this chapter under the heading "Images of the Eucharist."

A. INSTITUTION OF THE EUCHARIST

From the very beginning of the Church, Christians have come together to celebrate God's saving acts in Christ by sharing a meal. Immediately after Pentecost "they broke bread in their homes and ate together with glad and sincere hearts, praising God" (Acts 2:46-47). In doing so, they were following the example set by Jesus when He ate meals with His followers on various occasions even previous to the final meal of the Last Supper. But doubtless when they ate together, they also had that final meal in mind and were aware that they were obeying a mandate: "Do this." They were also passing on the mandate to succeeding generations.

The last supper of Jesus with His disciples is mentioned five times in the New Testament—in all four Gospels and by Paul in 1 Corinthians 11. The account in the Fourth Gospel however, only records the fact that "the evening meal was being served" (13:2) and then passes quickly to the foot washing incident. John, therefore, tells us nothing about the institution of the Eucharist.[20]

To these accounts of the Last Supper may be added three more passages that yield valuable information concerning eating and drinking in New Testament times and thus, at least indirectly, add color to the picture of the Lord's Supper that has come down to us: Acts 2:42; 1 Cor. 10:16-17; and John 6:25-58, particularly verses 51-56. To understand fully the New Testament eucharistic teaching, one must consider, in addition to the above texts, the many instances where Jesus ate and drank with His disciples, as well as the parables that speak of eating and drinking in the kingdom of God.

It is in the Synoptic Gospels and in Paul that the accounts of the institution of the Lord's Supper are found. In each of

---

20. However, as we noted in chapter 4, some think it is precisely the foot washing that is instituted and mandated in John.

these four accounts (Matt. 26:26-30; Mark 14:22-26; Luke 22:14-20; and 1 Cor. 11:23-26), all the main features of the meal are included. The accounts of Matthew and Mark are similar, except that Matthew's version places slightly more weight on the participation of the disciples, and the explicit command to eat and drink, and stresses the point that the covenant is for the forgiveness of sins.

Paul's account is considerably different. It includes the command to "do this in remembrance of me," which Matthew and Mark omit. In its place, Matthew and Mark include the phrase "poured out for many" after the reference to the "blood of the covenant." In place of the declaration of Jesus in the Synoptics that He will not drink the cup again until He drinks it in the kingdom of God, Paul refers to the proclaiming of the Lord's death "until he comes."

Luke's account differs from the others in some respects, the main difference being the fact that both a longer and a shorter version are found in the ancient manuscripts. The shorter version ends in the middle of Luke 22:19, with the words, "This is my body." The longer version continues with "given for you; do this in remembrance of me" and goes to the end of verse 20. A majority of exegetes believe the long text to be the original, although only the short form is found in the so-called Western text.

The variations between texts, which can be confusing, should not cause us to overlook the important facts that the New Testament witnesses have in common: At the final meal that Jesus ate with His disciples, He distributes bread and wine and relates these elements to His body and blood (the two components of a human being whose dissolution spells death). Jesus relates His shedding of blood (the surrender of life) to a new covenant that is constituted by that very act, possibly in an allusion to Exod. 24:8 (where the covenant was made by the sprinkling of blood), following which a covenantal meal took place at Mount Sinai (v. 11).

Against this background of what the New Testament accounts have in common, one can see the different emphases given by each writer. In Matthew and Mark, there is more focus on the future meal in the kingdom of God. In Paul, the death of

Jesus is central. In Luke both aspects are found. In both Paul and Luke the emphasis on the death of Jesus is related to His instructions to "do this in remembrance."[21]

Besides problems of how to harmonize and interpret the different accounts, other questions present themselves. One is the problem of *date*. This is tied to the issue whether or not the Last Supper was a Passover meal. The Gospels themselves seem to disagree on the point. The Synoptics lead up to the story of the Last Supper by describing the preparation for the Passover that Jesus desired to eat with His disciples (see Mark 14:14; Matthew's and Luke's accounts are similar). But in John 18:28 it is explicitly stated that the Passover *followed* the arrest of Jesus. According to John, the final dramatic events took place on the 14th of Nisan, the day before the Passover feast.

The evidence is confusing, and different conclusions have quite understandably been drawn by different scholars. The most natural reading of the Synoptics shows the Last Supper to be the Passover meal. The most natural reading of John, on the other hand, shows Jesus as crucified at the very time the Passover lambs were being slain in the Temple.

A number of solutions have been proposed. One possibility is that the Last Supper was not a Passover meal, but a kind of solemn-fellowship meal that Jesus and His disciples were in the habit of sharing. Another view seeks to harmonize the accounts by holding that the meal Jesus ate with His disciples was a Passover, but held a day earlier than the official one, perhaps because different calendars were used by different Jewish groups.[22] Still another solution is that the Synoptic account is the correct one, and that the Fourth Gospel has altered the timetable in order to connect the Crucifixion with the Passover and to highlight the meaning of Jesus as the new Passover Lamb. Within each of these proposals there are different subproposals, all attempting to solve the problem.[23] Without being dogmatic re-

---

21. The meaning of this "remembrance" will be discussed in section C of this chapter.

22. This view was put forth by P. Billerbeck and is adopted by Marshall in his excellent study, 75.

23. A concise but fairly complete summary of the different solutions is found in Leon Morris, *The Gospel According to John,* in *The New International Commentary on the*

garding the details we are persuaded that the Lord's Supper was a Passover meal of some kind.

Another problem concerns the relation between early celebrations of the Eucharist and ordinary meals. In the Early Church meals were held in a liturgical setting. This is the so-called Agape or "love feast" (Jude 12). These were apparently held with regularity in the congregations as occasions of Christian fellowship and worship. In the "Epistle of Ignatius to the Smyrnaeans," the Eucharist and the Agape appear to be practically synonymous, or at least held in conjunction with each other.[24] These events were intended to supply a free meal to the poorer members. It appears, from the available evidence, that the sacramental meal and the social meal were originally one. Before many generations had passed, the Eucharist and the Agape were entirely separated, and the latter disappeared altogether, due to abuses such as those already found by Paul in the church at Corinth (1 Cor. 11:20 ff.). In the *Didache*[25] they are still together, but the social meals began to disappear as the congregations grew. Thus the Eucharist became less and less a real meal.

The medieval Roman Catholic Mass was an example of the great distance separating the Eucharist from the Agape feast, the sacramental from the social, the vertical from the horizontal. Protestantism has not closed the gap more than halfway. Recent moves in sacramental theology to close the gap further have much to commend them.

Again we must mention the two broad perspectives on the Lord's Supper found in the New Testament itself. In the Synoptic Gospels the Eucharist has links in two directions: On the one hand is its connection with the earlier meals Jesus and His disciples shared, and on the other hand is its link with the future banquet in the final Kingdom of which Jesus taught in parables. In Paul, the link is almost altogether with the death of Jesus on the Cross. It has been suggested that this difference in perspective is due to the different cultural environments in which each perspective was developed. The ideas of covenant, covenantal meal, and acted parable were familiar in the Palestinian setting of the Synoptics, whereas Paul's Hellenistic environment, with its familiarity with the mystery religions, made ideas of sacrifice quite understandable. Berkhof suggests that what Paul meant as a contrast or antithesis (1 Cor. 10:14-22) between the Eucharist and these Hellenistic ideas was eventually turned into a parallelism, in which the meal, originally meant to be a *remembrance* of Christ's sacrifice, became itself a *repetition* of His sacrifice.[26] We see the end of this development in the medieval Roman Catholic Mass. But even Protestantism keeps "looking one-sidedly to the sacrifice of the cross at the expense of the meal and the eschaton."[27]

The Synoptic and the Pauline traditions need to be once again combined so that they can complement each other. The same can be said for the variety of interpretations given to all the problems discussed above. Without being irresponsibly eclectic, we can assimilate whatever light is shed on the Eucharist by each approach to it that has been made by biblical scholarship. In the final analysis, our reception of the grace given to us through the means of the Lord's Supper will best be enhanced, not by having to choose between various options presented by biblical criticism, but by our openness to the images of the Eucharist reflected to us by the New Testament. This will be explored in section C. But first we must survey the four major historical interpretations of the Eucharist, in order to compare the divergent traditions and gain from each of them any aid they may offer toward giving us a deeper understanding of this hallowed means of grace.

B. INTERPRETATIONS OF THE EUCHARIST

One of the issues most vehemently debated throughout the centuries centers around the meaning of Jesus' words of institution at the Last Supper: "This is my body" and "This is my blood." What did our Lord mean by those words? Philosophical-

---

26. Hendrikus Berkhof, *Christian Faith,* trans. Sierd Woudstra (Grand Rapids: Wm. B. Eerdmans Publishing Co., 1979), 367.
27. Ibid.

ly, the question is that of the relationship between the "sign" *(signum)* and the "thing signified" *(res)*. More simply, the question is: How are we to understand the "is" in Jesus' words "This *is* my body"? How can it be said that bread *is* the body of Christ and the cup *is* His blood? Inseparable from those questions is this one: What is meant by the word "this" in the words of institution? Did Jesus refer solely to the bread and wine, or was He speaking of their *use* in the entire *action* surrounding the eating of the meal as part of the table fellowship in the Upper Room?

In continental Europe at the time of the Protestant Reformation, four different interpretations vied for acceptance: *transubstantiation* (the Roman Catholic position), *consubstantiation* (the Lutheran position), *spiritual presence* (the Reformed, or Calvinist, view), and the *memorialist* view (which is that of Zwingli). The above order reflects the degree of literalness with which the different views take the words of Jesus, "This *is* my body," the Roman Catholic view taking the "is" most literally, and Zwingli's position taking it least so. Or, put another way, this order might be said to reflect the degree to which the concept of "Real Presence" is proclaimed in each view.

In our discussion, we will reverse the order of the last two positions, treating Zwingli's before Calvin's. This is a more correct chronological order (Zwingli's work was as old as Luther's and older than Calvin's). Also, since the sacramental perspective of this book is Wesleyan,[28] this is best reflected in such an order, since Wesley was arguably closer to Calvin's view than to the others. Our listing, then, will reflect, in an ascending order, the degree to which Wesley may be said to be in agreement with the various positions.

This "Wesleyan connection" is the primary reason the differing positions are examined here. In one sense these 16th-century debates may seem like outdated relics of a bygone era. Present-day sacramental theology has moved beyond these issues as it has recognized that the philosophical ground on which the debates were staged has shifted during the intervening centuries. In spite of this, however, an important ques-

---

28. Although, as stated in the Preface, this is not a book purely about John Wesley's theology of sacraments.

tion still remains: Exactly what is happening—to the elements, to the participants, to Christ, and to the Church—when we celebrate the Eucharist? On that question, the 16th-century discussions still have some light to shed. Theology must move beyond the past, but it dare not ignore it.

1. *Transubstantiation.* Of the four viewpoints, the Roman Catholic position, which began to emerge in the 9th century and was first clearly stated in the 11th,[29] takes the "is" most literally. The word *transubstantiation* means the change of one substance into another. Alexander of Hales defined it as the action "by which an actual being, without being destroyed or annihilated, is changed according to its whole substance into another actual being."[30]

To many Protestant laypersons, transubstantiation has seemed like a superstitious bit of magic.[31] But the theory is much more sophisticated than that. It is based on a philosophical understanding that goes back to Aristotle's distinction between *substance* and *accidents.*[32] This distinction is central to the scholastic doctrine of the Eucharist as elaborated by Thomas Aquinas. The accidents of a thing are the qualities that can be empirically observed, while the substance is the underlying essence. Take, for example, a chair. The chair's accidents may be the number of its legs, its color, shape, and size, and even the material out of which it is made, such as wood, steel, or plastic. But none of these constitutes its "substance." The substance is that which underlies the accidents of the chair (its "chairness"). In Aristotelian (and hence, Scholastic) thought, the chair's substance is an entity that "stands under" the accidents, is separable from them, and is actually more real than the accidents, even

29. By the Second Council of Rome in 1079, in the "Confession for Berengar." The doctrine was elevated to the status of official dogma by the Fourth Lateran Council in 1215, was confirmed by the Council of Trent (1545-63), and was reaffirmed as late as 1965 in the encyclical *Mysterium fidei.*

30. Quoted by Englebert Gutwenger in "Transubstantiation," in *Encyclopedia of Theology: The Concise Sacramentum Mundi,* ed. Karl Rahner (New York: Seabury Press, 1975), 1752.

31. The extent of such a perception is seen in the fact that the term *hocus-pocus* is an alteration of the Latin words *hoc est corpus.* The full phrase, *hoc est corpus meum,* is the Latin translation of Jesus' words, "This is my body."

32. The accidents may also be called "attributes" or "properties."

though not empirically observable.[33] Another chair might have different accidents (a different number of legs, different color, shape, and size, and made from a different material), but it would share the same "substance" (i.e., chairness).

Modern thought largely dismisses the idea of substance for the simple reason that it is not an object of experience; one can never "get hold" of it. Instead, a chair is understood to be precisely the sum of its accidents or properties. This chair that I sit on as I write has no other entity or substance called "chair" that underlies it and is separable from it. This chair I am sitting on (which is the sum of all its accidents) is the only chair in the room. Nevertheless, the doctrine of transubstantiation rests upon this Aristotelian distinction between substance and accidents.

In the doctrine of transubstantiation, bread has certain "accidents"—taste, color, texture, smell, etc. As the bread of the Eucharist is consecrated, the accidents remain the same. But the substance is no longer that of bread but of the body of Christ. The same can be said of the wine; its color, taste, smell, etc., remain, but its substance has become the blood of the Lord. Hence when we partake of the elements, we are not partaking of bread and wine at all but of the body and blood of Christ. As Alexander of Hales would describe the action, one actual being (bread), without being destroyed or annihilated (i.e., it does not disappear but becomes something else), has been changed according to its whole substance (none of the substance of bread remains, only its accidents) into another actual being (the body of Christ).

According to Aquinas, this can happen only by a miracle, a new miracle at each Mass.[34] But such a miracle must not happen willy-nilly, controlled solely by the Spirit, who is like the wind, which blows where it wishes (John 3:8).

---

33. Akin to this, and perhaps making it more understandable, is the doctrine of the immortality of the soul (which is more Greek than biblical), in which a substantial, detachable soul is understood to be the real essence of the person, the body being merely an unnecessary "accidental" appendage. New Testament Christianity steers away from such a notion in its doctrine of the resurrection of the body. In the New Testament, therefore, the *whole person*, and not merely some underlying "spiritual" part, has an eternal destiny.

34. *Summa Theologica* 3, 75, 4.

> It must be a predictable miracle; we must know where to find it. This is guaranteed by the existence of the church. . . . God grants to the church, through its own sacramental structure, the authority to make the miracle, to say "This is my body" and have it become true.[35]

Transubstantiation fixes Christ's presence in the elements themselves, separate from the fellowship of the meal and from any interpersonal encounter, giving them an *ex opere operato* efficacy. In this Aristotelian-Scholastic theory the Supper has for centuries been one-sidedly understood in a substantialistic sense.

Another aspect of the Roman Catholic Mass, as understood by the Thomists,[36] was the idea of sacrifice. In every celebration of the Mass, Christ's body and blood were offered anew as a repetition of the atoning sacrifice of the Cross. From the Protestant perspective, this amounts to works-righteousness. We come to God as those who would perform a good work for Him, giving as a good work the very thing we receive as a gift.

John Wesley rejects transubstantiation. He calls it a "senseless opinion."[37] It is against Scripture, antiquity, reason, and the senses.[38] It is "attended with consequences hurtful to piety."[39] In his Articles of Religion for the Methodists, Wesley takes over verbatim the Anglican Article 28, which reads in part: "Transubstantiation, or the change of the substance of bread and wine in the supper of the Lord, cannot be proved by holy writ; but is repugnant to the plain words of Scripture, overthroweth the nature of a sacrament, and hath given occasion to many superstitions."[40] To the claim that Christ's words, "This is my body," demand the doctrine of transubstantiation, Wesley replies:

> We answer: No such change of the bread into the body of Christ can be inferred from his words, "This is my body."

---

35. Carl E. Braaten and Robert W. Jenson, eds., *Christian Dogmatics*, 2 vols. (Philadelphia: Fortress Press, 1984), 2:356.

36. I.e., those who follow the teachings of Thomas Aquinas, or St. Thomas, as he is also known in church history.

37. *Works* 7:64.

38. Ibid. 10:151-52. Note that here Wesley brings the "Quadrilateral" (Scripture, tradition, reason, and experience) to bear against transubstantiation.

39. Ibid. 9:278.

40. *John Wesley's Sunday Service*, 312.

> For it is not said, "This is *changed* into my body," but, "This *is*
> my body;" which, if it were to be taken literally, would rather
> prove the substance of the bread to be his body. But that they
> are not to be taken literally is manifest from the words of St.
> Paul, who calls it bread, not only before, but likewise after,
> the consecration. (1 Cor. x. 17; xi. 26-28.) Here we see, that
> what was called his body, was bread at the same time. And
> accordingly these elements are called by the Fathers, "the im-
> ages, the symbols, the figure, of Christ's body and blood."[41]

Fortunately, the medieval Scholastic doctrine of transubstantiation is today undergoing creative reinterpretations by Roman Catholic scholars, which make it more palatable, if still not
fully acceptable, to Wesleyan theology. These reinterpretations
are being done along relational and personalistic lines. Roman
Catholic theologians from the Netherlands are in the forefront
of this effort. Edward Schillebeeckx, for example, sees the sacraments as the historical, and therefore embodied, aspect of our
personal encounter with God in Christ. His understanding is
thus Christological—sacraments are the means by which the ascended Christ maintains personal communion with us.[42] It is
also eschatological. In the sacrament the "thing signified" (the
res) is the eschaton, and sacraments are needed precisely because Christ is already glorified but our glorification is yet to
come.[43]

These new approaches to transubstantiation attempt to preserve the intent of the medieval doctrine but understand it in
terms more conducive to modern modes of thought. The older
substantialist models became untenable in a world where metaphysics is understood in existential, personalistic, relational, and
phenomenological ways, and where the newer physics is also
understood relationally. In these new ways of thinking about
transubstantiation, a change of substance still occurs (bread and
wine are still changed into the body and blood of Christ), but

---

41. *Works* 10:151.
42. Edward Schillebeeckx, O.P., *Christ the Sacrament of the Encounter with God* (New York: Sheed and Ward, 1963), 54-65.
43. Edward Schillebeeckx, "The Sacraments: An Encounter with God," in *Edward Schillebeeckx, OP,* ed. M. Redefern (New York and London: Sheed and Ward, 1972), 22-25.

the change is understood differently. The substance of a thing is no longer seen as some actual entity underlying the accidents, but rather is understood to be identical to the meaning and purpose of the thing. The following statement of Englebert Gutwenger shows how this applies to the Eucharist:

> The meaning of a thing can be changed without detriment to its matter. A house, for instance, consists of a certain arrangement of materials and has a clearly established nature and a clearly established purpose. If the house is demolished and the materials used for building a bridge, a change of nature or essence has intervened. Something completely different is there. The meaning has been changed, since a house is meant to be lived in and a bridge is used to cross a depression. But there has been no loss of material. In an analogous way, the meaning of the bread has been changed through the consecration. Something which formerly served profane use now becomes the dwelling-place and the symbol of Christ who is present and gives himself to his own. This means that an ontological change has taken place in the bread.[44]

One might wonder whether John Wesley's condemnation of the doctrine of transubstantiation would have been so strong if such a relational reinterpretation of it had been possible in his day and available to him. But that would be needless speculation. Doubtless he would have believed there was a still better way to understand the Eucharist.

2. *Consubstantiation.* In opposition to the Roman Catholic theory, Martin Luther formulated a position that is one step removed from the literalism of transubstantiation. Concerned to preserve the idea of "Real Presence" found in the Roman position, and to take with equal seriousness the words of institution, he developed a theory known as *consubstantiation.* In this theory, the bread and wine do not miraculously become the body and blood of Christ. They remain what they are—bread and wine. But in the Lord's Supper, the presence of Christ is *in, with,* and *under* the elements. When we receive the elements, we also receive the body and blood of Christ, which comes "with" them (hence "con-substantiation," i.e., "with the substance"[45]).

---

44. *Encyclopedia of Theology,* 1754.
45. *Com* is the more usual prefix meaning "with," but the dictionary gives *con* as a

Luther meant that Christ is present in the elements *bodily,* not merely in some "spiritual" sense. How can this be? Is not the exalted Christ bodily present in heaven at the right hand of God and not at the Communion table? Luther did not have at hand a neat philosophical basis for his view as the Roman Catholics had for theirs in the thought of Aristotle. But he rejected the Aristotelian-Thomistic position with great vehemence in his hard-hitting treatise, *The Babylonian Captivity of the Church.*[46] Instead, he based his position on the idea of the *ubiquity* (omnipresence) of Christ's body. But how can Christ be present everywhere in bodily form? Is it not a preposterous notion? Luther knows that it transcends reason—we cannot understand how Christ can be physically present both in heaven and at the table. But Luther wants to show that Christ is no less present with us when we receive the bread and wine than He was present with His disciples in the Upper Room at the Last Supper. There Christ was certainly present bodily. And He is bodily present with us also in, with, and under the bread and wine, so that when we partake of these elements, we partake also of Him. Luther simply asserts that Christ's risen body is not separated from any reality; Christ has indeed risen bodily to be where God is, and God is everywhere!

Luther was convinced that after the elements were consecrated in the Mass, they remained bread and wine. It was not merely their accidents that were present on the altar. But he believed that Christ's "real presence" was there also, with the bread and wine, to be received by the communicants. He says:

> After floating in a sea of doubt, I at last found rest for my conscience in the . . . view that it is real bread and real wine, in which Christ's real flesh and real blood are present in no other way and to no less a degree than the others assert them to be under their accidents.[47]

Luther is aware that such a position is not easily demonstrated rationally. But he castigates the Thomists for having no support in either reason or Scripture for *their* view. He accuses

---

variant of *com.* Both are from Latin.
    46. *Luther's Works* 36:27 ff.
    47. Ibid., 29.

them of misusing Aristotle, who held that the accidents of a
thing could not be separated from the thing itself.[48]

> Let us not dabble too much in philosophy. . . . For my
> part, if I cannot fathom how the bread is the body of Christ,
> yet I will take my reason captive to the obedience of Christ (2
> Cor. 10:5), and clinging simply to his words, firmly believe
> not only that the body of Christ is in the bread, but that the
> bread is the body of Christ. . . . What does it matter if philos-
> ophy cannot fathom this? The Holy Spirit is greater than
> Aristotle.[49]

For his doctrine of consubstantiation, Luther finds a parallel
in Christology. The doctrine of the *communicatio idiomatum*
("communication of properties") holds that the deity of Christ
shared the properties of His humanity, and the humanity shared
those of His deity. He holds that it was not necessary for human
nature to be changed in substance before it could be the bodily
dwelling of the divine. Nor was it necessary for the divine nature to be "contained under the accidents of the human nature."
Both natures are there in their entirety, and it can be truly said:
"This man is God; this God is man."[50]

> In like manner, it is not necessary in the sacrament that
> the bread and wine be transubstantiated and that Christ be
> contained under their accidents in order that the real body
> and real blood be present. Both remain there at the same
> time, and it is truly said: "This bread is my body; this wine is
> my blood," and vice versa.[51]

For Luther, Christ's risen body has no location in heaven
that is distinct from its location on the table. There is no need
therefore for Luther to overcome a spatial separation between
Christ's body in heaven and the bread and wine on the table. In
his *Confession Concerning Christ's Supper*,[52] written in 1528, he
distinguishes three ways in which something can be present
somewhere. First, a material element, like water in a bottle, may
be present by occupying all the space in the bottle. In that sense,

---

48. Ibid.
49. Ibid., 34.
50. Ibid., 35.
51. Ibid.
52. Ibid. 37:161 ff.

God and Christ are not present anywhere. Second, a *person* may be in a place as a subject—the place is the place that person apprehends and addresses, the place *before* that person, just as a priest or pastor standing in the pulpit may be said to be present in the church building. In this way, says Luther, all the universe is one place for God, and also for the risen Christ whose location is precisely God's right hand of omnipotence. Or, third, a person may be somewhere in that he or she is *available* there, just as we might say to someone, "I am here if you need me." In this way, Christ's body is where the bread and cup are. In short, for Luther, the bodily risen Christ actually has no other body than the embodiment of the gospel.[53] For Luther, once the miracle of resurrection and ascension are posited, no further miracle is necessary for Christ to be present in the bread and the cup. Robert W. Jenson insightfully suggests that Luther's view anticipates the concept of personal being as understood in modern biblical studies, in existential thought, and in phenomenology. He says:

> This drastic solution reworks the notion of "body," detaching it from definitions by "materiality" and defining it instead phenomenologically: Whatever makes a person available to and intendable by other people *is* that person's body. . . . Whatever makes a person available to others is *truly* that person's body if it does the same for him or her, that is, if it also lets the person see who and what he or she is.[54]

Just as in the case of transubstantiation, one might wonder if such a phenomenological understanding of Luther's view would have made consubstantiation more acceptable to Wesley if it had been possible in his day. But this too would be speculative. As it is, we know that he disagreed with Luther's position almost as strongly as he had rejected transubstantiation.[55] In a passage that may be seen as refuting both positions, Wesley insists that "it is grossly absurd, to suppose that Christ speaks of what he then held in his hands, as his real, natural body. . . .

---

53. Cf. Braaten and Jenson 2:359.
54. Ibid. See also Jenson's *Visible Words*, 111.
55. Franz Hildebrandt, *From Luther to Wesley* (London: Lutterworth Press, 1951) sees in Wesley many parallels with Luther's eucharistic theology, but such claims have been adequately countered by Borgen, 61-69.

The sense of, 'This is my body,' may be clearly explained by other scriptures, where the like forms of speech are used."[56] These "like forms of speech" found in other scriptures (he appeals to Gen. 40:12; Gal. 4:24; and Exod. 12:11) show Wesley that "*this* bread *is*, that is, signifies or represents, *my body*, according to the style of the sacred writers."[57]

Wesley asserts that Christ is bodily present only in heaven. There is no local presence of Christ in the elements of the Supper. Wesley's position relative to Luther's is correctly summarized in these words of Borgen:

> Wesley rejects the Lutheran views of consubstantiation and ubiquity, which require a communicating of the properties of the divine nature to the human. Christ is only omnipresent according to his divine nature; therefore, in order to communicate the benefits of his human life and death to us, these must be, as it were, at the disposal of Christ as omnipresent God. According to Wesley, no corporeal, carnal, material, substantial or localized presence of Christ in the sacrament can be accepted.[58]

3. *The Memorialist View*. Luther's main opponent among the Reformers was Ulrich Zwingli (1484-1531), whose reforming activity in the German-speaking part of Switzerland was as old as Luther's in Germany. Among the Protestant Reformers, Luther stayed closest to the spirit of the Middle Ages, with his view of consubstantiation underpinned by the Scholastic conception of the "communication of properties." But behind it all was his passion to keep grace inviolate, not subject to our subjective moods and inner struggles. In contrast, Zwingli understood the Lord's Supper from the standpoint of the worshiping believer who in the sacrament commemorates Christ's death and its benefits and openly gives expression to personal faith.[59]

While as opposed to Rome as was Luther, Zwingli approached theology from the standpoint of Christian humanism, having been influenced by Erasmus. He did not become a Reformer as a result of soul-wrenching religious experiences, as

---

56. *Works* 9:278.
57. *NT Notes*, Matt. 26:26, cf. 28.
58. Borgen, p. 65.
59. Cf. Berkhof, 367-68.

did Luther. Instead, it was his classical and biblical studies that influenced him most.

As a predestinarian, Zwingli believed the sacraments could not communicate assurance to the believer, for the elect are already assured of their salvation. Thus the sacraments did not convey grace for salvation but were a sign of grace that had already been received by the individual through faith. They constitute a public confession of faith and of allegiance to the church. They have no supernatural content but are merely an external sign of something that has already been accomplished inwardly.

The Eucharist, for Zwingli, was a fellowship meal with Christ and with fellow believers. His theory is a simple one. Bread and wine are *signs* of the body and blood of Christ and thus remind us of His redemptive act. The words of Jesus, "This is my body," are therefore equivalent to "This *signifies* my body." Only faith can appropriate salvation; but faith has to do with spiritual entities. Therefore the eating of the body of Christ can signify only the appropriation in faith of the salvation secured for us by the sacrifice of that body. Christ is present in the Supper, not in essence or reality, but only by the contemplation of faith. We "eat" the body of Christ when we believe. If we were to take the "eating" of Christ's body more literally, we would come into conflict with the Johannine assertion that "the flesh counts for nothing" (John 6:63).

Just as Luther called into service his Christology for support for his view of the Eucharist, so does Zwingli. But whereas Luther argued from the *communicatio idiomatum,* Zwingli falls back on his doctrine of Christ's two natures, revealing a Nestorian tendency.[60] He also rejected Luther's idea of ubiquity. The humanity of Christ was limited to a definite place in heaven. He cannot be present in the Supper in His human nature because in this He is at the right hand of God. If Luther's Christology is akin to the unification type found at Alexandria in the early centuries, Zwingli's is more like the separation type found at An-

---

60. A dualism runs through much of Zwingli's thought, as seen in his concept of God's Word as both inward and outward, the Church as both visible and invisible, and the means of grace as having both an external form and an inward grace given by the Holy Spirit.

tioch. Given their divergent viewpoints, it is not surprising that Luther and Zwingli, in spite of their shared zeal for reforming the church, could not reach agreement regarding the Eucharist at the Marburg Colloquy in 1529.

According to Zwingli, the Lord's Supper is (1) a profession of adherence to Christ in the presence of the congregation, and thus the assuming of an obligation to lead a Christian life, and (2) a memorial designed to remind us of the redemption accomplished by the death of Christ. However, when we speak of his as a "memorialist view," we must not think that it is merely a *mental* remembering that is carried on in one's head. The sacrament would not be necessary for that. He understands that the sacrament with its actions, rituals, and words of promise is important for the remembering. It is a remembrance by reenactment. We gather at the table as the disciples did in the Upper Room, remembering what happened on that night by eating and drinking as they had done. Zwingli knows the reenacting is important for the remembering.

But reenactment did not, for him, mean "Real Presence." Although the common caricature of Zwingli as teaching the "real absence" of Christ is unfair to him, he did fail to see the Supper as a real feeding on Christ, as a real means of grace. What was lacking was an understanding that at the table there is a real communion with the living Christ, and a real reception of the body and blood of Christ, albeit in a spiritual, and not physical, manner. Such a view was to be supplied by Calvin.

In spite of a great deal of "memorialist" language found in John Wesley's eucharistic teachings, he does not fit into a Zwinglian mold. His emphasis upon the presence of Christ in the Lord's Supper *in His divinity but not in His humanity* might seem Zwinglian, but this is countered by his strong insistence that the sacraments are real means of grace. Much of the eucharistic teaching of the Wesleys is found in the volume of *Hymns on the Lord's Supper*,[61] first published in 1745 (seven years *after* Wesley's Aldersgate experience, as Borgen reminds us[62]).

---

61. G. Osborn, ed., *The Poetical Works of John and Charles Wesley* (London: Wesleyan-Methodist Conference Office, 1869), 3:181-342.

62. Borgen, 16.

As a preface to that publication, Wesley printed an abridgment of Daniel Brevint's *Christian Sacrament and Sacrifice*.[63] The structure of the treatise forms the outline for the grouping of the hymns. By virtue of Wesley's use of Brevint, the latter's ideas can be considered Wesley's also. Brevint decries the attempts of men to make the Lord's Supper "an empty ceremony," calling such attempts the work of the devil.[64] Brevint (and hence Wesley) describes the Eucharist under three categories: a memorial of Christ's *past* sufferings, a means of *present* graces, and a pledge of *future* glory. If the first seems Zwinglian, the other two counter that impression. Wesley agrees with his mother when she says that "the consecrated bread" is "more than a sign of Christ's body," and that in the sacrament "we receive not only the sign, but with it the thing signified, all the benefits of his incarnation and passion!"[65] For Wesley, a purely memorialist conception of the sacraments was inadequate.

Then, if Wesley disagreed with both transubstantiation and consubstantiation on the one hand, and with a memorialist view on the other hand, where do we place him in his eucharistic doctrine? Although there are differences, Wesley's views come closest to those of Calvin.

4. *Spiritual Presence.* Among the Reformers, John Calvin (1509-64) seeks to avoid the Roman Catholic and Lutheran positions on one hand and that of Zwingli on the other. His position appears therefore to be a mediating position between those two, but it is actually an independent position.[66] Against Zwingli (and also against the Anabaptists), Calvin argues that the sacraments are efficacious, although not in an *ex opere operato* manner. It is the Spirit who makes them efficacious, just as the Spirit makes the Word efficacious.[67] It is true that one of the functions of a sacrament is to serve as a testimonial before the world, but this

---

63. Brevint, who like Wesley later was a fellow of Oxford, was a pastor in France for a time. Returning to England in 1661, he was appointed dean of Lincoln (in the region of Wesley's childhood years at Epworth). He died there in 1695.

64. Osborn, 3:185-86.

65. *Methodist Magazine*, 1844, 818. Quoted by Borgen, 68.

66. M. E. Osterhaven, "Lord's Supper, Views of," in *Evangelical Dictionary of Theology*, ed. Walter A. Elwell (Grand Rapids: Baker Book House, 1984), 655.

67. *Institutes* 4.14.7, 9-10.

in only a secondary function. The primary purpose is to serve and fortify the faith of the partaker.

On the other hand, those are mistaken who claim that the sacraments, in themselves, have power to bestow grace. Their mistake is to confuse the figure of the sacrament with the truth in it.

> For the distinction signifies not only that the figure and the truth are contained in the sacrament, but that they are not so linked that they cannot be separated; and that even in the union itself the matter must always be distinguished from the sign, that we may not transfer to the one what belongs to the other.[68]

Not only did Calvin reject Zwingli's "memorialism," he condemns Luther's doctrine of ubiquity, calling it a "monstrous notion."[69] But with Zwingli, he maintained that after the Ascension, Christ retained a real body that is located in heaven.[70] Nevertheless, there is a real reception of the body and blood of Christ in the Lord's Supper, but they are received *in a spiritual manner.* He discusses the "spiritual, and hence, actual partaking of Christ." To the Lutherans who "enclose Christ in bread" and claim that talk of a spiritual eating is no eating at all, Calvin replies: "For us the manner is spiritual because the secret power of the Spirit is the bond of our union with Christ."[71] With Luther, he believed that the elements of the Supper are signs that *exhibit* the fact that Christ is truly present, and he rejected Zwingli's belief that these elements are signs that only *represent* Christ, who is in heaven.

Calvin held that the physical body of Christ is itself of little value, since it "had its origin from earth, and underwent death."[72] The essence of Christ's body is its power. The Holy Spirit, who gave Christ a body, communicates its power to us so that in the Supper we receive the whole Christ. "We say Christ descends to us both by the outward symbol and by his Spirit,

---

68. Ibid. 4.14.15 (*LCC* 21:1290).
69. *Institutes* 4.17.30 (*LCC* 21:1401).
70. *Institutes* 4.17.19 (*LCC* 21:1381).
71. *Institutes* 4.17.33 (*LCC* 21:1405).
72. *Institutes* 4.17.24 (*LCC* 21:1390).

that he may truly quicken our souls by the substance of his flesh and his blood."[73]

Since the doctrine of the "real presence" of Christ in the Eucharist was the key issue in the eucharistic controversy, it is obvious that Calvin agreed with Luther more than with Zwingli. As we have seen, Zwingli understood that Christ's presence was by the contemplation of faith and not in essence or reality. For Luther and Calvin it is communion with a present Christ who actually feeds believers with His body and blood that makes the Eucharist a sacrament. The issue was the manner in which Christ's body exists, is present in the Supper, and given to believers. Unlike Luther, Calvin believed that Christ is bodily in heaven, but distance is overcome by the Holy Spirit, so that the Supper is a true communion with Christ, who feeds us with His body and His blood. But just as Luther insisted that there is mystery involved in his theory of ubiquity, so Calvin appeals to mystery also: "Now, if anyone should ask me how this takes place, I shall not be ashamed to confess that it is a secret too lofty for either my mind to comprehend or my words to declare. And, to speak more plainly, I rather experience than understand it."[74]

5. *Wesley's Understanding.* We have suggested that John Wesley was closer to Calvin in his view of the Lord's Supper than to the other historical views discussed above.[75] But this does not mean that he was in total agreement. In fact, there are some significant differences. He does have a doctrine of "Real Presence" that is closer to Calvin's than to Luther's. He follows Calvin in holding that Christ's body is present only in heaven,[76] and, unlike Luther, he refuses to accept any local presence of Christ in the elements. Like Calvin, he holds to a *spiritual presence* of Christ in the Lord's Supper, but his conception of this differs from Calvin's. Whereas Calvin speaks of the presence of

---

73. Ibid.

74. *Institutes* 4.17.32 (LCC 21:1403).

75. A number of Wesley scholars have so thought, e.g., J. Ernest Rattenbury, John Deschner, A. W. Harrison, and Paul S. Sanders. See Borgen, 67 n. 64.

76. Borgen asserts that the evidence is "almost overwhelming" that Wesley held the doctrine that Christ's body, or human nature, is present in heaven. See Borgen, 59 n. 35, for a listing of such evidence.

Christ's body in terms of "power," mediated by the Holy Spirit, Wesley stresses the presence of Christ in terms of His *divinity*. In fact, the whole Trinity is present, bestowing the benefits of Christ's redemptive act.[77]

In summary, Wesley believed in the "real presence" of Christ in the Eucharist. But his was more than a "memorialist" view. He does not, however, tie his idea of Real Presence to any concept of Christ's corporeal, physical, bodily, or localized presence on the Communion table that is subsumed under the elements of bread and wine. The Real Presence is a spiritual and not a bodily presence. The sign and the thing signified (*signum* and *res*) are closely related, but Christ's presence in the sacrament is not something static or organic. Wesley's view of the Real Presence is what Borgen calls "Dynamic" in that it is related to God's action. "Where God acts, there he is." It is "real" presence because it is "Living Presence."[78] Thus the objective presence of Christ in the Supper "cannot be thought of as the static presence of an object, but rather as that of a living and acting person *working* through the means."[79]

It only needs to be added that such a conception answers the question of what to do with unused elements after the Supper. Although ecumenical interests may be compelled to see otherwise,[80] there would seem to be no absolute necessity to preserve remaining elements for future celebrations of the sacrament, as if they were sacred objects. As Borgen rightly says, "This would impose a form of necessity upon God."[81]

Although Wesley states his agreement with Calvin on the doctrines of original sin and justification by faith,[82] he never re-

---

77. Cf. *Hymns on the Lord's Supper,* no. 53 (Osborn 3:252), and no. 155 (Osborn 3:333).

78. Cf. Borgen, 68-69.

79. Ibid., 69.

80. Cf. Braaten and Jenson 2:361.

81. Borgen, 68. Dunning seems to think a "Tillichian" concept of symbol, such as that discussed in chapter 2, applied to sacraments, might at least raise such a question, since a symbol "shares in the reality to which it points and thus has a sacred character within itself insofar as it is sacramentally intended." P. 543; cf. n. 14. But it seems to this writer that Dunning answers his own question in the phrase "insofar as it is sacramentally intended." It is not the elements themselves, merely as bread and wine, that are symbols, but rather their use within the whole eucharistic action. Their "sacred character" is not something that clings to the elements apart from the whole action, but arises from the concept of "Dynamic" or "Living Presence."

82. *Works* 10:391; *Letters* 4:298.

fers to Calvin in his discussions of the sacraments. Several scholars have attempted to show Wesley's indebtedness to Luther and Calvin.[83] But Outler is more correct when he says: "There are a few instructive parallels between Wesley in the eighteenth century and Luther and Calvin in the sixteenth, but it is highly misleading to interpret him as their conscious debtor."[84] Wesley's chief influences are Anglican. Nevertheless, when compared with the four eucharistic theories that swirled in the maelstrom of the Continental Reformation at the time of Protestantism's beginnings, his views have more affinities with those of Calvin than with the others.

C. IMAGES OF THE EUCHARIST

There are several images by which the Eucharist was understood in the Early Church. None of them constitutes a technical rational explanation of exactly what is taking place in the Supper. Instead, metaphorical and pictorial language is used. In terms of our discussion in chapter 2, the words used to describe the Eucharist fall more in the category of *mythos* than of *logos.* These images are not the result of logical deductions, although they have sometimes been treated as such in the history of Christian thought, as the discussion in the previous section has shown. Rather they are images that arose out of the religious imagination of the early Christians as they worshiped together. The New Testament gives us only glimpses of the way Christians celebrated the Lord's Supper in a variety of localities around the eastern Mediterranean. James F. White says:

> Never does the New Testament give us a treatise on the meaning of the Lord's Supper, but it does allow us to look over the shoulders of those who were experiencing it daily or weekly and to learn what we can from their experiences. Even their casual comments give insight into what these celebrations meant for them, expressed in images they apparently found adequate for expressing what they were experiencing.[85]

---

83. E.g., George Croft Cell, *The Rediscovery of John Wesley* (New York: Henry Holt and Co., 1935); Williams; and Hildebrandt, both mentioned earlier.

84. Outler, 119-20. He says the attempt to make Wesley the theological heir of Continental Protestantism is "a notion that would have astonished Wesley." P. 120 n. 2.

85. *Sacraments,* 53.

What were the images that expressed the meaning the Supper had for them? There are several. In chapter 5, we discussed five different aspects of baptism that were interrelated but distinguishable. Likewise, we will discuss the Eucharist in light of five different images that are also interrelated but distinguishable from one another: (1) thanksgiving to the Father, (2) commemoration of Christ, (3) sacrifice of ourselves, (4) fellowship of the faithful, and (5) foretaste of the Kingdom.[86] Although the Eucharist is one whole action, each of these five images reveals a different aspect of its meaning. There are overlappings and crossovers between some of these, and it is difficult to discuss one in isolation from the others. But, as in the case of baptism, there are important theological nuances in each that might be missed if they are not treated separately.

1. *Thanksgiving to the Father.* This image arises from the word Eucharist itself, which simply means "thanksgiving" and is from the Greek verb *eucharistein,* "to be thankful." A form of the word is found in each of the four New Testament accounts of the Last Supper (Matt. 26:26-30; Mark 14:22-26; Luke 22:14-20; 1 Cor. 11:23-26), where Jesus gave thanks for the bread and wine before giving it to the disciples.

In the New Testament origins of the Supper the giving of thanks was a matter of joyful celebration. This was the case whenever Christians ate together, not only in the Eucharist itself but also at other times of fellowship with one another. "They broke bread in their homes and ate together with glad and sincere hearts, praising God and enjoying the favor of all the people" (Acts 2:46-47).[87]

The Eucharist was not a solemn, mournful occasion, but a festive one. At least by the time of the late Middle Ages the mournful note had become the dominant one, and unfortunate-

---

86. Cf. *Baptism, Eucharist, and Ministry,* Faith and Order Paper No. 111 (Geneva: World Council of Churches, 1982), 10-15, where the meaning of the Eucharist is discussed under five headings similar to these, except for "sacrifice," which is discussed within the memorial or commemoration image. Another image is included, namely that of "invocation of the Spirit." Since this is not a biblical idea, it is not discussed here (although it is found in the early fathers and known as the *epiklēsis*). Our description of Eucharist as the sacrament of sanctification would see this as the all-embracing category that includes *all* the images.

87. Many scholars, although not all, understand this statement in Acts to be a reference to the Lord's Supper.

ly this note has persisted far too long in many churches, both Catholic and Protestant, although happily it is rapidly disappearing in most work being done today in eucharistic theology. As we noted in chapter 3, the Lord's Supper represents *fiesta,* not *funeral.* For happy families, mealtime is a joyful time. It should be even more so when the family of God gathers for the Lord's Supper.

The Church in the New Testament followed the example of Jesus in giving thanks by the use of bread and wine, probably following a Jewish pattern of praise, thanksgiving, and supplication. To its own detriment, the Church has sometimes forgotten the influence of Jewish worship on Christian eucharistic thought and practice. When this has occurred, Christian worship has tended to become weak and sentimental, losing its robustness.[88] Just as the Jews celebrated God's mighty redemptive acts in their various festivals, so in the Eucharist Christians proclaim and celebrate the work of God in His acts of redemption. It is thanksgiving for all that God has accomplished in the history of salvation. It is thanksgiving for what God is accomplishing now in the world and in the Church. And it is thanksgiving for the future fulfillment of God's kingdom we anticipate each time we gather at the Lord's table.

We learn from the writings of the Apostolic Fathers that the New Testament note of thanksgiving continued to be sounded in connection with the Eucharist in post-New Testament times. In these writings we find the first eucharistic prayers that have come down to us. They are prayers of thanksgiving. In the *Didache,* an early Christian document dating from the late first or early second century, are these instructions to the Church:

> Now about the Eucharist: This is how to *give thanks:*
> First in connection with the cup:
> "*We thank you, our Father,* for the holy vine of David, your child, which you have revealed through Jesus your child. To you be glory forever."
> Then in connection with the piece [broken off the loaf]:
> "*We thank you, our Father,* for the life and knowledge

---

88. James F. White, *Sacraments,* 54-55.

which you have revealed through Jesus, your child. To you be glory forever.

"As this piece [of bread] was scattered over the hills and then was brought together and made one, so let your Church be brought together from the ends of the earth into your Kingdom. For yours is the glory and the power through Jesus Christ forever."[89]

The *Didache* continues:

After you have finished your meal, say grace,[90] in this way:

"*We thank you, holy Father,* for your sacred name which you have lodged in our hearts, and for the knowledge and faith and immortality which you have revealed through Jesus, your child. To you be glory forever."[91]

In the "Epistle of Ignatius to the Ephesians" is this admonition:

Try to gather together more frequently to celebrate God's Eucharist and to praise him. For when you meet with frequency, Satan's powers are overthrown and his destructiveness is undone by the unanimity of your faith.[92]

And Justin Martyr, in the second century, writes that before the distribution of the bread and wine the one presiding at the Lord's Supper "sends up prayers and thanksgivings to the best of his ability, and the congregation assents, saying the Amen."[93]

The Eucharist, then, is the time for celebration, for praise, and for thanksgiving to God for His works in creation and in redemption. In the Eucharist, the Church speaks on behalf of the whole creation, for the world that God has created is represented at every Supper. It is represented in the bread and the wine, fruits of the earth and of human labor; and in the persons of the faithful, who make intercession for all humanity. The Eu-

---

89. Cyril C. Richardson, ed., "The Teaching of the Twelve Apostles, Commonly Called the Didache," 9:1-2, in *Early Christian Fathers*, vol. 1 of *Library of Christian Classics* (Philadelphia: Westminster Press, 1953), 175, italics mine.

90. Cyril Richardson notes that the term Eucharist or "the Thanksgiving," in its verb form, might be rendered "say grace," because "it was out of the Jewish forms for grace before and after meals (accompanied in the one instance by the breaking of bread and in the other by sharing a common cup of wine) that the Christian thanksgivings of the Lord's Supper developed." Ibid., n. 47.

91. Cyril Richardson, 177, italics mine.

92. Ignatius, "To the Ephesians," 13:1, in Cyril Richardson, 91.

93. Justin Martyr, "First Apology," 67, in Cyril Richardson, 287.

charist thus signifies what is God's purpose for the whole world to become—"an offering and hymn of praise to the Creator, a universal communion in the body of Christ, a kingdom of justice, love and peace in the Holy Spirit."[94]

2. *Commemoration of Christ.* A second image of the Eucharist is that of commemoration, memorial, or remembrance. Barclay calls the Eucharist "the sacrament of memory."[95] Luke's and Paul's accounts of the Last Supper contain the mandate: "Do this in remembrance of me" (Luke 22:19; 1 Cor. 11:24, cf. 25). The words could be translated, "Do this as a memorial of me." Some scholars prefer to translate the phrase, "Do this for my remembrance." This has implications, as we shall see a little later.

The key word in this command is the Greek *anamnēsis.* John F. White says the term is "exasperatingly difficult to translate" and suggests that "it might be easier just to leave *anamnesis* in Greek and educate congregations as to its meaning instead!"[96] Basically, however, the word has to do with remembering. We know what *amnesia* is—the loss of memory sometimes suffered by persons who have experienced shock, brain injury, or psychological disturbance. When the prefix *an* (the Greek negative) is added to *amnēsis,* the compound word means "not forgetting," hence "remembering."

Remembering is important in the Old Testament. The people are continually admonished not to forget God's mighty acts of deliverance in bringing them out of bondage and into the Land of Promise. Most of the Jewish festivals were designed as aids to remembering.[97] One outstanding example is the Passover, at the observance of which the Lord's Supper was probably instituted. "Do this in remembrance of me" is the only definite command we are given by Jesus regarding the Lord's Supper.

If the image of *remembrance* is taken as the main theme of the Eucharist, Zwingli's memorialist view might appear to be the

---

94. *Baptism, Eucharist, and Ministry,* 11.
95. William Barclay, *The Lord's Supper* (Nashville: Abingdon Press, 1967), 110.
96. *Sacraments,* 55.
97. A more somber side of Jewish remembering is the concern of today's Jews that the world "not forget" the Holocaust of World War II, a concern shared also by Christians everywhere.

correct one. But even with Zwingli, remembering was not a simple matter of mental recall. As we noted earlier, the entire action surrounding the sacrament, including the ritual and the words of promise, as well as the eating and drinking, were all a part of the remembering. It was remembering by reenacting.

Perhaps an illustration will help to explain a reenacted remembrance: A young couple, after 12 years of marriage, was contemplating divorce. They had two lovely children, a nice home, and outwardly appeared to be an ideal couple. He was quite successful in a growing business and began to spend more and more time away from the family. She began to find fault with his neglect of the children, and he accused her of not being interested in his success. No infidelity was involved; it was just a matter of failing to put first things first—for both of them. They drew farther and farther apart and had mutually agreed to get a divorce. In trying to save the marriage, their pastor suggested to them that they needed a vacation. He advised them to go away for two weeks for what he happened to call a "second honeymoon." Those words stuck in their minds, and they decided to give it a try. Leaving the children with grandparents, they went away for two weeks—to the same little seacoast town where they had spent their honeymoon 12 years earlier. And something happened there—at first almost against their will. Staying in the same hotel, dining in the same restaurants where they had dined on their honeymoon, strolling once again along the beach hand in hand in the moonlight, feeling the salty spray in their faces, and getting close to each other, both physically and spiritually, as they had not done in many months, they began to feel love again and decided their marriage was worth saving.

Now, in that story, what happened? They remembered their happier days, but it was more than a mental remembering. Of course they could have stayed home and mentally recalled their honeymoon. But that would not have worked; the marriage was too far gone for that to have been effective. Their marriage was saved by a *reenacted remembrance!* All the senses were brought into the act of remembering. It is something like this that Jesus must have had in mind for His disciples in the Upper Room. He knew that they—and we—would be prone to forget the first love. He wanted them to remember Him, but not merely by

mental recall. So He commanded them—and us—to act out that
final scene around the table. It was to be done by eating and
drinking together, just as they had done when He was still with
them. Interestingly, Jesus did not propose that He be remembered by some strange, bizarre, or esoteric act that was performed at no other time or place in our everyday lives. On the
contrary, He told us to remember Him by the very act of doing
what we do three times a day—eating and drinking! This would
enable us to remember. The Christ of the Communion table
wants also to be the Christ of the breakfast table, the lunch table, and the dinner table.

Still, this is not quite enough. Zwingli did not have an adequate doctrine of "Real Presence." When at the Eucharist we remember Jesus Christ, it is not as if we remember someone who
was here in the past but is now gone. Rather, when we "do this,"
we experience the "real presence" of the living Savior.

> Christ is again present to give himself to us through our
> re-experiencing his past works. Past events are made con-
> temporary; we have overcome time. We engage in a time
> mystery where past events become present with all their
> power to save. Thus, the dynamic of the original event—
> Christ giving himself for us—exists once again whenever we
> make eucharist.[98]

We still lack an adequate view of *anamnēsis* if we think that
we are to remember (and reenact) only the Supper in the Upper
Room, or even only the events of Passion Week. The entire work
of God from creation to the eschaton is remembered in the Eucharist. We remember not only backward but forward as well;
we remember the promise of the Second Coming. In this sacrament, as Paul reminds us, we "proclaim the Lord's death *until he
comes*" (1 Cor. 11:26, italics mine). The celebration of the Eucharist in the Eastern churches has incorporated this wider vision all along, and Western Christianity has recently begun to
emphasize creation as well as redemption, and God's works under the old covenant as well as the new, in its eucharistic theology and liturgies.

Thus far our discussion of *anamnēsis* has proceeded on the

---

98. James F. White, *Sacraments*, 55.

assumption that Jesus commands us to remember *Him* in the Eucharist. This is how the command has most often been understood. But another interpretation has been put forth that has some plausibility when the words of Jesus are translated, "Do this *for my remembrance.*" Joachim Jeremias suggests that the one to do the remembering is *God.* Thus we are to observe the Eucharist in order to remind *God* about *Jesus* and what He has done for our salvation.[99] According to this interpretation of the words of institution ("Do this for my remembrance"), the command of Jesus is: "Do this so that *God* will remember *me.*"

This is not so strange to anyone familiar with the Old Testament. There God's remembering is an important theological factor in Israel's salvation. "God heard their groaning and he remembered his covenant with Abraham, with Isaac and with Jacob" (Exod. 2:24). Prayers are offered in order to remind God of what He has committed himself to do for the people. "Remember, O Lord, your great mercy and love, for they are from of old" (Ps. 25:6). Jeremias contends that the remembrance passages in the Old Testament and in Palestinian Judaism speak for the most part of *God's* remembrance rather than human remembrance.[100]

In this interpretation, we come to the Lord's Supper to remind God that the only basis for our hope and salvation is Jesus, whose body was broken and whose blood was shed for us. Philosophically, one might argue that since God is omniscient, we cannot "remind" Him of anything. But such a view is foreign to biblical religion. At the Lord's Supper we are reminding all who are addressed (both God and the people) of what God has done through Jesus and of the work to which He has thereby committed himself. In one form or another, we are to pray: "Remember, O God, the sacrifice of Your Son, and hasten to bring to all peoples the salvation for which He died." For Jeremias, the Palestinian usage of *anamnēsis* designates "always, and without exception, *a presentation before God intended to induce God to act.*"[101]

---

99. *Eucharistic Words,* 237-55.
100. Ibid., 247-48.
101. Ibid., 249.

Which understanding of "remembrance" shall we adopt? Both have important insights to contribute. Can we not allow both interpretations to speak to us? Undoubtedly Jenson is correct when he says: "What is remarkable is how little difference the argument makes for the sense of the mandate."[102] Our major concern should be to "do this."

3. *Sacrifice of Ourselves.* Closely related both to the image of thanksgiving and to that of commemoration is that of *sacrifice.* The concept of the Eucharist as a sacrifice has occasioned untold controversy in the history of the church. At the time of the Reformation it was a matter of sharp contention between Luther and Rome. In recent years, however, sacramental theology has been able to sweep away much of the fog surrounding the controversies of the 16th century and focus more intently on the witness of Scripture. The result has been a recognition that the Reformation debates were locked into a very restricted understanding of the sacrifice that occurs in the Eucharist, an understanding in which much of the biblical witness was not heard.

The image of sacrifice was extremely significant in the religion of Israel. It is also pervasive in the New Testament. Sacrificial imagery abounds in the Epistle to the Hebrews. Christ is compared both to the high priest who offers the sacrifice and to the victim that is offered. "He sacrificed for their sins once for all when he offered himself" (7:27). As Priest, Christ "offered for all time one sacrifice for sins . . . by one sacrifice he has made perfect forever those who are being made holy" (10:12, 14).

The image of sacrifice permeates the very language used by Jesus in the institution of the Supper in the Upper Room. "This is my blood of the covenant, which is poured out for many for the forgiveness of sins" (Matt. 26:28; cf. Mark 14:24). "This cup is the new covenant in my blood, which is poured out for you" (Luke 22:20; cf. 1 Cor. 11:25). By using the language of sacrifice in the context of the Jewish Passover festival, Jesus made crystal clear the meaning of the Supper for first-century Jews, for

---

102. Braaten and Jenson 2:362 n. 9.

whom the covenant on Mount Sinai was ratified by the pouring out of blood (Exod. 24:6-8).[103]

From the *Didache,* we learn that the Church soon began to apply the words about sacrifice in Mal. 1:11-14 to the Lord's Supper. The Sunday Eucharist was the believers' "sacrifice."[104] Writing before the end of the first century, Clement of Rome, in his "First Letter to the Corinthians," says that Christ "ordered sacrifices and services to be performed in a regular and orderly manner."[105]

Thus in the Early Church the idea of sacrifice was one of the images by which Christians described what they were experiencing in the Eucharist. But this raises questions: Sacrifice *of what?* And sacrifice *by whom?*

In our discussion of transubstantiation we saw how medieval theology asserted that in every celebration of the Mass, Christ's body and blood were offered anew as a repetition of the atoning sacrifice of the Cross. The Reformation rejected this, seeing it as an idolatrous form of works-righteousness. In the *Treatise on the New Testament, That is, the Holy Mass,* Luther says it would be permissible to call the Eucharist a "sacrifice" if we did not presume to give God something in the sacrament, when it is He who in the Eucharist gives us all things. External sacrifices have ceased. Instead, we are to bring "spiritual sacrifices" and offer "ourselves, and all that we have, with constant prayer."[106] Expounding on the intercessory priesthood of the ascended Christ, as taught in Hebrews and in Romans, he says:

> From these words we learn that we do not offer Christ as a sacrifice, but that Christ offers us. And in this way it is permissible, yes, profitable, to call the mass a sacrifice; not on its own account, but because we offer ourselves as a sacrifice along with Christ. That is, we lay ourselves on Christ by a firm faith in his testament and do not otherwise appear before God with our prayer, praise, and sacrifice except through Christ and his mediation.[107]

---

103. Cf. James F. White, *Sacraments,* 57.
104. *Didache,* 14:1-3, in Cyril Richardson, 178.
105. Clement's "First Letter," 40:2, in Cyril Richardson, 62.
106. *Luther's Works* 35:98.
107. Ibid., 99.

Like Luther, Wesley rejects the Mass as a continual offering up of Christ. Christ's sacrifice on the Cross is finished; no other sacrifice need be made to bring about atonement for sin. And yet, as Dunning correctly notes, there is in Wesley's thought an unfinished aspect of Christ's work represented by His intercession at the right hand of God, and this work is ongoing.[108] "There is a sense in which . . . the great High Priest continually presents himself as sacrifice to the Father, not as a repetition but as symbolizing the ongoing efficacy of the Atonement."[109] We do not offer up Christ; He offers up himself.

In the above discussion of *anamnēsis* ("remembering"), we took note of Jeremias' notion that in the Eucharist we implore *God* to remember the work of Jesus on our behalf. From that perspective, the sacrifice we offer in the Eucharist is a memorial of Christ that we make by reminding God that Jesus Christ is for us. We have nothing to offer God but Jesus Christ.

> *I need no other argument,*
> *I need no other plea,*
> *It is enough that Jesus died,*
> *And that He died for me.*
> —Lidie H. Edmunds

All we have to offer to God is the atoning work of Christ, but that is all we need.

> *In my hand no price I bring;*
> *Simply to Thy cross I cling.*
> —Augustus M. Toplady

From this viewpoint, the sacrifice we make in the Eucharist is not our work at all but Christ's alone. This truth lies at the heart of the gospel.

However, in one sense we do offer something else to God. The *Book of Common Prayer*, with which Wesley was intimately familiar, uses Heb. 13:15-16, in connection with the Lord's Supper:[110]

> Through Jesus, therefore, let us continually offer to God
> a sacrifice of praise—the fruit of lips that confess his name.

---

108. Dunning, 562.
109. Ibid.
110. No direct connection is made in Hebrews itself, however.

> And do not forget to do good and to share with others, for
> with such sacrifices God is pleased.

All our worship should be regarded as an offering to God. This
is fully consistent with the Reformation's rejection of the sacrifice of the Mass, and also with the Reformation principle of the
"priesthood of believers." We are to be "a holy priesthood, offering spiritual sacrifices acceptable to God through Jesus Christ" (1
Pet. 2:5). The Westminster Shorter Catechism defines prayer as
"an offering up of our desires unto God, for things agreeable to
his will, in the name of Christ, with confession of our sins, and
thankful acknowledgement of his mercies."[111] But these spiritual
sacrifices that we offer (prayer, praise, and the like) are not
something that *we* offer by our own initiative and in our own
power. Wesley's doctrine of prevenient grace helps to avoid that
misunderstanding. It is only by grace that we are enabled to offer the sacrifice of praise. Hence, in that sense, the insight of
Jeremias is correct—to God we can only offer Christ. Not that
we sacrifice Him continually in the Eucharist, but that in the Eucharist we come before God acknowledging that Christ is our
only salvation.

In the image of sacrifice we encounter the full force of the
Wesleyan doctrine of sanctification.[112] In this chapter, we have
called the Lord's Supper "the sacrament of sanctification." Central to that doctrine is the New Testament imperative of sacrifice.
Paul urges us: "Offer yourselves to God, as those who have
been brought from death to life" (Rom. 6:13). And again: "Offer
your bodies as living sacrifices, holy and pleasing to God—this
is your spiritual act of worship" (12:1). Wesley tells us that his
quest for holiness began in earnest when, upon reading the
writings of Jeremy Taylor, he instantly resolved to dedicate all
his life to God, being convinced that there was no middle
ground between making his entire life a sacrifice to God, or to
himself, which would, in effect, be a sacrifice to the devil.[113]

But what is the connection between such offering of self

---

111. Question no. 98.
112. Cf. Dunning, 564, where he also makes note of this.
113. *Works* 11:366.

and the sacrament of the Lord's Supper? The reader is referred back to the beginning of this chapter, where we saw that Wesley believed the Lord's Supper was ordained by God to be a means of conveying sanctifying grace.[114] "As our bodies are strengthened by bread and wine, so are our souls by these tokens of the body and the blood of Christ. This is the food of our souls: This gives strength to perform our duty, *and leads us on to perfection.*"[115] In Wesleyan theology, therefore, the Lord's table is a place where we can come and offer ourselves as "living sacrifices," thereby receiving sanctifying grace.

4. *Fellowship of the Faithful.* Another New Testament image of the Eucharist is that of fellowship or communion. The key word is the Greek *koinōnia.* Variously translated as fellowship, communion, participation, and sharing, the word has a richer meaning than any of these English words can fully capture. *Koinōnia* in the New Testament is more than mere human friendship or conviviality. Fellowship among Christians is derived from the unity we have in Christ.

The Eucharist is described as *koinōnia* in 1 Corinthians 10. Writing about the Lord's Supper, Paul says: "Is not the cup of thanksgiving for which we give thanks a participation *[koinōnia]* in the blood of Christ? And is not the bread that we break a participation *[koinōnia]* in the body of Christ?" (v. 16). He continues by speaking of the unity Christians have with one another, which derives from their participation, or sharing, in the body and blood of Christ: "Because there is one loaf, we, who are many, are one body, for we all partake of the one loaf" (v. 17).

In all cultures, the meal speaks a language of its own. Festive and joyful occasions, in particular, are probably best celebrated with a meal. At a meal a person can relax, find acceptance, and enjoy the fellowship of other like-minded persons. There is something about a meal that binds the participants together. At least this is what meals should be. In today's fast-paced society, with its busy schedules, working mothers, and latchkey children, mealtime family fellowship is often disrupted,

---

114. See n. 7 above.
115. See n. 8 above.

sometimes of necessity. But for Jewish households in biblical times, meals were understood as events that bound family members together. Paul builds upon this understanding in the next verse: "Consider the people of Israel: Do not those who eat the sacrifices participate in the altar?" Since for Paul it is a truism that eating together means participation, fellowship, communion (i.e., *koinōnia*), he pursues the idea still farther in order to warn against the *wrong kind* of fellowship, namely fellowship with idols (v. 19). "I do not want you to be participants with demons. You cannot drink the cup of the Lord and the cup of demons too; you cannot have a part in both the Lord's table and the table of demons" (vv. 20-21). The Eucharist fellowship excludes all compromise with evil!

This idea is reflected in the *Didache* where these instructions are found: "You must not let anyone eat or drink your Eucharist except those baptized in the Lord's name. For in reference to this the Lord said, 'Do not give what is sacred to dogs.'"[116] After the Supper was eaten, this prayer was to be prayed: "Remember, Lord, your Church, to save it from all evil and to make it perfect by your love."[117]

We see, then, that for Paul and the Early Church the Lord's Supper meant fellowship among the faithful and the exclusion of idolatry and evil. This thought is carried still further by the apostle as he warns against unworthy participation in the Eucharist. He says: "Whoever eats the bread or drinks the cup of the Lord in an unworthy manner will be guilty of sinning against the body and blood of the Lord" (1 Cor. 11:27). Tragically, the failure to understand Paul's meaning has kept many a sensitive Christian away from the Lord's table! Being convinced that one should not partake without measuring up to a certain standard of righteousness, such persons cheat themselves out of great blessing. The truth of the gospel is that *none of us is ever really worthy!* If our own worthiness were the entrance requirement to the Lord's Supper, none of us would ever partake.

It is necessary to understand the context of Paul's remarks. He is discussing propriety in worship. He had heard that in the

---

116. *Didache* 9:5, in Cyril Richardson, 175.
117. *Didache* 10:5, in Cyril Richardson, 176.

church at Corinth there were divisions. Among other things, the Lord's Supper had become an occasion for the *absence* of fellowship. The unity of the church was threatened. Apparently at this early period, the Eucharist was still combined with the Agape, or love feast. The Corinthian believers were behaving quite selfishly. "Each of you goes ahead without waiting for anybody else" (1 Cor. 11:21). Those who arrived early (or crowded to the front of the line?) ate up all the food, while others remained hungry. The spirit of true sharing was missing. So Paul urges: "When you come together to eat, wait for each other" (v. 33).

Set down between those two verses (21 and 33) is Paul's account of the institution of the Lord's Supper, which he "received from the Lord" (v. 23). What does it mean to eat and drink "unworthily" (vv. 27, 29, KJV)? He tells us in plain words. It is to eat and drink *"without recognizing the body of the Lord"* (v. 29, italics mine). In some of the oldest and most authoritative manuscripts, the words "of the Lord" are not found; they were quite likely not a part of the original text. The text then simply reads "not recognizing the body."

The person Paul condemns is not the one who fails to understand that the elements of bread and wine are the body and blood of Christ (that would almost be a condemnation of those who reject transubstantiation!). The person Paul condemns is the one who does not discern that Christians are the Body of Christ. Eating and drinking "in an unworthy manner" (v. 27) means to violate *koinōnia*. "In that the bread and cup are given, there is a body present that is Jesus, and there is a body present that is the community, and a person's relation to the one is not distinguishable from that person's relation to the other."[118] Christians are to be in unity before they approach the sacrament. This sacrament is Christ's own Supper. He it is who invites the guests. His invitation is as open and universal as His death "for many" at Calvary. The hands that invite us to the table are the outstretched nail-scarred hands of the Crucified One. "The only qualification for acceptance of this open invitation is that we recognize the Giver of the feast."[119] When we truly rec-

---

118. Braaten and Jenson, 2:346-47.
119. Jürgen Moltmann, "The Life Signs of the Spirit in the Fellowship Community

ognize Him for who He is, all human divisions and disagreements seem unimportant, and He is able to create *koinōnia* among us.

5. *Foretaste of the Kingdom.* The final image to be considered is that of the Eucharist as a preview of the final consummation of all things, a foretaste of the Heavenly Banquet to which we are invited. From a biblical perspective, this is probably the most significant image of all. In the Eucharist we proclaim the Lord's death "until he comes" (1 Cor. 11:26), looking forward to the day "when the times will have reached their fulfillment—to bring all things in heaven and on earth together under one head, even Christ" (Eph. 1:10). In ringing tones, the Eucharist celebrates the eschatological hope of the Christian. In this sacrament we both remember the past sacrifice of our Lord at Calvary and express our confidence in His future triumph. "There is nothing in Christian worship which so looks to the past, the present and the future, as the sacrament of the Lord's Supper does."[120]

In recent years the eschatological dimension of the Eucharist has come to the forefront and occupied a degree of theological interest not seen for centuries. In 1926 Hans Lietzmann, a German scholar, paved the way for an understanding of the Eucharist as grounded in the idea of the kingdom of God.[121] He identified two distinct types of eucharistic worship in the Early Church. One type centered on the death of Christ and the institution of the Supper in the Upper Room. This type has been preserved for us in *The Apostolic Tradition* of Hippolytus. The other type focused on the return of Christ and the idea of community. It has been preserved in the *Didache*. Lietzmann claims to trace the first type back to its ultimate source in Paul (1 Corinthians 10 and 11), and the second type to the fellowship meals Jesus had with His disciples during His lifetime and continued after the Resurrection. Interest in the second type has increased since Lietzmann's analysis.

---

of Christ," in *Hope for the Church*, ed. Theodore Runyon (Nashville: Abingdon Press, 1979), 52.

120. Barclay, 110.

121. Hans Lietzmann, *Mass and Lord's Supper*, trans. Dorothea H. G. Reeve (Leiden: E. J. Brill, 1979); English translation of *Messe und Herrenmahl* (Berlin: Walter de Gruyter, 1926).

Oscar Cullmann has shown that there is more in the New Testament that informs us about the Eucharist than merely the accounts of the Upper Room. He relates the Eucharist to the resurrection appearances of Jesus and the eschatological significance of eating and drinking with Christ and shows their relation to early Christian liturgy.[122] Cullmann insists that the ancient prayer, *"Maranatha!"* ("Lord, come!") ought to characterize celebrations of the Eucharist, as it once did, and "should express the double desire, which was realized for the early Christians, of seeing Christ descend into the midst of the faithful gathered in His name and of discovering for themselves, in that coming, an anticipation of his final messianic return."[123] Jürgen Moltmann and others who have written on the "theology of hope" also emphasize this facet of eucharistic theology. Perhaps the most complete and systematic treatment of these themes has been given by Geoffrey Wainwright.[124] Examining all the relevant scriptural texts and early Christian literature, he uses three biblical images to depict the Eucharist—the messianic feast, the expectation of Christ's return, and the firstfruits of the Kingdom.

This recently recovered eschatological dimension can be seen most graphically when the newer characterizations of the Eucharist are contrasted with the older images. Browning and Reed list six emphases in each. The "inherited liturgical imagery common to most Christian traditions" has emphasized

1. The cross and the death of Jesus

2. Sacrifice as the theme of the atoning, saving death of Jesus

3. Memorial and recollection as modes of our participation

4. The past and our sin and guilt, which are relieved by Jesus' sacrificial death

5. Communion as personal meeting with Christ

6. The supper as a somber event where we recall death on the Cross, our sin, and costly salvation[125]

---

122. "The Meaning of the Lord's Supper in Primitive Christianity," in Oscar Cullmann and F. J. Leenhardt, *Essays on the Lord's Supper,* trans. J. G. Davies (London: Lutterworth Press, 1971).
123. Ibid., 23.
124. Geoffrey Wainwright, *Eucharist and Eschatology* (New York: Oxford University Press, 1981).
125. Browning and Reed, 168.

According to these authors, a contrasting imagery has been rediscovered and introduced by recent historical and liturgical scholarship, whose characteristics are

1. Resurrection, emphasizing the risen Christ
2. Banquet of joy and festivity
3. The presence of Christ as the host of a present celebration
4. The future and the coming kingdom of God
5. Communion as fellowship, our meeting together in Christ
6. The supper as a luminous, happy event where we celebrate in a festive mood[126]

This change of emphases has been brought about by "the discovery of eschatology as a key to understanding the essential character of the Lord's Supper."[127] It is imperative that we understand that the second set of emphases does not cancel out the first set of more traditional themes. Each set of images complements the other.

There can be no doubt that eschatology is a prominent biblical theme. In the Old Testament, the Passover was celebrated as a commemoration of God's mighty redemptive acts in the *past*. But the Jews also viewed the Passover meal as an anticipation of the Messianic Banquet when God's will would be finally accomplished through the coming of the Messiah. If the Last Supper that Jesus ate with His disciples was some kind of Passover meal (which we have concluded as being likely), then Jesus builds upon both past and future as He institutes the Eucharist. One can say, with Berkhof, that "God's way with Israel was from one meal to the other"—from the Passover meal, where the deliverance from Egypt was celebrated each year, to the "meal of the great future" where God will abolish death, wipe away all tears, and prepare His rich banquet on Mount Zion (Isaiah 25).[128] One of Wainwright's designations for the Lord's Supper is "antepast of heaven."[129] We may call it the "appetizer" for the Messianic Banquet!

---

126. Ibid.
127. Ibid., 168-69.
128. Berkhof, 362.
129. Wainwright, chap. 2.

The Old Testament opens the way for our understanding of the eschatological significance of the Lord's Supper. At the making of the covenant at Mount Sinai, which was sealed with the sprinkling of blood, there was eating and drinking afterward (Exod. 24:8-11). In a statement rich with meaning, it is said that Israel's leaders "saw God, and they ate and drank," yet God was not displeased (v. 11). The relation between the covenant made on Mount Sinai and the new covenant is seen in the words of Jesus: "This is my blood of the covenant" (Matt. 26:28; Mark 14:24).

In the Pentateuch, the historical books, and in the wisdom literature, there are various references to eating and drinking in connection with religious rites. In most of them the feasting in God's presence takes place in the *present*. But in the prophets such eating and drinking takes on a *future* reference.

In Isaiah 49 and 55 and Ezekiel 34, God will feed His people during their deliverance from Babylonian captivity and restoration to their homeland. The same note is heard in Zech. 9:16-17, and Isaiah 25 speaks of "a *future* feast for *all peoples*, in a context of *the abolition of death* and a *day of salvation and rejoicing*."[130] Similar themes are found in the intertestamental literature, with strong eschatological significance.[131]

In the New Testament, Jesus speaks about eating and drinking in the kingdom of God and relates this to the Eucharist. In passages such as Matt. 8:11 and Luke 13:29, Jesus uses the image of eating and drinking to picture the future salvation in the Kingdom. In Luke 12:35-38, a parable urging vigilance, most likely pointing to His second coming, the servants are commended whom the master finds awake when he comes from the marriage feast.

Such teachings as these (of which there are many more examples) are acted out during the ministry of Jesus on the many occasions when He participated in a meal. Such meals formed a focus of fellowship between Him and His disciples while He was still with them. "Can you make the guests of the bridegroom fast while he is with them?" (Luke 5:34). But Jesus also

---

130. Ibid., 21.
131. Cf. ibid., 21-25.

ate deliberately with tax collectors and sinners. His invitation to eat with Him was universal, and often sinners sought to eat with Him. But merely dining with Jesus was no guarantee of admission to the feast of the Kingdom. Rather, sinners were invited *to repent* (Luke 13:25-27). The miracle of the feeding of the 5,000 is given messianic significance in the Fourth Gospel, even though the people interpreted it in political terms (John 6: 14-15). These are only a few examples of the meals of Jesus' ministry.[132]

Is there a relation between the meals Jesus ate during His earthly ministry and the sacrament of the Lord's Supper? Whether or not the Last Supper was a Passover meal, it was a fellowship meal Jesus ate with His chosen disciples—the last of a series of meals they had taken together, the last meal before the Bridegroom was to be removed from His friends (Mark 2:19), the last time He would drink the fruit of the vine until He drank it new with them in the Kingdom (Matt. 26:29). "The Last Supper was apparently intended to be the last of the parabolic meal-signs dispensed by the man who had come eating and drinking, and next would come the full feasting of the kingdom."[133] Thus it was both the *fulfillment* of the meal-signs of the coming Kingdom that Jesus had given during His ministry, and a sign *pointing toward* the future Messianic Banquet of the Kingdom. The first is a taste of the second; it is a *real* taste, but not the *full* taste. It is Christ who feeds us when we come to His table, but His glory is not directly seen or comprehended. The Kingdom is both "already" and "not yet." In the words of one of the eucharistic hymns of the Wesleys,

> *Come, let us join with one accord*
> *Who share the supper of the Lord,*
> *   Our Lord and Master's praise to sing;*
> *Nourish'd on earth with living bread,*
> *We now are at His table fed,*
> *   But wait to see our heavenly King;*

---

132. The reader is referred to Wainwright for an exhaustive treatment of all the relevant texts, in which no stone is left unturned in the search for the significance of these meals for the *future* Kingdom.

133. Ibid., 35.

> *To see the great Invisible*
> *Without a sacramental veil,*
>   *With all His robes of glory on,*
> *In rapturous joy and love and praise*
> *Him to behold with open face,*
>   *High on His everlasting throne.* [134]

This clear eschatological note of the Eucharist, so obvious in the New Testament, was scarcely heard at all during the Protestant Reformation. Demanding most attention were the debates with Rome concerning the repeated sacrifice of Christ in the Mass and the internal disputes regarding the nature of Christ's presence in the Eucharist. Wainwright correctly observes that it was not until the Wesleys published their *Hymns on the Lord's Supper* in 1745 that "the Western church achieved again a rich appreciation of the eucharist as the sign of the future banquet of the heavenly kingdom."[135] These hymns (166 of them in all) constitute a valuable but sadly neglected resource for celebrations of the Lord's Supper in Wesleyan/holiness churches.

The eschatological perspective of the Eucharist is closely related to our designation of the Lord's Supper as "the sacrament of sanctification." Wesley spoke of justification and sanctification as "those two grand branches" of salvation.[136] Justification is what God does for us by His Son, and sanctification is what God works in us by His Spirit.[137] Thus justification looks *backward* to Christ's first coming and is an appropriation by faith of what He did for us in the Cross. Although sanctification also is provided by the Blood of atonement, its focus is on the *future.* That is, it anticipates the kingdom of God and experiences it proleptically. To live in this world through the power of the Spirit is to live the life of eternity, the life of the Kingdom. Although sanctification, in Wesley's understanding, has instantaneous as well as gradual aspects, it is never, as we have already pointed out, a static state that "does not admit of a continual increase."[138] The life of Christian perfection is an "already, but

---

134. *Hymns on the Lord's Supper,* no. 93; Osborn 3:283-84.
135. Wainwright, 56.
136. *Works* 6:509.
137. Ibid. 5:56.
138. Ibid. 6:5.

not yet" life. Sanctification belongs to the eschaton, but this eschatological reality may be received proleptically (and always only approximately) in the midst of our personal history. The Eucharist, the meal of the Kingdom, opens up the vision of the divine rule that has been promised as the final renewal of the creation, and is a foretaste of it. This promised divine rule is cosmic, communal, and personal. Sanctification is occurring when we are opening ourselves to that divine rule. We open ourselves to that divine rule when we "draw near . . . in full assurance of faith" (Heb. 10:22) and receive the bread and the cup.

Chapter Eight

EUCHARIST AND EVANGELISM

Another topic clamors for attention in a study of the place of sacraments in Wesleyan spirituality, due to the importance given to evangelism within the Wesleyan/holiness tradition. Although the treatment of this topic can be brief, it is sufficiently important to merit a chapter of its own.

A. A CONVERTING ORDINANCE

To speak of Eucharist as the "sacrament of sanctification," as we have done in the preceding chapter, may seem to undercut the present topic. For Wesley, the Lord's Supper was also a *converting* ordinance. For some Wesleyans this may seem to be a contradiction. But it is a problem only for those Wesleyans who have a static, "wooden" concept of both conversion and sanctification and who fail to appreciate Wesley's dynamic understanding of each. For Wesley, salvation was "not a once-for-all experience but a dynamic relation needing moment-by-moment cultivation."[1]

To call the Eucharist a converting ordinance might appear, on the surface, to be a contradiction for denominations such as the Church of the Nazarene, whose ritual for the Lord's Supper invites to the table only those "who have with true repentance

---

1. Dunning, 560.

251

forsaken their sins" (past tense). It is less a problem in The Wesleyan Church and the Free Methodist church, whose invitations are to those who "truly and earnestly repent" (present tense). But in each case the problem is more imagined than real, as we shall see. We must not forget that the stipulation about repentance in these invitations is essentially identical to that of the Methodist and Anglican rituals, from which, of course, it is copied.

In some Wesleyan/holiness denominations, especially the Church of the Nazarene, evangelism and church growth have been overarching concerns in recent years, having almost become the proverbial tail that wags the dog. Attention was called to this in chapter 1. Such concerns receive far more official attention than concern for worship and sacraments. *There is a supreme irony in the spectacle of present-day Wesleyans, with great concern for evangelism, plainly neglecting one of the most meaningful tools for evangelism ever conceived within their own tradition!*[2]

To understand this aspect of Wesley's doctrine of the Lord's Supper, it is necessary to see the importance of this sacrament in his soteriology as a whole, and the position it occupies in his *ordo salutis* ("order of salvation"). He explains "that the Lord's Supper was ordained by God, to be a means of conveying to men either *preventing,* or *justifying,* or *sanctifying* grace, according to their several necessities."[3]

We will consider these different stages of grace in reverse order. In the preceding chapter we took note of Wesley's belief that the Eucharist conveyed *sanctifying* grace, and this needs no further attention here. But he believed the Eucharist conveyed *justifying* grace also, and the sacrament could thus be called a converting ordinance. The evidence for this is abundant and unmistakable. He was persuaded of it by the testimony of both experience and Scripture. Against the argument that only those who were converted and were "believers in the full sense" should communicate,[4] he appeals to the scriptural account of the Last Supper and to the experience recorded there.

---

2. At least one cause of this neglect is the misunderstanding, discussed earlier, of Paul's words about eating and drinking "in an unworthy manner." See chapter 7, section D, on "Fellowship of the Faithful."

3. *Works* 1:280, italics mine. A similar statement is made in Wesley's discussion of all "The Means of Grace" in the sermon by that title, ibid. 5:187.

4. The term, in this context, means "to receive Communion."

"The falsehood of the . . . assertion appears both from Scripture precept and example. Our Lord commanded those very men who were then unconverted, who had not yet received the Holy Ghost, who (in the full sense of the word) were not believers, to do this 'in remembrance of' him. Here the precept is clear. And to these he delivered the elements with his own hands. Here is example equally indisputable."[5]

He understood justification and the new birth to be concomitant, and these were part of being converted in the "full sense." This is obvious from the above assessment of the disciples' spiritual state at the Last Supper. That Wesley viewed them as "unconverted" and "not believers" has puzzled many in the Wesleyan/holiness tradition, who have tended to look upon those men as believers. The matter becomes clear if two things are understood: (1) For Wesley, there are degrees in every aspect of spirituality—degrees of faith, of love, of assurance, of holiness, of perfection. He does not deny that the disciples were believers in some sense, as the parenthetical words in his statement show. For him, "conversion" meant faith in the "full sense." This is explained by the next point: (2) For Wesley, the "converted" person, the "believer in the full sense" was one who had received the Holy Spirit. Therefore he can say, "The Apostles themselves had not the proper Christian faith till after the day of Pentecost."[6]

He could say the same for the spiritual state of Cornelius previous to Peter's visit and the outpouring of the Holy Spirit on all the Gentiles present: "It is certain, in the Christian sense, Cornelius was then an unbeliever. He had not then faith in Christ."[7] In the sermon "Salvation by Faith," Wesley holds that "the faith through which we are saved . . . is not barely that which the Apostles themselves had while Christ was yet upon earth" but is a faith that "acknowledges the necessity and merit of his death, and the power of his resurrection."[8] "Conversion,"

---

5. *Works* 1:279-80.
6. Ibid. 8:291. As we have noted in chapter 5, Wesley did not distinguish between "receiving the Spirit" and "being filled with the Spirit," as many of his followers have tended to do. For him the expressions were synonymous.
7. *NT Notes,* Acts 10:4.
8. *Works* 5:9.

to Wesley, meant *evangelical* conversion—having the "faith of a son," not merely the "faith of a servant." The pre-Pentecost disciples, though "unconverted" and not believers in the full sense (having only the "faith of a servant"), were nevertheless "justified" under the terms of the old covenant.[9]

What Wesley learned from these New Testament examples was doubtless augmented by the experience of his own mother. Susanna Wesley gave testimony that she was brought to the full assurance of faith while partaking of the Lord's Supper. She was 70 years old at the time. It was not long after the Aldersgate experience of her son John and the similar "heartwarming" experience of her son Charles just a few days earlier. Of course, she had long lived a life of devotion and spiritual discipline, and at first had been skeptical of these inward experiences of her sons. But she had her own "warmed heart" experience at a Communion service while her son-in-law Hall, an Anglican clergyman, was pronouncing the words "The blood of our Lord Jesus Christ, which was given for thee." Those words, she says, "struck through my heart, and I knew God for Christ's sake had forgiven *me* all *my* sins."[10]

It is clear, therefore, that Wesley viewed the Eucharist as a converting ordinance at least in a somewhat restricted and relative sense. At the Lord's table a person with weak faith (that is, one not yet converted in the full new covenant sense) could be "converted" to faith "in the full sense."

But did he believe it to be also a converting ordinance for those with no faith at all, who were not believers in any sense? Appealing to the authority of experience, he tells of a woman who,

> when many . . . laboured to persuade her she had no faith, replied, with a spirit they were not able to resist, "I know that the life which I now live, I live by faith in the Son of God, who loved me, and gave himself for me: And He has never left me one moment, since the hour *He was made known to me in the breaking of bread.*"[11]

---

9. Cf. his comments on John 14:23 and 15:3, in *NT Notes.*
10. *Works,* 1:222.
11. Ibid., 1:248, italics mine.

From this "undeniable matter of fact," Wesley infers:

> (1) That there are means of grace, that is, outward ordinances, whereby the inward grace of God is ordinarily conveyed to man; whereby the faith that brings salvation is conveyed to them who before had it not. (2) That one of these means is the Lord's Supper. And, (3) That he who has not this faith ought to wait for it, in the use both of this, and of the other means which God hath ordained.[12]

At first glance, the third inference seems to contain an ambiguity. He speaks of *not having faith* and of *waiting for it* at the same time. This raises the question: Does not "waiting for" faith, while using the means of grace, imply that some degree of faith already exists? Wesley would undoubtedly say yes. Again the key to understanding lies in his concept of "degrees" of faith. In this case the degree of faith present when one is "waiting for it" is something less than "the faith that brings salvation."

In countering those who asserted that the Lord's Supper is not a converting ordinance, but only a confirming one, Wesley replies:

> But experience shows the gross falsehood of that assertion. . . . Ye are the witnesses. For many now present know, the very beginning of your conversion to God (perhaps, in some, the first deep conviction) was wrought at the Lord's Supper. Now, one single instance of this kind overthrows the whole assertion.[13]

Thus it is clear that Wesley believed the Eucharist conveyed not only sanctifying grace but, prior to that, justifying grace also.[14]

But how are we to understand his assertion that the Lord's Supper conveys *preventing* (or prevenient) grace, which is prior even to justification? Since prevenient grace is the grace that "comes before" justification, does Wesley intend for the unbeliever to be invited to the table to receive it? And if prevenient grace needs to be received, does this mean that such a person does not now have it?

---

12. Ibid.
13. Ibid., 279.
14. Although sanctification, for Wesley, begins in the moment of justification, the latter is theologically prior, being the ground of the former. One factor in the rise of

These questions create certain problems for the student of Wesley. Since he insists that all living persons have prevenient grace, unless they have quenched the Spirit,[15] the necessity of having this grace bestowed in the Lord's Supper would seem to imply that it has been lost by quenching the Spirit. This would in turn imply a lack of any thirst for spiritual things. But in the same passage where prevenient grace is included in those graces given in the Lord's Supper, Wesley states as conditions for receiving the sacrament "a desire to receive whatsoever he pleases to give . . . a sense of our state, of our utter sinfulness and helplessness."[16] These conditions, by Wesley's own definitions, are incapable of being fulfilled by one who is without prevenient grace. They would seem, therefore, to exclude such a one from the Lord's table.

However, when he was challenged on this point by Thomas Church, in an attempt to prove that Wesley did not preach faith to be necessary in the recipient at the Lord's Supper, Wesley replies, "But I include abundantly more in that desire than you seem to apprehend," for "neither can this sense of our utter helplessness subsist without earnest desires of universal holiness."[17] Once more, Wesley's concept of "degrees" comes into play.[18] Regardless of the measure of prevenient grace we have been given, if we respond positively to the grace that we have, we will be given more grace and will be moved further along the road toward the point where we can believe for salvation. We must not, therefore, misconstrue his insistence that the Eucharist may be a converting ordinance to imply that the sacrament conveys saving grace without any faith at all on the part of the recipient.

> *Gross misconceit be far away!*
> *Through faith we on His body feed;*
> *Faith only doth the Spirit convey*

Methodism, he says, was the discovery by Charles and himself "that men are justified before they are sanctified." Ibid. 8:300. Of course, when *entire* sanctification is under discussion, justification's priority is also *chronological* as well as theological.

15. Ibid. 6:512; 7:374.
16. Ibid. 1:280. Cf. Borgen's more detailed discussion of these problems, 195 ff.
17. *Letters* 2:231.
18. Cf. Borgen, 196.

> *And fills our souls with living bread,*
> *The effects of Jesu's death imparts,*
> *And pours His blood into our hearts.* [19]

And again,

> *Lift your eyes of faith, and look*
> *On the signs He did ordain!*
> *Thus the Bread of Life was broke,*
> *Thus the Lamb of God was slain,*
> *Thus was shed on Calvary*
> *His last drop of blood for me!*
>
> *See the slaughter's Sacrifice,*
> *See the altar stain'd with blood!*
> *Crucified before our eyes*
> *Faith discerns the dying God,*
> *Dying that our souls might live,*
> *Gasping at His death, Forgive!* [20]

In the sermon "On Working Out Our Own Salvation," Wesley delineates the steps that lead to salvation:

> Salvation begins with what is usually termed (and very properly) *preventing grace;* including the first wish to please God, the first dawn of light concerning his will, and the first slight transient conviction of having sinned against him. All these imply some tendency toward life; some degree of salvation; the beginning of a deliverance from a blind, unfeeling heart, quite insensible of God and the things of God. Salvation is carried on by *convincing grace,* usually in Scripture termed *repentance;* which brings a larger measure of self-knowledge, and a farther deliverance from the heart of stone. Afterwards we experience the proper Christian salvation; whereby, "through grace," we "are saved by faith;" consisting of those two grand branches, justification and sanctification. [21]

Since there are several degrees of faith, one need not have the "full assurance of faith" in order to receive these several sac-

---

19. *Hymns on the Lord's Supper,* no. 71; Osborn 3:266.
20. *Hymns on the Lord's Supper,* no. 18; Osborn 3:227-28.
21. *Works* 6:509.

ramental graces. If the seeker is sincere and comes to the Lord's table with a genuine "desire" for God's grace, a sense of helplessness and need before Christ, it is sufficient.[22] But what about the person without any desire for God at all, that is, the one who has quenched the Spirit? To be sure, Wesley refuses Communion to the hardened, impenitent, and inveterate sinner:

> How dreadful is the Mystery,
> Which instituted, Lord, by Thee,
>   Or life or death conveys!
> Death to the impious and profane;
> Nor shall our faith in Thee be vain,
>   Who here expect Thy grace.[23]

But on the basis of all he says on the matter, Wesley undoubtedly believed that if a person responded to the invitation to the Lord's table, with no intent of hypocrisy or mockery, even this meager response would be evidence of desire, repentance, and faith—in some small degree—and such a person Christ would not turn away. Deciding whether another person (or even oneself) has any desire or even any faith is a tricky question. It depends on the perspective. One is reminded of the words of George Macdonald (1824-1905), who was the spiritual mentor of C. S. Lewis: "That man is perfect in faith who can come to God in the utter dearth of his feelings and desires, without a glow or an aspiration, with the weight of low thoughts, failures, neglects, and wandering forgetfulness, and say to Him, 'Thou art my refuge.'"[24]

Viewing faith in this manner, we can understand the contradiction seemingly implied in Wesley's insistence (1) that a person could come to the Eucharist without any faith, and (2) that one must have faith for the Eucharist to be effective. For Wesley, one without saving faith may, in spite of appearances, still have a "degree" of faith. Such faith "as a grain of mustard seed" is enough for one to bring to the table of the Lord.

The persons for whom the Lord's Supper was ordained, ac-

---

22. Ibid. 1:280.
23. *Hymns on the Lord's Supper,* no. 56; Osborn 3:255.
24. C. S. Lewis, ed., *George Macdonald: An Anthology* (Garden City, N.Y.: Doubleday and Co., 1962), 31.

cording to Wesley, "are all those who know and feel that they want the grace of God, either to restrain them from sin, or to show their sins forgiven, or to renew their souls in the image of God."[25] Here we see how Wesley defines the three graces receivable in the Eucharist:

Prevenient grace—to restrain from sin

Justifying grace—to show their sins forgiven

Sanctifying grace—to renew their souls in the image of God

All three, he insists, are available at the table of the Lord. Those who have found reconciliation through Christ and are "perfecting holiness out of reverence for God" (2 Cor. 7:1) are invited to come. Those who are still without saving faith but have ever so slight a desire for it are invited to come. With this latter conviction of their progenitor, present-day Wesleyans may not feel altogether comfortable, but Wesleyanism in its classical form knows it must keep the table open.

B. THE OPEN TABLE

Churches in the Wesleyan/holiness tradition have never practiced "closed Communion" in the sense of barring from the sacrament those from other denominations, traditions, or theological persuasions. All are invited who "truly and earnestly repent" of their sins. It is at the point of inviting those who have *not yet* "believed in Christ unto salvation" that many present-day Wesleyans may be prone to drag their feet, thus diverging from Wesley. The open invitation to sinners is expressed in this Wesley hymn:

> *Come, to the supper come,*
> *Sinners, there still is room;*
> *Every soul may be His guest,*
> *Jesus gives the general word;*
> *Share the monumental feast,*
> *Eat the supper of our Lord.*[26]

---

25. *Works* 1:280. The word "want" in this statement may be understood either as "desire" or "lack." Either dictionary definition fits the context. But since "desire" is a prominent word used by Wesley elsewhere, and since he often uses "want" to mean "lack," it is safe to conclude that it has the latter meaning here.

26. *Hymns on the Lord's Supper,* no. 8; Osborn 3:221.

And in this one:

> *Sinner, with awe draw near,*
> *And find thy Saviour here,*
> *In His ordinances still,*
>   *Touch His sacramental clothes;*
> *Present in His power to heal,*
>   *Virtue from His body flows.* [27]

This emphasis on an open invitation to sinners grows out of the eschatological understanding of the Lord's Supper and is its natural consequence. At the end of the preceding chapter we discussed the Eucharist under the eschatological image, "Foretaste of the Kingdom," and noted that this is a prominent theme in contemporary sacramental theology. It is found also in the thought of Wesley and deserves renewed consideration by Wesley's "grandchildren" in the Wesleyan/holiness churches.

The theme of banqueting with Jesus as a prelude to the Heavenly Banquet in the kingdom of God is found in another of the Wesley hymns:

> *Did Jesus ordain*
> *His supper in vain,*
> *And furnish a feast*
> *For none but His earliest servants to taste?*
>
> *Nay, but this is His will,*
> *(We know it and feel,)*
> *That we should partake*
> *The banquet for all He so freely did make.*
>
> *O that all men would haste*
> *To the spiritual feast,*
> *At Jesus' word*
> *Do this, and be fed with the love of our Lord!*
>
> *Bring near the glad day*
> *When all shall obey*
> *Thy dying request,*
> *And eat of Thy supper, and lean on Thy breast.*

---

27. *Hymns on the Lord's Supper,* no. 39; Osborn 3:243-44.

Then, then let us see
Thy glory, and be
Caught up in the air,
This heavenly supper in heaven to share.[28]

God's call to salvation is universal. He has invited everyone to feast with Him in His final Kingdom. And the invitation to the sacramental Supper, which is the foretaste of that final feast, must therefore likewise be universal. The universality of the invitation makes of every eucharistic celebration an evangelistic or missionary event.[29] It is the offer of salvation to all who will accept; and, as Wainwright says, "On the shadow side, those who will not yet, or who will no longer, accept the invitation are choosing death rather than life, are excluding themselves from salvation."[30]

A parable in the Gospel of Luke sheds light upon this aspect of the Lord's Supper. In Luke 14:7-24, while eating in the house of a prominent Pharisee, Jesus tells two parables about banquets. In each, it is the poor, the crippled, the lame, and the blind who are invited, which causes great surprise at who finally accepts the invitation. The lesson is clear: In God's kingdom our human values are turned upside down.

In Luke 12:35-37 Jesus uses the imagery of a banquet to teach that the time of the Kingdom's advent is unknown; it may come when we least expect it, and we must be always ready and watching. Like the guests in 14:24, these also are surprised. Their surprise occurs when the Master dresses himself to serve, has them recline at the table, and comes to serve them. As Browning and Reed say, "The new time of God is not only a banquet . . . where common values may be turned upside down, it is a meal where the messiah waits upon the tables."[31]

In those two passages, and in many others, the kingdom of God is pictured by Jesus as "a happy fulfillment, as food and drink enough, a banquet where the Christ serves, a banquet hosted, strange to say, by the one who serves."[32]

---

28. *Hymns on the Lord's Supper,* no. 92; Osborn 3:282.
29. Cf. Wainwright, 130.
30. Ibid.
31. Browning and Reed, 170-71.
32. Ibid., 171.

According to Isaiah 25, the kingdom of God is the great banquet of joy in Zion for all nations. According to Luke 13:29, "People will come from east and west and north and south, and will take their places at the feast in the kingdom of God." The meals Jesus ate with His disciples were not exclusive meals of the righteous elite, but meals of the friends of Jesus who share His mission "to seek and to save what was lost" (19:10). Our Christian table fellowship at the Supper should recapture the three factors which, according to Moltmann, characterized Jesus' eating and drinking with His disciples: "(1) The last meal of Jesus with his disciples which anticipated his death on the cross, (2) the table fellowship of Jesus with the poor, and with sinners and publicans, and (3) the prophetic hope for the great banquet of all peoples in Zion."[33] In the light of all this, the table of the Lord must certainly be an open one.

Since God invites everyone to the feast in the final Kingdom, although many will refuse the invitation (Luke 14:18-20), the Church can be assured it is God's will that as many as possible should be brought to enjoy now the meal that is the sign and foretaste of that final feast. Commenting on verse 23, Wainwright finds it strange that the expression "compel them to come in" (KJV) has often inspired the Church in its missionary and evangelistic task, and yet the churches have often taken this mandate out of context, forgetting that it is a part of the parable of the great supper. He says:

> We have pressed them to come in . . . and then left them without food and drink at the meal which is the sign of the great supper of the final kingdom, telling them rather that they must wait several years until by their acquired knowledge and virtues they have earned the right . . . to baptism and, after a further interval, "confirmation" (by whatever name), and only then will they be admitted to the Lord's table.[34]

In the Wesleyan/holiness churches a personal conversion or public profession of faith by a comprehending adult or young person would answer to what Wainwright calls "confirmation

---

33. *Hope for the Church*, 54.
34. Wainwright, 130.

(by whatever name)." Although acknowledging that we have learned from Hippolytus that there was in the Roman church, at the beginning of the third century, a three-year period of preparation before one was baptized, Wainwright asks pointedly: "How long did the Philippian jailor have to wait before he was baptized . . . and the eucharistic table was spread (Acts 16:25-34)?"[35]

This raises another question—one already lurking in the Wesleyan conviction that the Eucharist may be a converting ordinance:

C. ANOTHER QUESTION ABOUT BAPTISM

Elsewhere in this book we have stated that the Lord's Supper is to be celebrated again and again from baptism until death. But what about the person who has never been baptized, who comes to genuinely experience the Eucharist as a converting ordinance? Here we can do no better than to quote Wainwright once again:

> The church must hope and expect that through the words and actions of the eucharistic sign which it performs before the world, God will arouse in those who have not so far committed themselves to His kingdom the desire to share in the blessings of salvation. *No one should be refused communion who has been moved by the celebration of the sign then in progress to seek saving fellowship with the Lord through eating the bread and drinking the wine.*[36]

He continues,

> But then he should be brought to *baptism,* and *soon.* For if he has on this first and exceptional occasion been drawn to the Lord's table as the recipient of a salvation to which he was hitherto a stranger, he has by the very reception of salvation been constituted a witness to the saving work of God: and the company of those who actively proclaim for others the salvation which they themselves receive is the church, to which the normal rite of admission, administered even, or

---

35. Ibid., 204 n. 428. Wainwright here assumes that the meal mentioned in verse 34 had some eucharistic meaning, an assumption that has gained widespread acceptance and which grows out of the contemporary eschatological understanding of the Eucharist.
36. Ibid., 134.

rather precisely, in the case of Cornelius (Acts 10:47f), is bap-tism.[37]

These remarks are especially pertinent to the Wesleyan/holiness churches, where many (if not most) of those who attend, but who make no profession of faith, were not baptized as infants. If and when such persons are moved by Christ's invitation to the Supper, let them be fed! Then *soon* let them be invited to baptism. If baptism is refused, then it is questionable if they are sincere in desiring to enter the Kingdom.[38] They should then be gently and lovingly dissuaded from partaking of the feast again until they are certain that they desire God's kingdom above all earthly ones. "Salvation scorned turns to judgment."[39]

Of course all who have been brought to repentance and faith, no matter by what method of evangelism, should be brought to baptism and Eucharist as soon as possible "so that they may already taste the feast of the future kingdom and share in celebrating the sign of the meal before the world."[40]

* * *

In this chapter we have dealt with a Wesleyan teaching that is largely forgotten by Wesley's "grandchildren" in the Wesleyan/holiness churches. In a day when some more traditional methods of public evangelism, because of past abuses, fail to attract significant numbers of persons to Christ, how meaningful it would be if the invitation to the Lord's table more pointedly included the "outsiders" of whom Jesus spoke in Luke 14:13! Here we are applying this to those who are outsiders to the gospel—those who have not yet "believed in Christ for salvation."

Such persons could be told that their very approach to the table (and receiving that which was broken and shed for them) could be an act of repentance on their part if they will make it so. Such persons Christ will not turn away. Nor should *we*.

---

37. Ibid., 134-35.
38. This follows from everything put forth in this book regarding the place of sacraments in a Wesleyan perspective. However, this is not to denigrate those whose traditions take a different view of sacraments. The truth of God, and of God's ways with us, is greater than any theological tradition can fully capture. We are only saying that if one is to be thoroughly Wesleyan, neither baptism nor Communion should be refused.
39. Wainwright, 135.
40. Ibid.

Chapter Nine

SACRAMENTAL PRACTICE: SOME SUGGESTIONS

The purpose of this chapter is to provide some usable suggestions for the practice of the sacraments. The intention here is to move beyond the theoretical considerations of the previous chapters to a simple list of "how to" suggestions.[1] Some of them may be more helpful than others, but all of them are consistent with the sacramental perspective developed in the previous chapters of this book. Suggestions for baptismal practice and for eucharistic practice will be listed separately. But first, we will consider some general norms by which sacramental practice should be guided.

A. NORMS FOR SACRAMENTAL PRACTICE

James F. White states that the practice of the sacraments should be based on three general norms—*pastoral, theological,* and *historical.* He suggests that a problem in any one of these areas will affect all decisions regarding sacramental practice.

> If one encounters serious problems in any one of these areas, it is time to reconsider before proceeding. One can imagine a triangle with checkpoints at each angle. A course

---

1. The idea for the format of this chapter is borrowed from that of chapter 6 in James F. White's *Sacraments as God's Self Giving,* titled "The Reform of Sacramental Practice." Although many of White's suggestions are not particularly usable in the Wesleyan/holiness churches, some of the following are adapted from White.

of action seems desirable if it can pass inspection at each of the three checkpoints: pastoral, theological, and historical. If so, then one is free to proceed. But if halted at any one angle, then the practice should be reconsidered.[2]

Although we would not follow White in the exact way he applies these norms, we agree that these norms should serve as checkpoints by which sacramental practice is evaluated. We will consider each norm, reversing the order in which they are listed by White.[3]

1. The HISTORICAL norm is that *sacramental decisions should not be made independently from the worship experiences of millions of Christians around the world over the course of 20 centuries.* For John Wesley and classical Wesleyanism, tradition was an authoritative source of religious truth; it was one of the four sides of the so-called Wesleyan Quadrilateral. An understanding of the historic Christian tradition can guide us in distinguishing what is primary from what is secondary, what is culturally conditioned from what is of permanent character. It helps us avoid highly individualistic interpretations that have no historical or biblical foundation. Those who do not learn from history are likely to repeat its mistakes. The sacramental beliefs and practices of people through the centuries cannot be justifiably ignored. Practices that have been tried and discarded in the past are not likely to be feasible in the present, but those that have been constant offer continued promise. This historical checkpoint, for example, alerts us to the fact that infant baptism has passed the test of time far more surely than has infant dedication. Thus the historical checkpoint has helped shape the conclusions about infant baptism stated in chapter 6. It is also the historical checkpoint that prevents the adoption of an exclusively immersionist position, as we will see below.

2. The THEOLOGICAL norm is that *sacramental action must reflect Christian faith.* The claim made in chapter 6 that the question of infant baptism must be decided on theological grounds was an application of the theological norm. Of course there is much doctrinal diversity within Christianity, and this is

2. Ibid., 121.
3. Cf. ibid., 121-24.

particularly true with regard to sacramental doctrine. But within this diversity there is much unity on the central truths. The theological norm prevents sacramental decisions from being made on the grounds of partisan proof-texting. The great central truths of the gospel are usually less subject to controversy than the more peripheral ones. For instance, the idea of *grace* is a central Christian truth, therefore we have allowed it to guide us in our claim in chapter 6 that baptism is an act of God and not merely a human act. Sacraments reflect our understanding of how God does His work in the world. Thus if any sacramental practice seems to conflict with the way Christians generally perceive the way God acts, such practice should be abandoned. For example, we would hold the idea of "closed Communion," in which only the members of a given local church or denomination are invited to the Lord's table, to be in conflict with the universality of the gospel. The theological checkpoint thus filters out practices that fail to truly reflect Christian faith.

   3. The PASTORAL norm is that *sacramental practice must fit the needs of actual people in a specific time and place.* The pastoral norm prompts us to make adjustments from time to time in our practices. For example, it has long been the custom in some communions to serve the wine of the Eucharist from a common chalice. Theologically, this is a better symbolism of the unity of all believers than the use of small individual cups, the latter tending to call attention to separation and stressing individualism rather than the solidarity inherent in the very meaning of the Church as the Body of Christ. But in light of cold viruses and other contagious diseases that may be spread through saliva, the use of individual cups may be preferred. This is an example in which a practice is modified at the pastoral checkpoint, which otherwise meets the theological and historical norms. In another example, which will be considered below (in suggestion number 6 on baptism), cases of "emergency baptism" present pastors with difficult choices. In most such cases, the theological and historical norms may need to be overridden by the pastoral norm, although these will usually be exceptions. At the least, the pastoral norm will require pastors to be sensitive to the way people understand worship and worship practices. This means knowing the people and respecting their cultural backgrounds

and tastes, even as one seeks to enrich the latter. The pastoral norm has a "situational" aspect that is essential for determining how to make sacraments most effective in a given context.

With these three norms in mind, we now offer several suggestions for sacramental practice, first on baptism and then on the Eucharist.

B. SUGGESTIONS FOR BAPTISMAL PRACTICE

1. *Infant baptism and infant dedication should not be confused.* This would appear to be obvious, but occasionally a Wesleyan/holiness minister will use water in dedicating a child, even when baptism is clearly not the choice. This is inappropriate. Water belongs to baptism, not dedication. When a minister is supposed to be dedicating a baby but uses water in the ceremony, it confuses the two rites. It probably confuses parents and congregation as well.

2. *Neither infant dedication nor infant baptism should be mixed with other ceremonial actions of doubtful meaning and value.* For example, in dedicating a child, some ministers have been known to sprinkle the child's head with a rose that has been dipped in a bowl of water. This is probably an attempt to avoid the appearance of baptism while coming as close to it as possible by the use of water! Or some ministers may use a rose in this manner when actually *baptizing* an infant. In any case, it is a dubious practice with no historical or theological meaning and should be avoided. Some may like to do it just because it "looks nice"—an extremely poor reason for performing a sacramental act whose meaning is identification with the death of Christ. The Crucifixion did not "look nice"! The result of such innovations is a profound sentimentalizing of the event. "The rose as symbol obscures and confuses water as symbol."[4]

Another confusing practice, which is seen occasionally when a child is dedicated, is that of anointing the child with oil. Historically, this practice is associated with the three Roman Catholic sacraments that are believed to convey a character, namely, baptism, confirmation, and ordination. Since dedication does not imply any conveyance of grace but is only a pledge on

---

4. Browning and Reed, 63.

the part of the parents, the use of oil can only confuse. Wesley did not believe in confirmation as a sacrament, and Wesleyan/holiness people do not practice it. Another use of oil is for the anointing of the sick, based on James 5:14. Certainly oil should not be associated with infant dedication. Then if not water and not oil, what "outward sign" should be used in dedication? The answer is: *None!* Dedication is not a sacrament, therefore it does not require an "outward sign." To use one is to presume to re-write Christian history!

3. *Infant baptism should be practiced only when the parent, parents, or guardians are professing Christians who promise to bring up the child in an environment of faith.* An exception might be made for a child when someone promises to be a sponsor as surrogate for the parents. But this is problematic, given the mobility of modern society. Baptism should not be practiced indiscriminately or promiscuously when there is little likelihood of many of them being brought to faith. Such practice is what Bonhoeffer called "cheap grace." Infant baptism, he insisted, should be administered "only where there is a firm faith present," otherwise it "is not only an abuse of the sacrament, it betokens a disgusting frivolity in dealing with the souls of the children themselves."[5] Such practice is one reason why the baptism of infants has fallen into disfavor in many churches and been criticized by theologians such as Karl Barth and Jürgen Moltmann. But, as we have said before, the misuse of a valid rite of the church does not invalidate its rightful use. If baptism is denied when parents are not practicing Christians, should they eventually become Christians, the children can always be baptized at a later date. As James F. White declares, "Baptizing without the likelihood of faith development makes baptism little more than a magical act, a talisman for protection."[6] Baptism is always an act that demands commitment, either from the candidates themselves or from someone who assumes responsibility for leading them toward maturity in faith. If baptism (or dedication, for that matter) should be requested by parents who themselves make

---

5. Dietrich Bonhoeffer, *The Cost of Discipleship*, trans. R. H. Fuller (New York: Macmillan Co., 1963), 261.

6. *Sacraments*, 126.

no profession of faith, the pastor is thereby presented with an excellent opportunity for counseling and for leading them to faith in Christ.

4. *Baptism, for either infants or adults, should be performed only when there is adequate instruction and counseling of the candidates or their parents.* It cannot be assumed that parents are fully aware of the responsibilities they undertake for their child in baptism. Nor can it be assumed that every youth or adult who requests baptism understands the ethical changes and creedal commitments that this act demands. Baptism is so important that it should not occur without adequate preparation. We learn from Hippolytus that the Early Church could require as long as three years of preparation for baptism.[7] Although this was quite rigorous, those who had been through it were willing to die (and often did) for their faith.

5. *A person who was baptized as an infant, upon coming to maturity and confessing personal faith in Christ, should be encouraged to publicly acknowledge and own the vows taken earlier on his or her behalf by the parents.* In some traditions this has been called "owning the covenant." The inappropriateness of rebaptism was discussed in chapter 6. Normally, baptism should never be repeated. Any practice that might be interpreted as rebaptism should be avoided. But it is appropriate that churches provide opportunity for the reaffirmation of one's baptismal vows. In the Wesleyan/holiness tradition this will usually involve a personal confession of faith by the baptized person when he or she reaches maturity (a personal conversion).[8] In this tradition, such an experience takes the place of confirmation. But along with this, and as soon after it as practicable, some type of public ritual would be appropriate by which one reaffirms for oneself the baptismal vows taken on his or her behalf by the parents during the person's infancy.

6. *Allowance should be made for special cases in the matter of baptism.* Stookey suggests two examples of such special cases: One special case is that of emergency baptism. "A distraught fa-

---

7. Dix, 28.
8. The word "usually" here allows for the kind of exception that is possible in Wesley's understanding. The reader is referred back to the section on "Baptismal Regeneration?" in chapter 6.

ther phones the pastor from the hospital. 'My wife just had a baby,' he says. 'The doctor tells us the baby probably will not live more than a few hours. Can you come over and baptize our child?'" Or the request may come from an older person: "My husband," says the caller, "was critically injured in an accident and is asking to be baptized. Will you come?" In the first example, says Stookey, "the theologically astute pastor can think of several reasons to decline the request." But he goes on to say, "Yet in both situations, the pastor usually honors the request. . . . There is such a thing as pastoral theology that draws upon systematic theology and yet knows that the textbooks on doctrine cannot cover all cases, and that the Gospel is offered to those in deep human need."[9] In these cases the pastoral norm tells us that the parents and the dying man need visible assurance of God's graciousness and of incorporation into a supporting community. The reasons for the requests may be misguided and even partly irrational. But in such instances, as Stookey says, "Neither reasoned systems of dogmatics nor exhortations on covenant responsibility will accomplish much. Pastoral instinct says, 'Go. Baptize. Explain and exhort later, if necessary.'"[10]

It is at the point of "explaining later" that many pastors fail their responsibility. Such failure has only increased the requests and misconceptions. If the baptized person dies, the pastor should help the family work through the grief process. If the person regains health, the implications of baptism need to be worked through. The baptized need to be presented to the congregation during a worship service, with the congregation pledging its commitment and support. A public reafffirmation of the baptismal covenant may be appropriate. Every effort should be made to integrate the baptized person into the life of the local church.

Whenever adults who do not know whether or not they were baptized as infants, and have no way of finding it out, seek baptism, the pastoral norm will usually dictate that baptism be administered in such cases.

7. *Although the historical and theological norms strongly cau-*

---

9. Stookey, 57.
10. Ibid., 58.

tion against rebaptism, there could possibly be cases where the pastoral norm requires it. In our earlier discussion, we attempted to present the best course of action in an ideal situation, based on theological grounds. But often situations arise that are not ideal. A person who was baptized as an infant, was away from the church for many years, and experiences a vital conversion may strongly desire to be baptized in a way that is meaningful to him or her *now.* The pastoral norm may cause the wish to be granted. But this should not be done lightly. Every attempt to counsel and instruct such a person should be made first. The meaning of baptism and the implications of rebaptism should be clarified for such a person. If the efforts at instruction and counseling still do not satisfy, and the person insists on adult baptism, the pastoral norm will allow the felt need to be met. It is better to bend theological rules than to hang a millstone around a convert's neck! Still, the pastor should understand that what he or she is doing is just that—bending the theological rules. It is an accommodation of the ideal.

8. *Every infant baptism should be a renewal of baptism for every baptized adult who is present.* It is not the minister who baptizes, but the church on whose behalf the minister acts. All baptized adults should see themselves as participating in the child's baptism. It should also be an occasion when they go back to the meaning of their own baptism and renew the spirit of it. Baptism is not only *by* the church but also *for* the church. The whole church utters its repentance, resolves anew, prays anew, to be faithful to the end. P. T. Forsyth says:

> In this high, true, practical sense the whole Church of the baptized undergo adult Baptism at each infant Baptism. They go through consciously what they were put through unconsciously at the first. They are not *spectators* of a Baptism—they *assist.* And they do not only assist, they *participate* in the Baptism.[11]

Infant baptism should thus be made an act of worship by the entire congregation. From this, there follows the next suggestion:

9. *Baptism should be a public event in the midst, and in full*

---

11. Forsyth, 182.

view, of the congregation. Almost as important as the use of water in baptism is the presence of a community of faith. As we noted in chapter 5, baptism incorporates a person into the Body of Christ. It is always into a community that one is baptized, and the presence and participation of that community is an essential part of the sacrament. James F. White says: "It is difficult to signify becoming part of 'a people claimed by God for his own' (1 Pet. 2:9) if that people is absent."[12]

10. *It should be made clear to adult candidates for baptism that they have a choice as to the mode of baptism.* Here, of course, we have in mind those churches in which the candidate does have a choice. These include most of the larger denominations in the Wesleyan/holiness tradition, and especially those that adhere most closely to their Methodist background. Pastors in these churches, especially those pastors whose personal preference is immersion, sometimes fail to inform new members of the available options. Three main modes have been practiced in the history of the church. They are *aspersion, affusion,* and *immersion*—the first two being more commonly called sprinkling and pouring, respectively.

Of course, Baptists insist that immersion is the only valid mode. In discussing the subject of infant baptism in chapter 6, we noted that it cannot be conclusively shown either that it *was* or *was not* practiced in the New Testament. The same is true with respect to the mode of baptism. The immersionist argument rests on two contentions: (1) that *baptizō* means to immerse, and (2) that passages like Rom. 6:3-6 and Col. 2:11-12 imply that the death and resurrection of Christ provide the pattern for immersion. As for the first argument, the Greek word *baptizō* and its cognates in the New Testament and in the Septuagint do not always refer exclusively to immersion, although that is one of the meanings.[13] In classical usage, *baptizein* generally meant "to dip," and this does not necessarily mean that the thing dipped was totally submerged (for example, the bread that Jesus dipped in the dish, in John 13:26). Due to geography and

---

12. *Sacraments,* 127.
13. Cf. Arndt and Gingrich, 131-32. For a concise but thorough discussion of the Greek words relevant to the mode of baptism, see John Murray, *Christian Baptism* (Nutley, N.J.: Presbyterian and Reformed Publishing Co., 1977), 9-33.

logistics, some of the baptisms recorded in the New Testament would have been rather difficult (although maybe not completely impossible) to administer by immersion—for example, the 3,000 on the Day of Pentecost, the Ethiopian eunuch in the middle of the desert, and the Philippian jailer. The examples we have are not conclusive. A case can be made for sprinkling from such New Testament references as Heb. 9:10, 13-14; 10:22; and from Ezek. 36:25 in the Old Testament. *Baptizein* can hardly mean immersion in Luke 11:38 and 1 Cor. 10:2.[14]

The second immersionist contention is that the symbolism of being "buried" and "raised" with Christ in Rom. 6:4 and Col. 2:12 implies immersion. But as we have already pointed out, this imagery does not bring to mind thoughts of water but of death and an empty tomb. To be facetious, one could say that those texts could be carried out more literally by shoveling dirt over a person, not submerging him or her in water! Water is a singularly unlikely symbol for the earth in which a dead person is buried.[15] Various images are used in the New Testament for baptism (fire, water, a grave, new birth, putting off old clothes and putting on new ones), and none of these images can legitimately be singled out as determining the mode. If these passages are to be taken as literally indicating a mode of baptism, why is 1 Cor. 12:13 not taken literally to mean that at Corinth baptism was administered by having the candidate drink a cup of water: "For we were all baptized by one Spirit into one body . . . and we were all given the one Spirit to drink"? In the New Testament references to baptism the primary symbolism of water is that of washing, not of burial. Paul's use of the burial imagery therefore must be understood figuratively rather than as literally dictating a mode—that is, in baptism (by any mode) the old sinful life is "buried" with Christ, and one is "raised" to a new life.

One of the New Testament uses of the word "baptism" is in

---

14. Since it is not the purpose of this book to argue for the exclusive priority of one mode of baptism over another, but only to point out the usefulness of some neglected modes, no attempt is made here to examine all the relevant biblical references.

15. Of course, in burials at sea, the dead person is "buried" in water, but this is an exception born of necessity, and hardly an image that Paul, a Jew, would have found attractive, since the Jews were not essentially a seafaring or sea-loving people. In John's vision of the new heaven and the new earth, "there was no longer any sea" (Rev. 21:1).

John the Baptist's promise of a baptism "with [or in] the Holy Spirit and with fire" (Matt. 3:11; Luke 3:16) and its fulfillment on the Day of Pentecost. If baptism means immersion then John's statement that Jesus would baptize with the Holy Spirit and fire must mean strictly, "He will *immerse* you with [or in] the Holy Spirit and with fire." But what we actually find in the records is that the baptism with the Holy Spirit is referred to in terms that contradict and preclude immersion. The images are those of the Holy Spirit "coming upon" them (Acts 1:8). In 2:17, 2:33, and 10:45, the Holy Spirit is "poured out." In 10:44 and 11:15, the Holy Spirit "falls" (KJV) or "comes on" the persons concerned. The terms are all those of affusion (pouring) and not of immersion. Yet this affusion is called a "baptism." It may be added that the Old Testament promises of the giving of the Spirit are stated in terms of pouring out and sprinkling (Isa. 32:15; Joel 2:28; Prov. 1:23; Ezek. 36:25-27). In short, *baptizō* and its cognates may be used to denote immersion, but they may also be used to denote an action that can be performed by different modes.

The preference for immersion basically rests on the idea that the more water there is, and the more of the body that is covered by it, the more valid the baptism is. Such symbolism seems more fitting than sprinkling or pouring. But, by the same logic, if more water meant better baptism, then in the Lord's Supper a scrumptious feast at a table loaded with food would seem to be a more fitting symbol of the coming Heavenly Banquet, of which the Eucharist is a foretaste, than the small amounts of bread and wine usually consumed by the communicant.[16] And it would be a better reenactment of the Last Supper if the communicants reclined on couches as they ate! Such literalistic thinking is a misunderstanding of the nature of symbolism. Implicit in our discussion of "Religious Symbolism" in chapter 2 was the idea that *quantity* or *amount* has no necessary relation to the validity of a symbol. If we may recall the example of a nation's flag as a symbol, it would be ludicrous for an

---

16. Of course, this argument is considered invalid by those who have argued that something more akin to a feast *should* be the norm for the way the Eucharist is celebrated.

American who raises a large flag on his lawn on the Fourth of July to make light of his neighbor's patriotism because the neighbor displays a smaller flag! The value of a symbol is determined not by *quantity* but by its *quality*—its power to unlock "dimensions and elements of our soul which correspond to the dimensions and levels of reality."[17]

Immersion, sprinkling, and pouring each symbolize an aspect of the meaning of baptism. Immersion, in spite of the reservations expressed above, comes closest to symbolizing our union with Christ in His death and resurrection. Sprinkling best symbolizes the cleansing of the heart "from a guilty conscience" (Heb. 10:22) described in 9:13, 19, 21. And baptism by pouring best symbolizes the Pentecostal outpouring of the Holy Spirit.

> Immersion, sprinkling, pouring—dying and rising with Christ, forgiveness, and the gift of the Holy Spirit—all are aspects of the work of Jesus Christ in saving us from death to life. In fact, *each* mode is a way of understanding the *whole* work of Jesus Christ as Savior. Therefore, each mode of baptism participates in the meaning of the other two, so it does not matter which mode is used.[18]

11. *A church's baptismal theology and liturgy should be reflected in the church's architecture.* For example, the Church of the Nazarene mentions in its article of faith on "Baptism" that it "may be administered by sprinkling, pouring, or immersion, according to the choice of the applicant."[19] But, ironically, most of the larger Nazarene church buildings have a baptistry to use for immersion, but one seldom sees in those churches a baptismal font to use for pouring or sprinkling. Instead, when sprinkling or pouring is administered, often some makeshift vessel (perhaps a candy dish!) is used and then hidden away out of sight. This is hardly the statement that a church ought to be making about its sacraments through its architecture! The Free Methodist church and The Wesleyan Church do not mention the mode of baptism in their doctrinal statements but do make the

---

17. Tillich, *DF,* 42.
18. Hardin, Quillian, and White, 112.
19. *Manual,* 1989, 36.

three options available in their rituals for baptism. In all such cases, where options are given, the architecture should reflect the doctrines and provide for *all* the authorized rituals.

12. *There are some practical advantages in promoting sprinkling or pouring as valid modes of baptism.* Most churches in the Wesleyan/holiness tradition allow the candidate to choose the mode of baptism. Where immersion is the prevailing mode, some difficulties are often encountered by the smaller congregations, many of which do not have baptistries in their church buildings. In such cases a neighboring church (perhaps of another denomination) must be borrowed. If that is not feasible, the baptismal services must be conducted in an outdoor body of water. In colder climates, when there are conversions during the winter months, the baptism must be postponed until warm weather permits baptism in a river, creek, lake, or swimming pool (or whatever). This violates the New Testament precedent of baptizing persons as soon after their conversion as possible. How simple it would be to solve such practical problems if sprinkling or pouring were more widely practiced! Most of the Wesleyan/holiness denominations allow a choice of modes anyway, and all that is needed is for those churches to begin to use their own doctrinal and liturgical resources! Then the baptism could be administered at the altar or Communion rail, as a much more integral portion of the worship service than immersion usually makes possible.[20]

13. *Affusion (pouring) should be given more consideration by the churches and their pastors.* Immersion seems to be the choice of most candidates in the Wesleyan/holiness churches. Sprinkling (aspersion) runs a distant second, and pouring (affusion) comes in as a very poor third. But pouring has a longer tradition

20. Although we have said that a church's baptismal theology should be reflected in the church's architecture, and although most Wesleyan/holiness churches recognize three modes of baptism, it might seem to be better stewardship to practice only pouring or sprinkling. Instead of the many thousands of dollars it costs to build a baptistry for immersion, a simple baptismal font can be provided much more economically and the money used for more worthy causes such as world missions or feeding the hungry! But to effect this would require changes in doctrine as well as in practice, in the case of those churches (such as the Church of the Nazarene) whose Articles of Faith mention the acceptability of all three modes. At present, this would appear an unlikely prospect!

behind it than sprinkling. In fact, some authorities believe it to be older than immersion, and the mode practiced in the New Testament. Much early Christian art portrays the candidate standing about knee-deep in water with water being scooped up by hand and poured over the head. It might be impractical to practice that today in most church buildings (although it could be done in the baptistry where immersions are usually administered). Since pouring normally requires more water than sprinkling, it could be a desirable compromise between immersion and sprinkling whenever the former is impossible or impractical and the latter is felt by the candidate to be "too little." Pouring can be administered in both infant and adult baptism. When it is adult baptism, a quantity of water should be used sufficient to be visible to the congregation, perhaps poured from a shell (an early Christian symbol) on the head of the candidate. The main concern should not be with physical appearance such as wet hair or shoulders (after all, baptism is a sacrament of the Church, not a fashion show!), but if desired, something may be draped over the shoulders to prevent undue wetting of clothing. Regardless of how the details are handled, affusion (pouring) should be given greater emphasis than it now enjoys in most Wesleyan/holiness churches. Baptism in this mode has the potential of being more meaningful to a congregation than either immersion or sprinkling.

The suggestion that pouring be given consideration as a more fitting mode than sprinkling may seem to conflict with the claim made above (in suggestion no. 10) that the amount of water does not determine the validity of a symbol. But the point is that the *amount* of water used is of less importance for the congregation than its *visibility*. Remember, sacraments are "visible words." To *see* the water being dipped up and poured out, and even to *hear* the sound of these actions, allows the people a greater participation in the rite (see suggestion no. 9 above). Furthermore, it would seem to avoid most of the objections to sprinkling, in which the amount of water is so small as to be scarcely *seen* by the congregation and *felt* only minimally by the baptizand.

Pouring would seem an especially fitting mode of baptism in the Wesleyan/holiness tradition because of the tradition's historic emphasis on the gift of the Holy Spirit, which was "poured out" on the Day of Pentecost.

14. *Whenever possible, baptism should be a part of the main worship service of the week.* In most Wesleyan/holiness churches this will be the Sunday morning worship service. With few exceptions, this is the service when most of the membership is present, and also when more guests are in attendance. It is important that both groups experience the sacraments being administered. It is one way to proclaim what the Church is all about. Neither sacrament should be "done in a corner," that is, consistently shunted to a service when fewer people are expected to be present. Having baptism in the Sunday morning service is another argument for the options of pouring or sprinkling, either of which can usually be incorporated into that service more easily than immersion. But there is no reason why immersion cannot be administered on Sunday morning also, in churches where there is a baptistry.

We turn now to some suggestions for the practice of the Eucharist.

C. SUGGESTIONS FOR EUCHARISTIC PRACTICE

1. *The Lord's Supper should always be celebrated in conjunction with the reading and preaching of the Word.* In chapter 4, we noted Augustine's description of a sacrament as a "visible word." When the Word of God is enacted visibly, it should also be proclaimed audibly. The Protestant Reformers were insistent that Word and sacrament belong together. This does not mean that the sermon should always take the form of a Communion meditation based on the New Testament "institution" texts. If a pastor's preaching program follows the lectionary readings, the sermon may be an exposition of any of the regular readings for the week. The important matter is that Word and sacrament not be torn asunder.

2. *An atmosphere of celebration, thanksgiving, and praise should characterize the Communion service.* We have already mentioned that often this aspect of the Supper is squelched in favor of a somber, solemn mood. The somber mood is not altogether wrong, in view of the Pauline admonition to remember Christ's death. But it needs to be balanced by the Synoptic picture of

Jesus eating with His disciples and by His parabolic teaching about feasting at the Heavenly Banquet of which the Eucharist is a foretaste. Unfortunately, the atmosphere prevailing at Communion services is sometimes more that of a funeral than of a feast! One way such an atmosphere is created is by having the elements on the table covered with a white linen cloth. Of course there is tradition behind this practice. It once may have reminded people of a meal. This was probably true for our grandparents or great-grandparents in the days before refrigeration when food from the noon meal was left on the table to be eaten at the evening meal. The cloth kept dust and insects away from the food! But it is doubtful if the cloth acts as a meal reminder today. Rather, when worshipers assemble in the church, the view of the table and the elements covered with a cloth may unconsciously give the impression of a funeral bier! At least the practice needs rethinking.

3. *The Supper should be celebrated in such a way as to give the greatest possible symbol value to the actions.* We have seen that the breaking of bread was an important event in the New Testament Church. It is a powerful sign of the unity of the Church and of our oneness in Christ of which the apostle Paul wrote: "Is not the cup of thanksgiving for which we give thanks a participation [koinōnia] in the blood of Christ? And is not the bread that we break a participation [koinōnia] in the body of Christ? Because there is one loaf, we, who are many, are one body, for we all partake of the one loaf" (1 Cor. 10:16-17). In the light of this, the symbol value of the eucharistic action would be enhanced by the breaking of one loaf by the minister in full view of the congregation before the pieces of bread are distributed. It should be a loaf of real unsliced bread. This would be a better "sign" than the distribution of tasteless manufactured wafers or tiny preshaped pieces of bread. Drinking from a common cup or chalice would also be a better sign of unity than the distribution of tiny individual cups, but the pastoral norm may dictate against this, as we mentioned above.

It must be granted that the argument for "real bread" could be used to argue also for "real wine." But the Wesleyan/holiness tradition opts for grape juice. It could ill afford to do otherwise in view of its consistent opposition to the consumption of alcoholic beverages, even though Wesley himself used real wine for the sacrament, and the use of grape juice is a relatively modern idea, first recommended for Methodists in the 1876 *Discipline*. In view of modern societal and familial evils issuing from over-indulgence in alcohol, the Wesleyan/holiness people believe the witness they give to the world by refraining from alcohol would be compromised by the use of real wine in the Eucharist.

4. *The Eucharist should be celebrated more often than is usually the case in most churches in the Wesleyan/holiness tradition.* John Wesley preached that every Christian should receive Communion as often as possible.[21] Several times a week were not too much for him. Some churches, such as the Disciples of Christ, Church of Christ, Roman Catholic, and Eastern Orthodox, observe this sacrament in the main service each week. The recommendation of most Wesleyan/holiness denominations that the Lord's Supper be celebrated at least once every three months seems to give it insufficient importance. Some of these churches have moved to a monthly celebration. Behind the reticence to celebrate it weekly lies the legitimate concern that it not become trite and mechanical, since, according to a well-known adage, "Familiarity breeds contempt." But the same reasoning could prohibit weekly preaching, or worship in general. A weekly Eucharist could be a great blessing, but only under certain conditions. James F. White says: "A weekly celebration of the eucharist under the spirit and form in which it is now performed monthly or occasionally in most Protestant churches would be an unmitigated disaster. . . . it is unduly long, unduly lugubrious, and unduly penitential."[22] If the celebration could emphasize more of the elements enumerated in our above discussion of "Images of the Eucharist," Communion could be observed much more often than at present, and with great benefit. From this follows the next suggestion:

5. *The Lord's Supper should be celebrated, at least some of the times, in the main worship service of the week.* In our suggestions for baptismal practice we said the same thing about the other

---

21. This was one of the two points he made in the sermon "The Duty of Constant Communion," in *Works* 7:147 ff.
22. *Sacraments*, 128.

sacrament. The main service will usually be Sunday morning worship. As noted earlier, this will be the service where the greatest number of church members will likely be present and also where more outsiders will be in attendance. It is important for both groups to *see* the gospel proclaimed visibly as well as to *hear* it proclaimed audibly. Especially in the Wesleyan/holiness tradition, where the doctrine of sanctification is a central tenet, the "sacrament of sanctification" should not be consistently administered in a service with fewer attendees than the main service of the week.

6. *Consideration might profitably be given to the restoration of the Early Church practice of celebrating the Eucharist in conjunction with an Agape meal or love feast.* This would bring into focus the eschatological aspect of the Eucharist that we discussed in chapter 7. We have called the Lord's Supper a foretaste of the *Heavenly* Banquet. But there is an *earthly* aspect to this banquet and the kingdom of God it symbolizes. Standing between our celebration of the Eucharist and the final Kingdom lies the hunger of the world. As a meal open to every Christian, and also open to penitent "publicans and sinners," the eucharistic meal demonstrates the eschatological hope for overcoming the world's hunger. This would be even more graphically demonstrated if poor and homeless people were brought in "from the highways and hedges" and fed a full meal as a true love-feast. One can imagine what an impact it would have on a church if such an Agape meal were served in the fellowship hall, not merely as a time for conviviality and frivolity, but in the spirit of true Christian fellowship and sharing, followed by adjournment to the sanctuary for a celebration of the Lord's Supper. Or the Lord's Supper could even be celebrated at the same tables where the meal has been eaten. To a degree, this would emulate the Last Supper, which was very likely instituted during the eating of a Passover meal. The more the Eucharist takes on the qualities of a meal, the more clearly it will reveal to those who witness it the qualities of the kingdom of God as Jesus described it.

7. *The Lord's Supper should always be a public event with a universal invitation.* This may seem so obvious as not to require mention. In the Early Church the Eucharist was sometimes celebrated behind closed doors, but the reasons for this (such as

persecution) exist hardly at all in places where it is celebrated today. Some rites in the Eastern church practice a form of private Mass by expelling the unbaptized before the Eucharist is celebrated. Roman Catholicism long practiced "private Masses," which were celebrations of the Supper by the priest only. This was one factor in the idea of the "sacrifice of the Mass" that the Reformation attacked so ardently. It is, of course, a disappearing practice. And yet, a type of "private Communion" (or semiprivate) is often seen at weddings in Wesleyan/holiness churches, where as part of the wedding ceremony only the bride and groom are served Communion. This is very improper—a contradiction of the very meaning of the Eucharist! No minister should agree to administer the Lord's Supper to the bride and groom unless every person in the congregation is also invited to participate. To partake of the Lord's Supper in full view of the congregation, while shutting everyone else out, appears a very selfish thing to do. No one will do it who really understands for whom Christ's body was broken and His blood was shed.

The case is a little different in situations where Communion is administered to sick and shut-in persons in their homes or in hospital rooms. Even there, however, all persons present should be given the opportunity to participate. One way to make such an occasion truly significant is for the Eucharist to be served to such persons immediately following a Communion service at the church. The pastor and some chosen representatives from the congregation could take to the sick person some of the same elements that were consecrated and served in church. This would make it an *extension* of the same Supper served at the church, and let the sick person know that he or she is still an integral part of the congregation and has been remembered at the table.

8. *If possible, the people should go forward to the Communion table or kneel at the Communion rail to receive the elements rather than being served in the pews.* In large churches this may not be practical, but the symbolism is better. Moving to assemble around a table or to kneel at a Communion rail signifies our response to Christ's invitation to the Supper. It is in keeping with Wesley and the Methodist tradition. In either method, however, logistics is a problem requiring attention. Order is important,

and yet too much regimentation detracts from the significance of the action. Many factors feed into this problem—the arrangement of the sanctuary, the space between pews, the space near the Communion table, and so forth. Planning is necessary, but "great art conceals art," and the smoothness of the operation should not detract from the freedom and spontaneity characterizing a true celebration. In some ways, and in some church buildings, it may be more meaningful for the people to come whenever they are ready, and from whatever part of the church, rather than being ushered forward pew by pew. But again, the layout of the nave of the church will be a factor. Instructions should be given about when to come forward.

When the bread and wine are served in the pews, the people are sometimes instructed to hold the elements until everyone partakes at the same time. This is one argument for Communion in the pews. There may be value in this—it may symbolize unity. But there is no compelling reason for it, and spills are more likely. As a sign of unity it is less effective than the breaking of bread from a single loaf, already mentioned. There is no special significance in everyone partaking at once. Perhaps a better symbolism is one that may remind us of the pictures we have seen on television newscasts of people in famine-stricken areas being given food from a relief truck. In such situations, no one waits on the others; each one eats when given food. Christians are those who "hunger and thirst for righteousness," and the promise of Jesus is that they will be filled. Does He ask us to wait? This is a different problem, of course, from that which Paul addresses in 1 Cor. 11:20-21 and which we have already discussed.

James White describes a method common in some churches where the people receive Communion, while standing, from ministers and assistants at several Communion stations at the head of each aisle. Then those receiving it may either return to their seats or kneel at the Communion rail to pray as long as they wish.[23] White believes that "nothing detracts from the service more than 'table dismissals'" and that their elimination re-

---

23. Ibid., 130.

duces the length of the service and does not result in fracturing the congregation.[24]

9. *The Lord's Supper should be celebrated in a way that symbolizes the gathering of minister and people around the Table.* This, of course, requires the Communion table to be as close to the people as feasible, and on the same level, and that the minister face the congregation. Until 1965, Roman Catholic priests followed the medieval pattern of celebrating with their back to the congregation as if God were "out there" remote from the people instead of "in the midst." One does not properly turn one's back on the family of God. Some Protestant ministers still follow this practice. It is out of place in Wesleyan/holiness churches. As we noted in the above suggestions on baptismal practice, the architecture of a church should reflect its theology. The architectural setting, including the arrangement and placement of the Communion table, may communicate the nature of the gospel more effectively than a sermon. "If the building contradicts the sermon, the building is more likely to win."[25]

10. A final suggestion could have been included here concerning the use of the Lord's Supper as a converting ordinance, but it has been mentioned in the chapter on "Eucharist and Evangelism." There it was suggested that, in keeping with Wesley's example, even unbelievers could be invited to the Lord's table under certain conditions. The reader is directed again to the last brief paragraph of chapter 8 and the suggestion that "such persons could be told that their very approach to the table . . . could be an act of repentance on their part if they will make it so." No one can lay down rigid rules on exactly how this should be done. But it will require careful explanation. Those ministers convinced that it is worth a try will find ways to make the call clear.

---

24. Ibid., 131.
25. Ibid., 130.

Chapter Ten

THE WESLEYAN DESIGN:
SPIRIT VIA STRUCTURE

In this final chapter little remains to be said. The conclusions have been drawn all along, step by step, and should be obvious at this point in our study.

Consider the title of this chapter as it compares with the title of the first chapter. We began by considering a Wesleyan dilemma. We must end by recognizing a Wesleyan design that has become apparent in our study. We began by characterizing present-day Wesleyan/holiness ambivalence on the sacraments as "spirit *versus* structure." But our study has shown the true Wesleyan way to be "spirit *via* structure."

The dilemma within the Wesleyan/holiness churches of today, described in the first chapter, is very real with regard to worship in general and sacraments in particular. What are we to do with sacraments? Should we give them greater place in the development of spirituality than we have hitherto given them? My answer, of course, is a resounding *yes*. I hope my efforts here will have helped others to share my concern.

The dilemma in Wesley's own thought is also real. We saw that he worked with two models of the church and sometimes struggled to gain a balance between his ingrained respect for things sacramental and corporate on the one hand and his fervent and intensely personal evangelical faith on the other.

And yet it is in this very balance he struggled to achieve

that we find his grand "design." *Both* spirit and structure were important, and they were not mutually exclusive. Structure was not opposed to spirit but was its very conduit. Forms of worship, ordered services, the *Book of Common Prayer,* hymns that directed the soul to God, ancient creeds, written prayers, and the like were the very channels through which God could send His convicting, regenerating, sanctifying Spirit. They were "means of grace." Foremost among the structures were the sacraments.

Around 1726-28, William Law, an Anglican writer of considerable stature, had great influence on John Wesley, helping to shape his doctrine of Christian perfection.[1] Wesley never forsook what he learned from Law on that score. But 30 years later Wesley took sharp issue with Law regarding sacraments and other means of grace. In reply to Law's claim that in the development of spirituality one should seek for no help from men or from books but "wholly leave yourself to God," Wesley asks: "But how can a man 'leave himself wholly to God' in the total neglect of His ordinances?" He insists that "all the externals of religion are in order to the renewal of our soul in righteousness and true holiness." He rejects the idea that the external way and the internal way are two different ways. "There is but one scriptural way wherein we receive inward grace—through the outward means which God hath appointed."[2]

Regarding public worship and sacraments, Law advocated a more mystical worship in which the Lord's Supper is a private affair observed within one's own inner being. He insisted that one well grounded in such inward worship would have no need of outward means and would have learned to "live unto God above time and place." But for Wesley, God's Word and His Spirit "act in connection with each other," and the Bible taught him that we are inwardly to worship God, not *above* time and place, but precisely at specific times and specific places.[3]

However, in seeing the Wesleyan design as "spirit *through* structure," we must not miss the point that what God gives through structure is *spirit.* This means more than a mood, atti-

---

1. *Works* 11:367.
2. *Letters* 3:366-67.
3. Ibid., 367.

tude, tone, or tenor. To be exact, it is *Spirit* (the *Holy* Spirit) that
God imparts through means of grace such as sacraments. Although God has tied himself to the sacraments, He has not *limited* himself to them. It is the Spirit that is sovereign, and not the
structures.

As our subtitle indicates, this book has been about the place
sacraments should have in the development of spirituality in a
Wesleyan mode. In the Preface we gave a brief preliminary definition of spirituality. Perhaps now we are in a position to say
more about it. It may be defined as the awareness of God and
the recognition of the holy in our life and in our world. Spirituality means that our awareness of the sacred has an impact on
our total lives, on the way we live and the choices we make. It
means that we sensitize ourselves to the pull of God and try to
align ourselves with this pull. Involved in spirituality is the understanding that the quest for meaning is our most important
pursuit.

This quest cannot be satisfied with the superficial, the shal-
low, and the subjective. Spirituality is more than emotional titil-
lation or release. Spirituality can be nurtured only on objective
reality, on every word that comes from the mouth of God—the
incarnate Word, the written Word, the preached Word, and the
"visible word" of sacrament. To know that one has been buried
with Christ in baptism and raised to newness of life—that is
spirituality! To eat the bread that is His body and drink the wine
that is His blood—that is spirituality! To "do this in remembrance" of Him who is our Redeemer and coming King, and to
do it with glad anticipation of that day when we shall sit down
with those who have come "from east and west and north and
south" to "take their places at the feast in the kingdom of God"
(Luke 13:29)—that is spirituality!

As I said in the Preface, my purpose in writing this book
was to help my fellow Christians in the Wesleyan/holiness tradition to better appreciate the sacraments and to show that a
clear sacramentalist vision can be a help to holy living. If my
efforts cause just a few persons to share that vision, I will have
been abundantly repaid.

Soli Deo gloria!

WORKS CITED

Aland, Kurt. *Did the Early Church Baptize Infants?* Translated by G. R. Beasley-Murray. Philadelphia: Westminster Press, 1963.

Althaus, Paul. *The Theology of Martin Luther.* Translated by Robert C. Schultz. Philadelphia: Fortress Press, 1966.

Ancient Christian Writers. Edited by Johannes Quasten and Joseph C. Plumpe. Westminster, Md.: Newman Press, 1953.

Aquinas, St. Thomas. *Summa Theologica.* 3 vols. Translated by Fathers of the English Dominican Province. New York: Benziger Brothers, 1947.

Arndt, W. F., and Gingrich, F. W. *A Greek-English Lexicon of the New Testament and Other Early Christian Literature.* Chicago: University of Chicago Press, 1957.

Augustine, St. "Tractus on the Gospel of John." 80.15.3. *Nicene and Post-Nicene Fathers.* 1st ser. Grand Rapids: Wm. B. Eerdmans Publishing Co., 1978.

Aulén, Gustaf. *The Faith of the Christian Church.* Translated by Eric H. Wahlstrom. Philadelphia: Muhlenberg Press, 1960.

Baillie, Donald M. *The Theology of the Sacraments.* New York: Charles Scribner's Sons, 1957.

Baker, Frank. *John Wesley and the Church of England.* Nashville: Abingdon Press, 1968.

Baptism, Eucharist, and Ministry. Faith and Order Paper No. 111. Geneva: World Council of Churches, 1982.

Barclay, William. *The Lord's Supper.* Nashville: Abingdon Press, 1967.

Barrett, C. K. *Church, Ministry, and Sacraments in the New Testament.* Grand Rapids: Wm. B. Eerdmans Publishing Co., 1985.

Bassett, Paul M. "The Fundamentalist Leavening of the Holiness Movement: 1914-1940." *Wesleyan Theological Journal,* Spring 1978.

Bassett, Paul M., and Greathouse, William M. *The Historical Development.* Vol. 2 of *Exploring Christian Holiness.* Kansas City: Beacon Hill Press of Kansas City, 1985.

Beasley-Murray, G. R. *Baptism in the New Testament.* Grand Rapids: Wm. B. Eerdmans Publishing Co., 1962.

Berkhof, Hendrikus. *Christian Faith.* Translated by Sierd Woudstra. Grand Rapids: Wm. B. Eerdmans Publishing Co., 1979.

Berkouwer, G. C. *The Sacraments.* Grand Rapids: Wm. B. Eerdmans Publishing Co., 1969.

Bonhoeffer, Dietrich. *The Cost of Discipleship.* Translated by R. H. Fuller. New York: Macmillan Co., 1963.

Borgen, Ole. *John Wesley on the Sacraments.* Nashville: Abingdon Press, 1972.

Braaten, Carl E., and Jenson, Robert W., eds. *Christian Dogmatics.* 2 vols. Philadelphia: Fortress Press, 1984.

Bromiley, G. W. *Sacramental Teaching and Practice in the Reformation Churches.* Grand Rapids: Wm. B. Eerdmans Publishing Co., 1957.

Browning, Robert L., and Reed, Roy A. *The Sacraments in Religious Education and Liturgy: An Ecumenical Model.* Birmingham, Ala.: Religious Education Press, 1985.

Calvin, John. *Institutes of the Christian Religion.* Volumes 20 and 21 of *The Library of Christian Classics.* Edited by John T. McNeill. Philadelphia: Westminster Press, 1960.

Cannon, William Ragsdale. *The Theology of John Wesley.* New York: Abingdon-Cokesbury Press, 1946.

Cell, George Croft. *The Rediscovery of John Wesley.* New York: Henry Holt and Co., 1935.

Chiles, Robert E. *Theological Transition in American Methodism: 1790-1935.* Nashville: Abingdon Press, 1965.

Cox, Harvey. *The Feast of Fools.* New York: Harper and Row, 1969.

Cullmann, Oscar. *Baptism in the New Testament.* Translated by J. K. S. Reid. London: SCM Press, 1950.

Cullmann, Oscar, and Leenhardt, F. J. *Essays on the Lord's Supper.* Translated by J. G. Davies. London: Lutterworth Press, 1971.

Cushman, Robert E. "Salvation for All." In *Methodism,* edited by William K. Anderson. Nashville: Methodist Publishing House, 1947.

Dinkler-Von Schubert, Erika. "Symbol." In *Handbook of Christian Theology,* edited by Marvin Halverson and Arthur A. Cohen. New York: World Publishing Co., 1958.

Dix, Gregory, ed. *The Treatise on the Apostolic Tradition of St. Hippolytus of Rome.* London: Society for Promoting Christian Knowledge, 1937.

Dunn, James D. G. *Baptism in the Holy Spirit.* Naperville, Ill.: Alec R. Allenson, 1970.

Dunning, H. Ray. *Grace, Faith, and Holiness: A Wesleyan Systematic Theology.* Kansas City: Beacon Hill Press of Kansas City, 1988.

Forsyth, P. T. *The Church and Sacraments.* London: Independent Press, 1917.

Gossip, Arthur John. *Experience Worketh Hope.* New York: Charles Scribner's Sons, 1945.

Greathouse, William M. "The Present Crisis in Our Worship." *Preacher's Magazine,* December, January, February 1989-90.

Green, Michael. *Baptism: Its Purpose, Practice, and Power.* Downers Grove, Ill.: InterVarsity Press, 1987.

Grider, J. Kenneth. *Entire Sanctification: The Distinctive Doctrine of Wesleyanism.* Kansas City: Beacon Hill Press of Kansas City, 1980.

Grimal, Pierre, ed. *Larousse World Mythology.* London: Hamlyn Publishing House, 1973.

Gutwenger, Englebert. "Transubstantiation." In *Encyclopedia of Theology: The Concise Sacramentum Mundi,* edited by Karl Rahner. New York: Seabury Press, 1975.

Hardin, H. Grady; Quillian, Joseph D.; and White, James F. *The Celebration of the Gospel.* Nashville: Abingdon Press, 1964.

Heron, Alasdair I. C. *Table and Tradition.* Philadelphia: Westminster Press, 1983.

Higgins, A. J. B. *The Lord's Supper in the New Testament.* Chicago: Alec R. Allenson, 1952.

Hildebrandt, Franz. *From Luther to Wesley.* London: Lutterworth Press, 1951.

Hordern, William. *Experience and Faith: The Significance of Luther for Understanding Today's Experiential Religion.* Minneapolis: Augsburg Publishing House, 1983.

Houston, J. M. "Spirituality." In *Evangelical Dictionary of Theology,* edited by Walter A. Elwell. Grand Rapids: Baker Book House, 1984.

Howard, Richard E. *Newness of Life: A Study in the Thought of Paul.* Kansas City: Beacon Hill Press of Kansas City, 1975.

Howard, Thomas. "The Idea of Sacrament: An Approach." *Reformed Journal,* February 1979.

———. "Imagination, Rites, and Mystery: Why Did Christ Institute Sacraments?" *Reformed Journal*, March 1979.

Jansen, John Frederick. *The Meaning of Baptism*. Philadelphia: Westminster Press, 1958.

Jenson, Robert W. *Visible Words: The Interpretation and Practice of Christian Sacraments*. Philadelphia: Fortress Press, 1978.

Jeremias, Joachim. *The Eucharistic Words of Jesus*. Translated by Norman Perrin. London: SCM Press, 1966.

———. *Infant Baptism in the First Four Centuries*. Translated by David Cairns. London: SCM Press, 1960.

———. *The Origins of Infant Baptism*. Translated by Dorothea M. Barton. Naperville, Ill.: Alec R. Allenson, 1963.

Jewett, Paul K. *Infant Baptism and the Covenant of Grace*. Grand Rapids: Wm. B. Eerdmans Publishing Co., 1978.

Johnston, Robert K. *The Christian at Play*. Grand Rapids: Wm. B. Eerdmans Publishing Co., 1983.

Kliever, Lonnie D. *The Shattered Spectrum*. Atlanta: John Knox Press, 1981.

Ladd, George Eldon. *A Theology of the New Testament*. Grand Rapids: Wm. B. Eerdmans Publishing Co., 1974.

Lawson, John. *Comprehensive Handbook of Christian Doctrine*. Englewood Cliffs, N.J.: Prentice-Hall, 1967.

Lewis, C. S., ed. *George Macdonald: An Anthology*. Garden City, N.Y.: Doubleday and Co., 1962.

Lietzmann, Hans. *Messe und Herrenmahl*. Berlin: Walter de Gruyter, 1926. English: *Mass and Lord's Supper*. Translated by Dorothea H. G. Reeve. Leiden: E. J. Brill, 1979.

Lindsell, Harold. *The Battle for the Bible*. Grand Rapids: Zondervan Publishing House, 1976.

———. *The Bible in the Balance*. Grand Rapids: Zondervan Publishing House, 1979.

Lindström, Harald. *Wesley and Sanctification*. London: Epworth Press, 1950.

Loewen, Harry. *Luther and the Radicals*. Waterloo, Ont.: Wilfrid Laurier University Press, 1974.

Luther, Martin. *D. Martin Luthers Werke*. Kritische Gesamtausgabe. Weimar: H. Böhlau, 1883—.

———. *Luther's Works*. Edited by Jaroslav Pelikan and Helmut T. Lehmann. 55 vols. Philadelphia: Muhlenberg Press, 1959.

McGonigle, Herbert. "Pneumatological Nomenclature in Early Methodism." *Wesleyan Theological Journal*, Spring 1973.

MacGregor, Geddes. *Introduction to Religious Philosophy*. Boston: Houghton Mifflin Co., 1959.

Macquarrie, John. *Principles of Christian Theology*. 2nd ed. New York: Charles Scribner's Sons, 1977.

Manual of the Church of the Nazarene. Kansas City: Nazarene Publishing House, 1989.

Marshall, I. Howard. *Last Supper and Lord's Supper*. Grand Rapids: Wm. B. Eerdmans Publishing Co., 1980.

Marty, Martin E. "Baptistification Takes Over." *Christianity Today*, September 2, 1983.

Miller, David L. *Gods and Games*. New York: Harper and Row, 1973.

Moltmann, Jürgen. *The Church in the Power of the Spirit*. Translated by Margaret Kohl. London: SCM Press, 1977.

———. "The Life Signs of the Spirit in the Fellowship Community of Christ." In *Hope for the Church*, edited by Theodore Runyon. Nashville: Abingdon Press, 1979.

Morris, Leon. *Jesus Is the Christ: Studies in the Theology of John.* Grand Rapids: Wm. B. Eerdmans Publishing Co., 1989.

————. *The Gospel According to John.* In *The New International Commentary on the New Testament.* Edited by F. F. Bruce. Grand Rapids: Wm. B. Eerdmans Publishing Co., 1971.

Murray, John. *Christian Baptism.* Nutley, N.J.: Presbyterian and Reformed Publishing Co., 1977.

Naglee, David Ingersoll. *From Font to Faith: John Wesley on Infant Baptism and the Nurture of Children.* New York: Peter Lang, 1987.

Niebuhr, Reinhold. *Essays in Applied Christianity.* Edited by D. B. Robertson. New York: Meredian Books, World Publishing Co., 1959.

Novak, Michael. *The Joy of Sports.* New York: Basic Books, 1976.

Osborn, G. *The Poetical Works of John and Charles Wesley.* London: Wesleyan-Methodist Conference Office, 1869.

Osterhaven, M. E. "Lord's Supper, Views of." In *Evangelical Dictionary of Theology,* edited by Walter A. Elwell. Grand Rapids: Baker Book House, 1984.

Outler, Albert C. *John Wesley.* New York: Oxford University Press, 1964.

Pannenberg, Wolfhart. *Anthropology in Theological Perspective.* Translated by Matthew J. O'Connell. Philadelphia: Westminster Press, 1985.

Patrick, St. *The Works of St. Patrick.* Translated and annotated by Ludwig Bieler. Vol. 17 of *Ancient Christian Writers.* Edited by Johannes Quasten and Joseph C. Plumpe. Westminster, Md.: Newman Press, 1953.

Pauck, Wilhelm. *Harnack and Troeltsch: Two Historical Theologians.* New York: Oxford University Press, 1968.

Rahner, Hugo. *Man at Play.* New York: Herder and Herder, 1972.

Rahner, Karl. "Penance." In *Encyclopedia of Theology: The Concise Sacramentum Mundi,* edited by Karl Rahner. New York: Seabury Press, 1975.

Ramshaw-Schmidt, Gail. *Christ in Sacred Speech.* Philadelphia: Fortress Press, 1986.

Rice, George W. *Susanna Wesley: A Remarkable Woman and Mother.* Kansas City: Beacon Hill Press of Kansas City, 1990.

Richardson, Alan. *An Introduction to the Theology of the New Testament.* New York: Harper and Brothers, 1958.

————. "Sacrament, Sacramental Theology." In *A Dictionary of Christian Theology,* edited by Alan Richardson. Philadelphia: Westminster Press, 1969.

Richardson, Cyril C., ed. and trans. *Early Christian Fathers.* Vol. 1 of *The Library of Christian Classics.* Edited by John Baillie, John T. McNeill, and Henry P. Van Dusen. Philadelphia: Westminster Press, 1953.

Schillebeeckx, Edward. *Christ the Sacrament of the Encounter with God.* New York: Sheed and Ward, 1963.

————. "The Sacraments: An Encounter with God." In *Edward Schillebeeckx, OP,* edited by M. Redefern. New York and London: Sheed and Ward, 1972.

Schulte, Raphael. "Sacraments." In *Encyclopedia of Theology: The Concise Sacramentum Mundi,* edited by Karl Rahner. New York: Seabury Press, 1975.

Shelton, R. Larry. "John Wesley's Approach to Scripture in Historical Perspective." *Wesleyan Theological Journal,* Spring 1981.

Stählin, G. "Mythos." In *Theological Dictionary of the New Testament,* edited by Gerhard Kittel, translated by Geoffrey Bromiley, 4:782. Grand Rapids: Wm. B. Eerdmans Publishing Co., 1967.

Staples, Rob L. "Dualism." In *Beacon Dictionary of Theology,* edited by Richard S. Taylor. Kansas City: Beacon Hill Press of Kansas City, 1983.

————. "John Wesley's Doctrine of the Holy Spirit." *Wesleyan Theological Journal* 21, nos. 1 and 2 (Spring—Fall 1986).

————. "Wesleyan Perspectives on the Doctrine of the Holy Spirit." In *The Spirit and the New Age*, edited by R. Larry Shelton and Alex R. G. Deasley. Wesleyan Theological Perspective Series, vol. 5. Anderson, Ind.: Warner Press, 1986.

Starkey, Lycurgus M., Jr. *The Work of the Holy Spirit: A Study in Wesleyan Theology.* New York: Abingdon Press, 1962.

Stevenson, Burton, ed. *The Home Book of Quotations.* 5th ed. New York: Dodd, Mead, and Co., 1947.

Stookey, Laurence Hull. *Baptism: Christ's Act in the Church.* Nashville: Abingdon Press, 1982.

Studdert-Kennedy, G. A. "Set Your Affections on Things Above." In *Rhymes.* London: Hodder and Stoughton, 1929.

Temple, William. *Nature, Man, and God.* London: Macmillan and Co., 1949.

Tillich, Paul. *Dynamics of Faith.* New York: Harper and Brothers, 1957.

————. *Systematic Theology.* 3 vols. Chicago: University of Chicago Press, 1951-63.

————. "Theology and Symbolism." In *Religious Symbolism*, edited by F. Earnest Johnson. Port Washington, N.Y.: Kennikat Press, 1955.

Todd, John M. *John Wesley and the Catholic Church.* London: Catholic Book Club, 1958.

Troeltsch, Ernst. *The Social Teaching of the Christian Churches.* Translated by Olive Wyon. 2 vols. New York: Harper and Brothers, 1960.

Wainwright, Geoffrey. *Eucharist and Eschatology.* New York: Oxford University Press, 1981.

Webber, Robert E. *Evangelicals on the Canterbury Trail.* Waco, Tex.: Word Books, 1985.

Welch, Claude. *Protestant Thought in the Nineteenth Century.* Vol. 2. New York: Yale University Press, 1985.

Wesley, John. *Explanatory Notes upon the New Testament.* 2 vols. London: Wesleyan Methodist Book Room, n.d. Reprint, Kansas City: Beacon Hill Press of Kansas City, 1981.

————. *Explanatory Notes upon the Old Testament.* 1765. Reprint, Salem, Ohio: Schmul Publishers, 1975.

————. *The Journal of the Rev. John Wesley, A.M.* Edited by Nehemiah Curnock. 8 vols. London: Epworth Press, 1916.

————. *The Letters of the Rev. John Wesley, A.M.* Edited by John Telford. 8 vols. London: Epworth Press, 1931.

————. *Sunday Service of the Methodists in North America.* With an introduction by James F. White. Methodist Bicentennial Commemorative Reprint. United Methodist Publishing House and the United Methodist Board of Higher Education and Ministry, 1984.

————. *The Works of John Wesley.* 3rd ed. 14 vols. London: Wesleyan Methodist Book Room, 1872. Reprint, Kansas City: Beacon Hill Press of Kansas City, 1978.

Westcott, B. F. *The Gospel According to St. John.* London: John Murray, Albermarle Street, 1889.

Whale, J. S. *Christian Doctrine.* Cambridge: Cambridge University Press, 1942.

White, Hugh Vernon. *Truth and the Person in Christian Theology.* New York: Oxford University Press, 1963.

White, James F. *Introduction to Christian Worship.* Nashville: Abingdon Press, 1981.

————. *Sacraments as God's Self Giving.* Nashville: Abingdon Press, 1983.

Wiley, H. Orton. *Christian Theology.* 3 vols. Kansas City: Beacon Hill Press, 1940-43.

Williams, Colin. *John Wesley's Theology Today.* New York: Abingdon Press, 1960.

Willimon, William H. *The Service of God.* Nashville: Abingdon Press, 1983.
———. *Word, Water, Wine, and Bread.* Valley Forge, Pa.: Judson Press, 1980.

SUBJECT INDEX

INDEX OF PERSONS

302